Praise For

It's On You

"Two of the leading scientists of human decision-making, on which the 'nudge' movement in behavioral economics is based, write that nudges have vastly overpromised and under-delivered. Instead of trying to solve big, systematic problems by marginally changing how individuals respond to perverse incentives, they persuasively advise us to systematically change those incentives with the tools of government and democracy."

—Alvin E. Roth, Nobel laureate and
author of *Who Gets What—and Why*

"This excellent book powerfully argues that focusing on individual psychology and incentives (and nudges) for tackling some of the most vexing problems of today—from obesity to climate change, health care, and inequality—is a losing proposition. Not only is it insufficient, but it shifts the blame onto the victims of systemic failures, often undergirded by political economy factors and excessive corporate power. From two experts in behavioral economics and social psychology, we have a master class on how to blend individual psychology with institutions, so that people are encouraged to get involved and develop solutions to our urgent problems via the democratic process."

—Daron Acemoglu, Nobel laureate and
coauthor of *Power and Progress*

"A wise and deeply researched book, and a stirring call to action. It is rare to see such expert thinkers reflect so profoundly on the risks of their own field."

—Tim Harford, author of *The Data Detective*

"This is an excellent book—engaging and well written. The authors convincingly show that in a system with complex interactions, nudge-style interventions at the individual level fail when the problem lies in the structure. They also reveal how large corporations play a key role in obscuring this fact."

—Nassim Nicholas Taleb, author of *Antifragile*

"If you believe corporate America, preventing a climate crisis is up to you. So is putting a halt to the obesity epidemic, stopping mass shootings, and fixing America's dysfunctional healthcare system, which delivers the poorest care in the affluent world at the highest cost. Chater and Loewenstein make a convincing case that this is little more than a self-serving lie. Indeed, the proposition that our greatest societal problems must be solved through individual action is leading America astray."

—Eduardo Porter, author of *American Poison*

IT'S ON YOU

How Corporations and Behavioral Scientists
Have Convinced Us That
We're to Blame for Society's Deepest Problems

NICK CHATER AND
GEORGE LOEWENSTEIN

BASIC

VENTURE

New York

Basic Venture
Hachette Book Group
1290 Avenue of the Americas, New York, NY 10104
www.basic-venture.com

Printed in Canada

First Edition: January 2026

Published by Basic Venture, an imprint of Hachette Book Group, Inc. The Basic Venture name and logo is a registered trademark of the Hachette Book Group.

Basic Venture books may be purchased in bulk for business, educational, or promotional use. For more information, please contact your local bookseller or the Hachette Book Group's Special Markets department at special.markets@hbgusa.com.

The Hachette Speakers Bureau provides a wide range of authors for speaking events. To find out more, go to hachettespeakersbureau.com or email HachetteSpeakers@hbgusa.com.

The publisher is not responsible for websites (or their content) that are not owned by the publisher.

Print book interior design by Amy Quinn.

Library of Congress Control Number: 2025940370

ISBNs: 9781541700116 (hardcover), 9781541700130 (ebook)

MRQ-T

10 9 8 7 6 5 4 3 2 1

CONTENTS

To Louie and Donna

Introduction

CHANGE THE GAME, NOT THE PLAYERS

An actor in a Native American costume paddles a birch bark canoe through a river clogged with floating trash. He pulls his boat ashore and walks toward a bustling freeway where a driver hurls a crumpled paper bag out a car window. As he turns toward the camera, a single teardrop is visible on his painted cheek. The advertisement concludes with a powerful message: *"People start pollution. People can stop it."*

Baby boomers in the US might recognize this as the famous "crying Indian" public service announcement, produced by a group called Keep America Beautiful and first aired on Earth Day in 1971. Beyond the irony that the Native American was actually an actor of Italian descent, the ad conveniently neglects to mention that both it, and Keep America Beautiful, were sponsored by beverage and packaging corporations such as the American Can Corporation and the Owens-Illinois Glass Company.

For decades, these companies broadcast the message that "people start pollution"—essentially shifting blame for a massive problem they created onto the public—while energetically fighting against any regulatory measure that would meaningfully reduce pollution, such as so-called bottle bills (laws requiring that people can get a deposit back when they return packaging). The "crying Indian" ad was finally retired in 2023, not because it was revealed to be a front for big business, but because it stereotyped Native Americans.

Yet the same tactic is still in wide use—and not only when it comes to pollution.

It may seem natural for us to feel a measure of personal responsibility for the many problems that plague society; or, if we ourselves don't feel personally responsible for them, to at least blame them on the actions of other individuals. We see an epidemic of obesity, for instance, and we focus on people's choices about their diet and exercise. We dread not having enough money for retirement and fault ourselves and other people for failing to put more aside. We see the threat of climate change, and we focus on the type of car we drive or the way we power and heat our home. But in these cases and many more, we have been led astray by the equivalent of a "crying Indian," misled into believing that individuals created these problems, and that individuals can fix them.

In this book, we will examine many daunting challenges that face our societies and troubled planet: from climate change to gun violence, from obesity to the opioid epidemic, from the crippling cost of health insurance in the US to global income inequality, from a spike in American traffic fatalities to a crisis in pensions and retirement savings. In every case we believe the only way to fix these problems is with a systemic approach, by changing *the rules of the game*: introducing regulations and taxes, removing perverse incentives, adding checks and balances, remaking infrastructure and redesigning institutions.

Yet over and over again, we will see how vested interests that have created the current situation—and benefit from it enormously—find ways of reframing the debate, whether it's the National Rifle Association telling us that "guns don't kill people; people kill people" or the oil giant BP cynically marketing the concept of the "individual carbon footprint" as it fights any and all measures to curb emissions caused by fossil fuels.

If players like these continue to set the rules of the game, the rest of us are bound to lose.

———

It's not only the occupants of the C-Suite (the CEO, CFO, etc.) and lobbyists in the halls of Congress who have distracted us from the real causes of the problems we face by focusing our attention on the flaws and failings of individuals. Over the last few decades, many psychologists and behavioral economists—including the psychologist and the behavioral economist who wrote this book— have also been focused on the shortcomings of individuals.[1]

We and many of our colleagues in the behavioral sciences have spent our careers running experiments and documenting the many "imperfections" of human judgment and decision-making. We have learned that people struggle to make sensible decisions involving risk and uncertainty; that they focus myopically on the short term; that they see patterns where none exist; that they fail to see patterns that *do* exist; that they unhelpfully divide the world into in-groups and out-groups (treating the latter with suspicion and hostility); and so on. Making matters worse, our collective research documents how profoundly people are influenced by their peers, whose attitudes, beliefs, and actions they often mimic without much in the way of rational deliberation. So not only do we have our own errors and biases to contend with, but we can inadvertently inherit the errors and biases of our friends, family, and colleagues as well.

With this intense focus on individual irrationality, it is perhaps unsurprising that a widely held view has come to dominate policy discussions—that many of society's, and the world's, problems stem from *individual failings*. We call this perspective on our social and environmental problems the *i-frame* (individual frame).

Standing in stark contrast to the i-frame perspective is the idea that social problems arise because there is something wrong with the *system* of complex and interlocking rules that govern our lives.

According to the *s-frame* (system frame) perspective, the outcomes we end up with depend on the rules of the game, not on the conduct of individual players. So when we see social problems that are either relatively new or have gotten much worse in recent years—whether it's obesity, income inequality, plastic waste, or gun violence—we should cast a critical eye on the playing field. What has changed about how the game is played? What new rules have been instituted (or, more likely, removed)—and at whose behest? What could be done to level the playing field? The mantra of the s-frame is *change the game, not the players*. And changing the game will usually involve the traditional levers of government: regulations, laws, taxes, incentives, and more.

The i-frame and s-frame perspectives are not, of course, mutually exclusive. The battle against smoking, as we'll see in Chapter 9, has deployed initiatives that target the i-frame (e.g., reducing or eliminating tobacco marketing; adding stark warnings on packaging; making tobacco products more difficult to obtain; public health campaigns) and the s-frame (e.g., regulating tar levels, ever-higher tobacco taxes, banning smoking in public places).[2] And, quite likely, i-frame and s-frame initiatives have been mutually reinforcing—e.g., public health messages may increase support for tough legislation, and tough legislation may reinforce our collective sense that smoking is a "bad thing" for ourselves and our loved ones. The i-frame and s-frame perspectives, however, lead us to search for solutions in very different directions. Thinking in terms of the i-frame, we take the rules of the game as fixed and ask how we can encourage or help the players to play the game better. Thinking in terms of the s-frame, we take human nature as fixed and ask how the rules of the game can be reshaped to produce better outcomes.

The i-frame perspective, we will see in this book, has some undeniably appealing features. It focuses on specific choices made by identifiable individuals; it adopts, as it were, a "person's-eye" view on social problems. When we see the world through the i-frame, diagnosing social problems by focusing on individual behavior, we tend to try to solve those problems by helping individuals make better choices: eat more healthily, exercise more, use less energy, recycle, avoid harmful addictions, put more money aside for a comfortable retirement, and so on. Self-help books, diet programs, fitness instructors, financial advisers, and life coaches stress how each of us can take control of our lives to be healthier, wealthier, and happier. Many religious traditions likewise focus, in diverse ways, on enjoining us to be better people and to lead better lives. Billions upon billions of better individual choices, the logic goes, will lead to a better world. All of this makes the i-frame perspective intuitively seductive: Individuals and their struggles are easy to relate to and empathize with. You can't relate to, or empathize with, a system.

With the i-frame perspective in the foreground, governments have attempted to create interventions that will help people make better choices, whether better for the specific individual (e.g., concerning health or savings), or better for the common good (e.g., concerning the environment).

One approach is to give people helpful *information*: calorie and nutrition labels on foods; clearly specified interest rates on loans; reminders that investments can go down as well as up.[3] A more general approach, along the same broad lines, involves *education*: training people to make better financial, health, or environmental decisions, often through some kind of financial or health "literacy" program. And policymakers also sometimes offer "personalized," often cleverly crafted, *incentives* to help specific groups of people, such as paying drug addicts to stay "clean."[4]

This all makes intuitive sense: If we are given better information, the education to make use of that information, and the ideal mix of carrots and sticks, surely we will be more likely to make the right choices. Or so one might expect, at least if people are thinking through their choices rationally, with suitable time, care, and attention. But here the catalog of biases and errors in human rationality—and the sheer volume and complexity of choices we have to make—raises the possibility that, even with the right information, education, and incentives, we may still make the wrong choices a lot of the time. Indeed, a large body of research on information disclosures such as product warnings suggests that, more often than not, such interventions yield disappointingly small, if any, benefits.[5] Calorie labeling, for example, has become ubiquitous at fast-food outlets, but a multitude of studies have shown that it only has a tiny impact on the body mass index of fast-food consumers. Worse, some studies find that this positive effect is concentrated among those who already have healthy body weight.[6] Other studies find that labeling can lead to a reduction in life satisfaction—due to an increase in guilt triggered by the information.[7]

Beyond providing people with better information to make better decisions, there are a variety of other i-frame interventions that promise to help by harnessing the quirks and foibles of human nature to the policymaker's advantage—an approach that has become remarkably influential. The basic idea is that we can help people make better choices through what are known as "nudges," a term that came to prominence after the publication of the 2008 book *Nudge* by the legal scholar Cass R. Sunstein and behavioral economist Richard Thaler. Nudging involves carefully arranging the choice options people face (rather grandly, the "choice architecture") so that the quirks of human nature propel us toward doing the right thing and steer us away from doing the wrong thing.

Some randomly chosen but fairly typical examples:

- Making sure that the "default" option—which kicks in if we do nothing—is mostly the "right" option, so that the lazy and inattentive are automatically "opted in" to get healthier food options, put more money aside for retirement, or receive their electricity from "green" providers.

- Exploiting the power of peer pressure by telling people who are doing the wrong thing (e.g., being late with their taxes, or running up big heating bills) about all those people who are doing the right thing.
- Making unhealthy things less accessible—moving candies, cigarettes, or alcohol away from the supermarket checkout; positioning healthier options at the top of the menu; reducing the sizes of portions and plates.

What is special about nudges, at least in theory, is that they tap into basic psychological mechanisms to help us behave in ways that benefit us irrespective of information, education, or carrots-and-sticks. And crucially, nudges don't require us to change the *actual choice options* at all—just the way in which those choice options are presented, which (according to the nudge approach) should help individuals "choose" the right options and promote their own or the greater good.

Nudging aims to go with the grain of human nature—to help each one of us, and by extension all of us, live better, one choice at a time. If billions of bad food choices make an obesity crisis, then billions of better food choices should unmake an obesity crisis. If each of us can be nudged to reduce our individual carbon footprint, then summing up our efforts should surely drive down the carbon footprint of the entire world. Following the i-frame logic, these better individual choices will add up to help mend a broken world.

Nudges are attractive to psychologists and behavioral economists because they seem to offer elegant solutions to the very shortcomings of human nature we've spent our careers documenting. Nudges also fit in with the individualistic ethos that is especially prominent in the US. And nudges are also attractive to policymakers in that they promise simple, effective, low-cost solutions for seemingly intractable social challenges—without, importantly, the need for fundamental systemic change.

While direct efforts to deal with policy problems such as obesity and poverty through public policy measures such as laws and taxes often get blocked by powerful interests or get ensnared in political thickets (especially in times of political polarization), i-frame policies such as nudges offer the promise of politically uncontroversial interventions. In fact, the attempt to reach out across the political spectrum was captured in the very titles of the two academic papers that launched the "nudge movement" in 2003: "Libertarian Paternalism" and "Regulation for Conservatives" (George was, in fact, a coauthor of this one).[8] The idea was that nudges retain the individual freedoms that are so important to people on the political right (because they don't actually restrict people's choice options). But they also enhance people's welfare, which is so important to those on the left, by designing the choice architecture so that people "naturally" tend to fall into choices that are best for them, and for society.

The nudge movement succeeded in breaking through political boundaries beyond its founders' wildest dreams. Indeed, political conservatives such as the former British prime minister David Cameron, who while in office in 2010 founded the UK Behavioural Insights Team, colloquially known as the "Nudge Unit," were some of the movement's most enthusiastic supporters. The hope, as eloquently expressed in the subtitle of a book by David Halpern, the first head of the UK Nudge Unit, was that "small changes can make a big difference."[9] Across the Atlantic, and on the opposite side of the political spectrum, President Barack Obama founded, in 2015, a similar behavioral insights team in the US. In the executive order establishing the Social and Behavioral Sciences Team (SBST), Obama noted that "a growing body of evidence demonstrates that behavioral science insights—research findings from fields such as behavioral economics and psychology about how people make decisions and act on them—can be used to design government policies to better serve the American people."[10] More broadly, nudge units, under various titles, have proliferated spectacularly across the globe—according to one estimate there were over four hundred by 2021.[11] And large numbers of corporations have also established behavioral insights teams, albeit often with goals very different from those of teams established in government (a point we return to in the second half of the book). The concept of a "nudge" itself, always somewhat ill-defined, has also steadily expanded.[12] As Sunstein recently noted, "A reminder is a nudge; so is a warning. A GPS [global positioning system] nudges; a default rule nudges. Some nudges are educative; consider labels and warnings. Other nudges are architectural; consider automatic enrollment or website design that places certain options first or in large font."[13] If GPS devices are counted as nudges, then the same is true for just about any aspect of technology, software, or design (or any aspect of education, public information, marketing, or advertising).

As it happens, and in hindsight perhaps not without irony, it was serving on the academic advisory board of the UK Nudge Unit that brought together the two of us, Nick Chater (a psychologist who cofounded Decision Technology, a behavioral science consultancy) and George Loewenstein (a behavioral economist, who has conducted extensive research on food choice, medication compliance, and health insurance). We met in December 2013 in London at a daylong Nudge Unit "retreat," held in a cubelike room, reached by a slender spiral staircase, atop the monumental Horse Guards building—once the main military headquarters of the British Empire—with spectacular views of Westminster. Chatting during the lunch break, and then at a nearby pub when the retreat disbanded, the two of us discovered that, while impressed with the Nudge Unit Team and its work, we shared increasing misgivings about "nudge" as an approach to public policy.

What was worrying us, exactly? It took a while for us to figure this out. We started working together on a variety of research topics, most of them completely unrelated to public policy, such as the "drive for sense-making" and the function served by boredom. But our many conversations kept returning to whether nudges were really an effective way of addressing social problems. We compared notes on our own disparate attempts to implement effective nudges, which had often proved disappointing. And our reading of the literature suggested that other researchers trying out different nudge interventions weren't faring much better. Based on these experiences and observations, and on looking over our shoulders at countries that seemed to be successfully solving the same problems through more substantive, systemic changes, our perspective on the limitations of the i-frame began to take shape. We started to worry that classic nudge interventions—such as showing people morphed images of themselves aging to get them to save more, painting perpendicular lines on highways to reduce speeding, or positioning healthy food first in cafeteria lines (the opening example in *Nudge*)—were unlikely to move the needle on the problems they aimed to address. Finally, we decided to try to crystallize our thoughts by writing this book.

The result was not at all what we expected when we began.

Perhaps most strikingly, when we discovered that an oil company had popularized the concept of the "carbon footprint," it felt like uncovering a trail of fingerprints at a crime scene. The more we investigated, the more we saw the marks of big business on nearly every problem we researched—hence the final title we settled on: *It's on You: How Corporations and Behavioral Scientists Have Convinced Us That We're to Blame for Society's Deepest Problems.* And, immersing ourselves in the recent public policy and political economy literature encompassing brilliant analyses such as historians Erik Conway and Naomi Oreskes's *The Big Myth: How American Business Taught Us to Loathe Government and Love the Free Market*, we gained a new perspective on the role that behavioral economics had inadvertently come to play in the "marketplace of ideas" influencing public policy.

Rather than i-frame policies arising organically by popular demand, or out of policymakers' natural inclinations, we found in case after case that there were *corporate interests* advancing i-frame solutions and perspectives. Corporations and whole industries that benefit from the status quo have figured out that they can effectively deflect pressure for systemic change that might threaten their business models—policy changes that might adversely affect their bottom line—by reframing problems from the s-frame to the i-frame. They have learned to publicly throw their considerable weight behind i-frame interventions—and in some cases behind the academics who back them—knowing full well that such measures are unlikely to have much impact on the problems they ostensibly target, and hence pose little threat to the corporate bottom line.

These and similar strategies—including Exxon's hiring of prominent economists, lawyers, and decision researchers to debunk methods of valuing environmental damages that would have led to huge punitive penalties for the 1989 *Exxon Valdez* disaster—go way back in time, and have worked surprisingly well. A variation is to increase the focus on individual solutions to social problems by implying that to advocate any change to the system (which is painted as having arisen spontaneously through the voluntary activities of free citizens) would lead to perverse and gruesome outcomes. Witness the repeated invocation of so-called death panels by opponents of the US Affordable Care Act (ACA, popularly known as "Obamacare"). Such panels, according to the former Alaska governor Sarah Palin, were bureaucratic committees that would be established as part of the ACA to decide whether elderly people or those with serious health conditions should receive care or die, "based on a subjective judgment of their 'level of productivity in society.'"[14] The actual proposal was very different: One provision of the ACA (which was dropped, in the wake of the "death panel" furor) simply allowed Medicare to reimburse doctors for counseling patients about end-of-life care options, such as completing a living will—a document in which individuals specify what actions should be taken for their health if they can no longer make decisions for themselves because of illness or incapacity. But the ominous "death panel" label gained huge political traction and still resonates to this day.

The pejorative term "socialized medicine" has been equally effective in the decades-long campaigning by the US health care industry to turn voters against any form of public health provision.[15] Indeed, the general tactic of painting any demand for better regulation or improved public provision of services as the first steps on an inexorable march to something close to a communist state has been widely and effectively deployed. The aim is to seed the idea that any s-frame reform is inevitably tainted, and that people should see the solutions to society's problems as the responsibility of individuals.

Of course, the corporations and other special interests pushing this i-frame viewpoint don't have to really believe that i-frame solutions can work. Indeed, in many cases, they are almost certainly banking on the fact that they won't work. If the fossil fuel, tobacco, or gambling industries, for example, really thought that individuals could radically cut fossil fuel use or break their smoking or gambling addictions, those industries would be far less keen to promote an i-frame perspective. But they are (rightly, as it turns out) confident that the resulting environmental and social problems can't and won't be solved, as it were, one person at a time. While publicly advocating the i-frame, corporations spend substantial resources on lobbying, funding think tanks, and sponsoring academic research to ensure that the game is, and remains, rigged in their favor. *This is the corporate sleight of hand: point to the i-frame act on the s-frame; rig the rules of the game, but blame individual citizens for any resulting social ills.*

Starting, in Chapter 1, with the fossil fuel industry's promotion of the carbon footprint—which reassigns responsibility for climate change from the perpetrators to the victims—we will see the same pattern of corporate interests aiming to focus public attention on the i-frame (often with the unwitting backing of academics) replicated in every policy domain we discuss.[16] Again and again, powerful commercial interests work tirelessly to block meaningful change, thereby preventing problems from being solved.

Examining a wide variety of social issues, we show that in almost every case the crux of the problem boils down to who—among the complex mix of corporations, billionaires, unions, government agencies, political parties, media, tech platforms, universities, lobbyists, think tanks, and, of course, individual citizens—controls the "rules of the game." In a perfect democracy, this would be the voters, who presumably would elect leaders who advocate policies that favor the common good rather than special interests. In practice, however, some players will inevitably have a lot more leverage than others.

More than half a century ago the political economist Mancur Olson, in his celebrated book *The Logic of Collective Action*, provided a crucial and insightful analysis of how conflicts between different interests are likely to play out.[17] Olson pointed out that in many policy domains there is a highly asymmetric battle between the concentrated interests of a small but well-organized and well-funded few who stand to benefit (or suffer) substantially from a particular government policy and the diffuse interests of the relatively unorganized many, each of whom may be impacted only slightly by that policy. Thus, a small number of large corporations might stand to lose substantially from tighter environmental standards; more severe regulations in consumer finance; changes to how prescription drugs are marketed, purchased, and prescribed; how health care is paid for; or restrictions on the marketing and sale of calorie-dense foods and drinks. According to Olson's logic, it is very much in the interests of large corporations in a sector to band together and oppose such policies. The benefits to the population that would result from reduced pollution and greenhouse gas emissions, improved health and well-being, and so on may be very much larger in total, but they are spread across millions and sometimes billions of people, none of whom individually has a strong incentive to push for change, or the resources or organizational support to help them do so.

It is worth stressing that Olson's arguments do not in and of themselves motivate an antibusiness agenda, because the interests of CEOs and billionaires are not necessarily—or at least not always—at odds with the common good. The remarkable success of market-oriented economies across the world in raising individual living standards and supporting public services such as education and health care provides compelling evidence that commercial and public interests are often aligned. Innovations that make money for their creators often provide huge social benefits. But when businesses can shape the rules of the game to their own benefit—as they will, of course, attempt to do—the result will often not be innovation for the benefit of all, but the extraction of profit at the expense of the public good.

The ability of firms and elites to extract value from economic activity, often in ways—e.g., by securing monopolies in key industries, obtaining tax breaks or government contracts, or weakening labor protections—that diminish long-term prosperity, is a central theme of the work of Daron Acemoglu, Simon Johnson, and James Robinson, whose shared Nobel Prize in economics was announced as we were putting the finishing touches on this book. Acemoglu and Robinson's 2012 book, *Why Nations Fail*, showed that the different institutions put in place when Europeans colonized large parts of the globe had profound consequences for economic prosperity that persist to current times. The key distinction, according to the authors, is that some institutions were aimed at exploiting indigenous populations and extracting resources, establishing patterns that persist to today, while other institutions, which upheld the rule of law and property rights, laid the foundations for the inclusive political and economic systems that have led to prosperity. Acemoglu's book with Johnson, *Power and Progress*, examines how technological innovations over the past thousand years have typically tended to benefit elites rather than creating prosperity for the populations at large. In media interviews following the announcement of the Nobel award, Acemoglu and his co-laureates cautioned that political polarization and the weakening of the clear, predictable, and impartial rule of law in the US (which restrains elite power) threaten to torpedo the inclusive institutions that are responsible for the country's immense prosperity. They argue further that without active regulatory intervention, the gains from AI—the latest revolutionary technological development—seem once again likely to accrue almost exclusively to a tiny economic elite.[18]

———

There is, on reflection, something decidedly odd about seeing individual psychological frailties as the root cause of the social problems that face us. After all, most of our pressing social problems of the moment are specific to time and place: The obesity crisis, for example, has emerged over the past few decades and has been very uneven across nations—witness the stark differences in obesity levels in the US and the UK (37 percent and 30 percent, respectively), in 2016, versus France (11 percent) and Japan (4 percent).[19] Human psychology (and physiology) is surely more or less the same across history and geography. What *has* changed, and is continuing to change, is (among other things) the nature of the complex commercial, economic, and technological systems that produce, distribute, and market the cheap ultra-processed and energy-dense foods that now make up a substantial part of our collective diet. The correct diagnosis, then, seems to be at the s-frame level, and any successful "treatment" will most naturally be directed at that level, too. The primary challenge is to fix broken or malfunctioning systems, rather than to circumvent flaws in human nature.

Take environmental challenges—from plastic waste, degraded soils, destruction of habitats, and loss of biodiversity to, most notably, the greenhouse gas emissions that are causing rapid heating of the earth's atmosphere. Blaming human shortsightedness or selfishness for ecologically unsustainable behavior can't be the right story, because humans with those very same psychological characteristics have successfully conserved farmland, forests, and fisheries over centuries and even millennia in many parts of the world.[20] Humans, it turns out, can be spectacularly good at organizing solutions to tricky governance problems—solutions that can and frequently do robustly overcome human shortsightedness and selfishness. Admittedly, the results have often been highly imperfect and inadequate; but there are numerous success stories to point to, including, perhaps most notably, the global banning of CFCs, the chemicals in aerosols and fridges responsible for the "ozone hole" over the South Pole reported by the British Antarctic Survey in 1985 and addressed by a comprehensive international agreement, the Montreal Protocol, which was adopted just two years later.

To see this point a bit more starkly, let us switch our focus for a moment away from humanity's manifold *psychological* limitations and frailties to our equally manifold *physiological* limitations and frailties. If we are vulnerable to psychological limitations, we are at least as vulnerable to physiological weaknesses, readily succumbing to cold, malnutrition, disease, predation, and violent conflict. An i-frame perspective on these problems would likely involve providing hints and tips to help individuals survive in a hostile world, and these might be helpful—on the margin. But human progress has arisen through s-frame changes—the invention and sharing of technologies (e.g., public water supplies) and the establishment of economic institutions and legal and political systems—which have, collectively, led to spectacular improvements in the material dimensions of life. The physiology of individual humans has changed little over time and across societies, but the systems of rules we live by have changed immeasurably. A continual process of creation, adjustment, and accumulation of s-frame changes—such as universal provision of medical care (in most advanced countries) and systems that provide for financial security in retirement—has transformed our ability collectively to overcome many of our physiological frailties by providing the food, clothing, shelter, and medicine that have enabled us to live ever-longer, healthier, and less perilous lives.

If i-frame interventions were as successful as many people seem to believe, perhaps systemic change, with all its inherent risks, would be unnecessary. Perhaps we could solve climate change by encouraging each individual to reduce their carbon footprint, ensure retirement security by inducing people to save more, eliminate obesity by figuring out clever interventions to promote dieting and exercise. Alas, a mountain of evidence shows that the impact of i-frame interventions—the nudges we have been told are so beneficial—has been disappointing, often showing small or even null results.

For example, one of the nudges that has received the most attention is the impact of defaults (choices that go into effect if one fails to make an explicit decision) on organ donation rates. The clever use of defaults—which are meant to automatically place people on a beneficial trajectory even if they take no action at all—has been the biggest apparent nudge success story, including when it comes to retirement savings (see Chapter 3). An important and hugely influential 2003 paper by Eric Johnson and Daniel Goldstein, published in the prestigious journal *Science*, reported the striking finding that most countries that adopted presumed-consent policies—in which individuals who failed to make an explicit choice (otherwise known as "opt out") were by default assumed to have opted in and consented to donate their organs—had consent rates for organ donation of greater than 90 percent, while in countries in which potential donors were required to "opt in" to organ donation, rates ranged between 4 percent and 28 percent.[21] Yet, more recent research has tempered expectations about the direct impact of defaults, leading some to conclude that opt-out policies may actually *reduce* ultimate organ donations. A 2022 study found, for example, that opt-in and opt-out policies have at best a tiny impact on actual donation rates, in part because families, who are often central to the decision over whether donation can go ahead, don't interpret a relative's failure to specify their preferences as communicating consent.[22] So the apparently stunningly successful nudge turns out to be frustratingly ineffective.[23]

Actually raising organ donation rates requires coordinated systemic change. Spain leads the world in rates of organ donations. How have they done it? A recent editorial in the leading medical journal, *The Lancet*, titled "Organ Donation: Lessons from the Spanish Model," explains that this success "is built on three components: a solid legislative framework, strong clinical leadership, and a highly organised logistics network overseen by the National Transplant Organization (ONT), whose creation led to a doubling of deceased donation activity in less than a decade." The popular podcast *If Books Could Kill* (which offers a two-episode critique of *Nudge*) reinforces the point.[24] Podcasters Michael Hobbes and Peter Shamshiri conclude that in order to emulate Spain's success, "You have to look at a system. You have to dedicate funding to it. You have to take the specifics seriously . . . that's how you solve problems."

Perhaps the most definitive study of the impacts of nudges, by Stefano DellaVigna and Elizabeth Linos, examined all the interventions conducted by two of the largest Nudge Units in the United States—a unique data set comprising 126 real-world experiments testing a total of 241 different nudges and involving a sample of a total of twenty-three million people.[25] These experiments tested a wide range of different types of nudges involving elements such as simplification, personalization, prompts, changing defaults, and providing information about what other people are doing. In one intervention, armed service members were sent a letter encouraging them to re-enroll in their Roth individual retirement account plans; another sent postcards to residents of a city encouraging them to fix up their homes to meet code regulations. Averaging over all 241 interventions, the observed effects turned out to be modest—a 1.4 percent change in the behaviors that the interventions targeted.

The authors also asked academics to predict the results; these predictions dramatically overestimated the impact of the nudges. Why this misperception? One factor may be the conclusions of an earlier, highly influential paper (with more than a thousand academic citations, so far) by Shlomo Benartzi and colleagues titled "Should Governments Invest More in Nudging?"[26] The article reviewed approximately one hundred nudges and found that they were largely effective (an average effect size of 8.7 percent), and especially—given the generally low cost of implementing nudges—that they were cost-effective. DellaVigna and Linos counter these and other optimistic findings by showing that they mainly resulted from "selection bias."[27] Selection bias arises because researchers often put aside studies in which nudges don't work, in part because journals are often reluctant to publish studies with effects that aren't strong and positive.[28] Such a bias is unsurprising: Who wants to publish a paper showing yet another failed behavioral intervention? Selection bias is sometimes known as the "file drawer" problem, because unsuccessful studies tend to end up in the filing cabinet instead of in academic journals. Researchers are aware of the problem of selection bias and often do seek to correct for it, but not nearly enough: DellaVigna and Linos found that academics, despite knowing about the file drawer problem, still radically overestimated the average impact of nudges.

Interestingly, however, responses to the same questions directed at a different sample—those working "on the ground" in behavioral insights teams across the world—revealed a far more realistic assessment of the impact of nudges. Perhaps this should not be surprising: These people have daily experience testing behavioral interventions and have a "bird's-eye" view of their mixed and modest (though sometimes nonetheless valuable) results. Academic researchers may be far more optimistic because their "sample" of studies comes from the published literature, which is skewed by publication bias. The hope of the nudge movement was, according to the Nobel Prize–winning psychologist Daniel Kahneman, that nudges can achieve "medium-sized gains by nano-sized invest-ments."[29] Alas, we have seen reasons to doubt that the medium-sized gains are so easy to come by. And not only that: Many scholars have recently been worried that the investments are often not quite as nano-sized as billed.[30] And even when they *are* shown to work successfully in initial trials, i-frame interventions are rarely scaled up, as would be required if they had any hope of making a dent on the social problems they target.[31]

If these were the only downsides of nudges, they might appear to be harmless at worst. But there is a more serious problem: They "crowd out" support for (and indeed attention to) much needed, more effective conventional system-changing policies. By promis-ing cheap and quick solutions to policy problems, diverse research suggests, the enormous publicity surrounding nudges convinces people that more fundamental policy change is unnecessary or at least not a top priority. At least, that's how the nudge agenda is often interpreted. As *If Books Could Kill* podcaster Shamshiri com-ments, nudge is "a framework for policy analysis where nothing large ever happens."[32] Hobbes responds, "Yes, . . . They don't want the government to do government stuff." In Chapter 1 we discuss a number of studies documenting this pattern.

Misattributing problems to individual weakness rather than to systemic factors has the further effect of implicitly blaming individuals—and encouraging them to blame themselves—for their inability to swim against powerful currents they have little hope of resisting.[33] Beyond the misery it causes by making people feel that they are the architects of their own problems, blaming the victim has myriad other consequences that we will discuss, such as contributing to the sky-high rates of eating disorders in the US population, and intensifying the stigma among drug addicts, which among other consequences leads many to hide their addic-tion and avoid asking for help.

For the two of us, as behavioral scientists, the really bad news is that the behavioral sciences, including some of our own work, may inadvertently be making matters worse. Starting with the premise that the human mind is inherently fallible and frail, many behavioral economists and psychologists (including ourselves) jumped on the i-frame bandwagon, enthusiastically attempting to find individual-level solutions to deal with society's woes. There is clear value to such efforts: Getting the "ergonomics" of policies right—designing them to go with the grain of human psychology—is as important when crafting government policy as it is when designing cell phones, computers, or aircraft cockpits. But, as we will argue, by adopting the i-frame, behavioral scientists have drawn attention away from the s-frame, where the real problems, and potential solutions, lie, and, as we discuss in detail in Chapter 9, have diverted huge amounts of researchers'—and to a lesser extent policymakers'—time, effort, and attention to interventions with demonstrably small impacts.

———

This book is divided into two parts. In Part One, we document how a strategy of misdirection—a diversion from the s-frame to the i-frame—has been applied methodically by powerful corporate interests across a wide variety of issues, from climate change to the obesity crisis, from poverty in retirement to the growth of inequality, and more. We describe different aspects of psychology that make this strategy work so well. We explain how well-intentioned researchers—including ourselves for more years than we care to remember—can get swept up in i-frame thinking and devote their time and attention to proposing misguided and ineffective solutions to problems. Indeed, psychologists and behavioral economists like us are particularly vulnerable to thinking that solving the world's problems depends on understanding, and perhaps helping to improve, individual human thinking and decision-making—because that is what we study.

In Part Two, we try to make sense of how we got into the situation of rampant dysfunction documented in Part One. We recount how the transition from the Great Society vision of government gave way to an antigovernment perspective—funded by powerful corporate interests and exemplified by the "Chicago school" of neoclassical economics—which culminated in the election of Ronald Reagan as president in 1980. The resulting "i-frame ideology" eschews all reforms and regulations and champions individual self-reliance and responsibility. A government-mandated cure, we're told, will always be worse than the disease.

We then document how the new discipline of behavioral economics, which emerged in the early 1980s as a reaction to the assumptions and policy positions of the Chicago school, ended up proposing equally individualistic solutions to public problems in lockstep with those advocated by the Chicago school.

We focus primarily on the US and, to a lesser degree, on the UK, as well as on other fairly rich nations possessing democratic political systems (indeed, the vulnerability of democracy to powerful interests will be a key theme). This is the geographic territory where we have direct experience and where behavioral science has been most extensively applied to public policy. Some of the problems we discuss, especially the cost of health care and the crisis in retirement savings, are particular to, and particularly acute in, the US. For readers outside the US and UK, we hope that both the contrasts and the parallels with their home country will be instructive.

This book does not attempt to outline detailed policy programs for each area we discuss; we don't have the expertise to do so in any case. But finding the right policies typically is rarely the main obstacle to change. In many areas, there is a fair degree of consensus among experts about the right direction for policy. But behavioral economics and psychology nonetheless have a crucial role to play, both by refocusing our collective attention on how and why so many social, political, and economic "games" have been rigged, and by helping to design, communicate, and implement s-frame policies that "change the game" while "going with the grain" of human nature.

S-frame change is essential, but it is no panacea. Yes, systemic solutions are the only way to make progress on a host of problems, but systems can and do go horribly wrong, leading to monstrous regimes, collective delusions, and human destruction and suffering on a vast scale, as history amply illustrates. In fact, seeing exactly how such systems have gone horribly wrong in the past only underlines the power of the s-frame—and the importance of getting it right.

Part One

FLAWED PLAYERS OR RIGGED GAMES?

Chapter 1

THE CORPORATE BOOT THAT MADE THE CARBON FOOTPRINT

[The fossil fuel interests are] deflecting attention away from the needed systemic solutions or policy solutions to [focus instead on] individual behavior. "Oh, it's just about us becoming vegans and not flying anymore." Well, individual action is important, it's part of the solution, but it's not a substitute for the needed systemic changes, changes that the fossil fuel industry, frankly, doesn't want to see happen.

—Michael Mann, author of *The New Climate War*, interviewed by Jeff Goodell in *Rolling Stone* magazine

In the early 2000s, the world's second-largest non-state-owned oil company, BP, began a massively funded media campaign—with the tagline "Beyond Petroleum"—to improve its environmental image. For years, BP and its fossil fuel allies had supported climate-change-doubting academics and mounted PR campaigns to discredit legitimate climate scientists, trying (often successfully, despite a mountain of evidence) to sow doubts about the reality of climate change. That was the *old* climate war. But, as documented by Michael Mann, in his book *The New Climate War*, in the face of an onslaught of climate-driven catastrophes that were unlikely to be ignored or misinterpreted by the general public, the oil companies shifted gears.[1] Rather than opposing climate science directly, they worked to reframe the problem of carbon reduction as a matter of individual responsibility. This is the *new* climate war: Promote the idea that addressing climate change is a problem of behavior change for each citizen, not a problem requiring systemic reform.

The "Beyond Petroleum" televised advertisements featured a baritone voice intoning *Brave New World*–reminiscent phrases like "Beyond darkness, there is light," "Beyond fear, there is courage," and "Beyond power, responsibility." The keystone of the campaign, however, was the development and marketing of the personal "carbon footprint"—a measure of the total amount of greenhouse gases produced by an individual.[2] BP developed its own carbon footprint calculator, which nearly three hundred thousand people completed in 2004, and the idea spread like a climate-change-induced wildfire.[3] Media organizations, governmental agencies, and even environmental groups such as The Nature Conservancy have all provided their constituents with access to carbon footprint calculators to help them reduce their impact on the planet.[4]

Examined superficially, BP's campaign seems benign and constructive. If we could just motivate people to decrease their personal carbon footprints, the implicit logic suggests, we could together substantially mitigate the problem of climate change. Indeed, behavioral scientists have stepped up to the task, most prominently with "green-energy nudges." The most popular of these involves showing people graphs that compare their own home energy use with that of their neighbors.[5] In a high-profile TED talk given in the year before he became the British prime minister, David Cameron extolled the virtues of this intervention.[6] "The best way to get someone to cut their electricity bill," according to Cameron, "is to show them their own spending, to show them what their neighbors are spending, and then show what an energy-conscious neighbor is spending." The apparent virtues of such an approach—which seemed simple, unobtrusive, and cheap—jibed nicely with Cameron's professed conservative values. "Behavioral economics," he continued, "can transform people's behavior in a way that all the bullying and all the information and all the badgering from a government cannot possibly achieve."

By "bullying" and "badgering," Cameron meant traditional regulatory policies such as mandated energy efficiency standards or targeted taxes designed to discourage energy use. The most prominent of these measures in the context of climate change are a carbon tax and a cap-and-trade policy. A carbon tax sets a fixed price on carbon emissions, making it costly to pollute and therefore incentivizing businesses and consumers to reduce their carbon footprint through market-driven decisions. A cap-and-trade system, by contrast, sets a total emissions limit (cap) and allows companies to buy and sell allowances, also creating a financial incentive for reducing emissions efficiently. Both policies aim to reduce greenhouse gas emissions by making pollution more costly, but a carbon tax provides price certainty, while cap-and-trade ensures a specific emissions reduction target. Both policies generate substantial public revenue, and both also encourage investment in technologies to reduce carbon emissions.

Indeed, Cameron seemed to suggest that such measures might not be necessary at all. Behavioral economics is thus portrayed as providing a different, effective, and less onerous route to help people lower their fuel bills and thus reduce their personal carbon footprints—a notion that BP had masterfully elevated to a central focus in the climate change debate.

The oil giant's "Beyond Petroleum" campaign may seem constructive or, at worst, innocuous. But Mann's analysis suggests that it was in fact a clever exercise in *framing*: deliberately describing a problem in a particular way in order to shift the debate and shape the solutions that come to mind.[7] BP's focus on individuals' carbon footprints encourages us to see the problem of carbon reduction as one of individual responsibility that should be solved

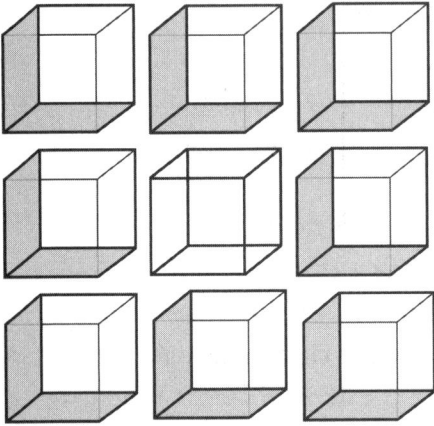

Figure 1.1. Nine boxes viewed from below.

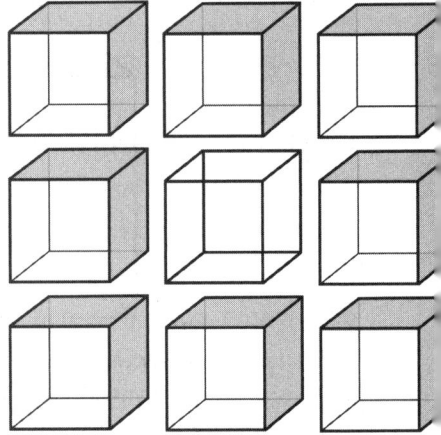

Figure 1.2. Nine boxes viewed from above.

by individual action. The trick works because of a key feature of human perception that is well illustrated by the "Necker cube," a visual illusion beloved by psychologists.

So named because it was created by Swiss scientist Louis Albert Necker in 1832, the Necker cube illustrates how easily our perception can flip between two entirely different interpretations. When Necker's ambiguous cube is depicted among clearly oriented versions, our brain is "lured" into interpreting it in a way that aligns with the dominant perspective of all the neighboring cubes.

To see the effect, first consider the nine boxes in Figure 1.1. Notice how all the cubes share the same orientation—they look as though you're viewing them from below and slightly to the left, with the boxes angled to the right. Now consider the nine boxes of Figure 1.2. Here, you'll see that the cubes are again uniformly oriented, but now they appear as though you're viewing them from above, with the boxes angled to the left. So far, everything seems straightforward. But now take a closer look at the central transparent box in each set. Surprisingly, although we interpret the two sets of cubes as very different 3D objects, these central cubes are actually the very same 2D image.

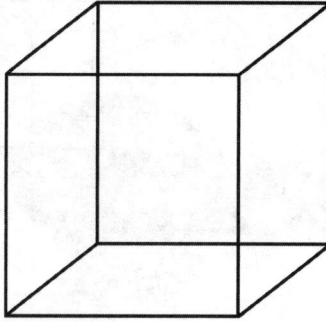

Figure 1.3. The Necker cube. In Figures 1.1 and 1.2 we see one 3D interpretation or the other (aligning with the 3D shapes of the surrounding boxes). But if you look at the Necker cube for a sustained period, you will likely find your interpretation "flipping" rather unpredictably. But we are only ever aware of one interpretation at a time.

What happens if we consider the Necker cube in isolation (see Figure 1.3)? Now you find that one or the other of these two possible 3D cubes will pop into your consciousness alternately, and somewhat unpredictably. When we shift between interpretations (the famous "Gestalt switch"), we have the feeling that something in the image must be changing—but the lines remain exactly the same. All that has changed, of course, is our interpretation. Oddly, though, when looking at the arrays of boxes, we typically have no idea that the central item *has* any other interpretation—it just seems unequivocally to align with the other boxes.

What these observations reveal is, on reflection, rather startling: Our brain seems unable to "see" the world in more than one way at a time—even when, as here, two potential ways of seeing are entirely possible. If we see one cube, the other vanishes; when the second interpretation bobs into consciousness, the first is obliterated. And if we are "lured" to latch onto one interpretation (as when we look at one of the surrounding cubes), the tendency to spontaneously see the other possible interpretation is suppressed. Indeed, if we're looking at the Necker cubes without much attention, we may not realize that another interpretation is even possible.

This phenomenon doesn't work just for cubes, of course. It's the same story for the interpretation of any kind of sensory

Figure 1.4. The famous duck-rabbit, a staple of psychological and philosophical discussion for more than a century. ("Kaninchen und Ente"—
rabbit and duck—first appeared in the October 23, 1892, issue of
Fliegende Blätter, a German humor magazine.)

information. Psychologists and artists have created all manner of
images that can, for example, be alternately seen as either ducks
or rabbits (see Figure 1.4, a duck facing left, or rabbit facing right).
Again, crucially, we only see one interpretation at a time; and
unless prompted to look carefully, we will think the first interpretation we see is the only possible interpretation.

We needn't rely only on visual examples. When you see the letters B-O-W, you might think of a word that rhymes with *cow* or
flow, but not both simultaneously; similarly, the letters B-A-R may
conjure up pubs, lawyers, iron rods, chocolate bars, salad bars,
sandbars, restrictions, and many more things—but only slowly,
one after the other.

Economists have explored a parallel phenomenon. In their
paper "Using Models to Persuade," Harvard's Joshua Schwartzstein and Adi Sunderam note that persuasion often doesn't involve
providing new data to make a point, but instead involves providing a "model" of the world—an interpretation of known data that
highlights a relationship between outcomes and data in a way
that leads the audience to adopt the interpretation favored by the

persuader.[8] As illustrated in Figure 1.5, the same bunch of dots plotting a company's performance over time can be used to argue for a variety of different trajectories; an ambiguous cloud of dots can seem to fit a variety of different models of the world—once we see the trajectory, we find ourselves easily convinced that our interpretation "emerges" from the dots themselves. Indeed, we find it difficult even to consider other interpretations of the data once a pattern has been suggested to us. Schwartzstein and Sunderam use their perspective to make sense of diverse examples of persuasion—e.g., so-called technical analysis of stocks, and methods that lawyers use to influence jurors.[9] The trick, in a nutshell, is, when faced with ambiguous information, to provide a story that alters our interpretation of the data—without our awareness. The possibility that there might be other, equally good stories/interpretations simply doesn't occur to us.

Researchers have extrapolated from these and many other examples to conclude that the human mind struggles to entertain more than one interpretation at a time of *anything*—including, of course, questions of politics and policy. And this really matters. In particular, it means that one interpretation of a policy problem will tend to *block* our mental access to other possible interpretations.

LINEAR   **ACCELERATING**   **DECELERATING**

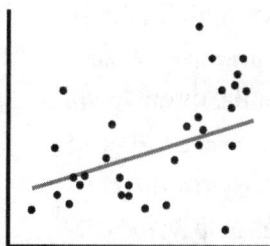

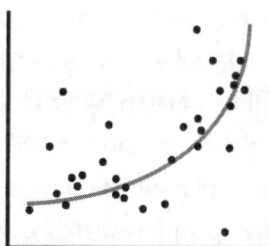

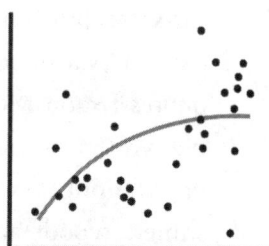

"Seems to be increasing steadily"   "Help, it's out of control!"   "Phew, it's tapering off"

Figure 1.5. When the data are highly ambiguous, almost any pattern can seem plausible. This example is inspired by a cartoon in the online comic *xkcd: A Webcomic of Romance, Sarcasm, Math, and Language*. (Randall Munroe, "Curve-Fitting Methods," *xkcd* no. 2048, March 5, 2019, https://xkcd.com/2048/.)

This provides a potentially powerful way to change people's minds without needing to resort to evidence or argument. To stop people "seeing a duck," we don't need to persuade them that no duck is present; we just need to find a way to make them see a rabbit—and the "duck" will vanish, at least as long as the rabbit is in view. This trick is known as "framing." By making one interpretation more salient, other interpretations are suppressed. Sometimes the effect is only temporary. But in other cases it is not. Once we've taken the path, we can walk for many miles before realizing we are heading in entirely the wrong direction—or never realize it at all. Once we are convinced by a clever framing trick that the person at the other end of the phone line is a police officer and not a scammer, we may unthinkingly give away our bank details; once we have succumbed to a conspiracy theory, the very idea that we have been duped may seem inconceivable.

The same phenomenon works, we suggest, for the i-frame and s-frame: Presenting a problem such as climate change as one that was caused—and can be fixed—by individual actions can block out thoughts of the role of systemic factors.

———

It is not just BP that has been focusing on individual responsibility for the climate crisis and deflecting attention from the radical systematic changes required—changes that will entail almost entirely phasing out fossil fuels. A 2024 piece in *Fortune* magazine quotes Exxon Mobil CEO Darren Woods to the effect that "people who are generating the emissions need to be aware . . . and pay the price," seemingly placing the blame squarely on the consumer. Woods adds that people must "be willing to pay for carbon reduction, because today we have opportunities to make fuels with lower carbon, but people aren't willing to spend the money to do that."[10] It seems that the "people" really need to step up—and pay up. According to Woods's account, the fossil fuel industry is willing, but largely powerless, to help. In short, Exxon Mobil portrays carbon reduction as an i-frame problem, while lobbying tirelessly against the s-frame regulations and international agreements that may actually reduce carbon emissions (and, of course, wreck the fossil fuel industry's business model), such as innovation and deployment of low-carbon energy and energy efficiency measures, powerful new regulations, and a carbon tax.[11]

The same pattern of disingenuously blaming the consumer for the status quo is revealed by systematic analysis of Exxon Mobil's internal and external documents by science historians Naomi Oreskes (whom we will meet later) and Geoffrey Supran.[12] Particularly telling illustrations are the company's "advertorials." For example, one in 2008 suggested that the "cars and trucks we drive aren't just vehicles, they're opportunities to solve the world's energy and environmental challenges." Another, in 2007, offered readers "simple steps" to combating climate change: "Be smart about electricity use"; "Heat and cool your home efficiently"; "Improve your gas mileage"; "Check your home's greenhouse gas emissions" using an online calculator. The oil companies present themselves as facilitating, and participating in, the fight against human-induced global warming. In the case of BP, its carbon footprint calculator included personal appeals, such as "It's time to go on a low carbon diet."[13]

But by continually presenting the challenge of combating climate change as a problem for individual citizens, the fossil fuel companies helped frame the conversation on their terms.[14] And they found unwitting allies in the media, even the more progressive media. *The Guardian* and *The New York Times* have published numerous articles focusing on how individual behavior—decisions about what to eat, how and where to travel, and how to heat and power your home—can combat climate change.[15]

We are not saying that the use of carbon footprints as a metric is misguided in every context; clearly, the measurement of individual carbon output is in many cases useful for academic researchers, governments, companies, and individuals. But by framing the problem of climate change as one of shrinking individual climate footprints, we may indeed be distracting ourselves from exploring systemic changes that are needed.

We've fallen into this trap ourselves. In consulting and advisory work, Nick, in particular, has spent years thinking about what kinds of interventions can help individuals reduce their use of heating, insulate their homes, and shift to low-carbon transport and more plant-based diets.[16] Upon reflection, however, we doubt that the problem of reducing carbon emissions can be solved or even noticeably alleviated by nudging individual behavior— whether these interventions involve giving people better or more transparent information, making them more aware of their own consumption and how they compare to their neighbors, or just defaulting them into buying green energy or auto-enrolling them into other climate-friendly programs.

Depressingly, in line with the pattern we mentioned in the Introduction, many nudges that seem at first to move the needle on climate change do a lot less than their proponents promise. For instance, consider the case of a "default" nudge, studied in a recent and impressively large-scale field trial in which Swiss consumers and businesses were defaulted into receiving electricity from renewable sources unless they actively opted out. At first sight, this nudge looked pretty effective (if rather heavy-handed): 85 percent of Swiss consumers and 75 percent of Swiss businesses stuck with this tariff over many years, despite the extra cost.[17] The authors of the paper evaluating the field trial estimate that nudging customers through this "green default" could yield very large carbon savings, especially if the program was scaled up.

In an optimistically titled commentary on this research ("Green Defaults Can Combat Climate Change"), Cass Sunstein (one of the authors of *Nudge*, and a frequent collaborator with George) directly contrasted i- and s-frame approaches to fighting climate change: "It has long been thought that to reduce environmental harm, the best approach is an economic incentive, perhaps a corrective tax. In recent years, however, increasing attention has been given to non-monetary interventions including 'nudges,' such as information disclosure, warnings, uses of social norms, and default rules. A potentially promising intervention would automatically enroll people in green energy, subject to opt-out."[18]

From an s-frame perspective, however, it becomes clear that the impact of such policies will be slight, at best. When a newly defaulted consumer switches to green energy, the system does not respond by instantaneously producing more green energy. Instead, someone in a back office (or nowadays probably a piece of accounting software) simply changes a spreadsheet so that existing green energy is reallocated to the newly green consumer— so one consumer gets greener, another gets browner, and there is no overall impact on the energy mix.[19] So, contrary to Sunstein's optimistic appraisal, this type of i-frame intervention does not, in reality, provide a real alternative to the s-frame regulatory and fiscal measures that are already decarbonizing the power systems in several countries (including, for example, the UK, France, and the Scandinavian countries—and in the US, the Biden administration's curiously named Inflation Reduction Act pursued this approach).

If defaults—arguably the most iconic, and effective, type of nudge—have limited potential to combat climate change, results are arguably still more dispiriting for other types of climate-related nudges, such as having people make commitments to change their behavior, providing people with diverse kinds of information (e.g., about the impact of their activities on the climate), and providing real-time feedback about energy use.[20] A comprehensive recent survey of eighty-three different randomized controlled trials (the type of experimental field trials often viewed as a gold standard of scientific rigor) of climate-change-targeting nudges of all sorts, comprising over three million individual observations, concludes that nudges "promote climate change mitigation to a very small degree while the intervention lasts, with no evidence of sustained positive effects once the intervention ends."[21] Our behaviors are determined, in large part, by the complex economic and social systems of which we are a part—we don't have a lot of wiggle room, it seems. And when a nudge "wiggles" our behavior momentarily, its impact doesn't last long.

Beyond the paucity of their likely cumulative effects, climate change nudges provide perhaps the best illustration of another pitfall of nudges—their propensity to "crowd out" support for more substantive policies. A series of experiments by George and his colleagues David Hagmann and Emily Ho illustrates this point: They show that merely alerting people (including policymakers in one study) to the potential of implementing an i-frame intervention (the green-energy nudge, discussed earlier in this chapter, which defaults residential consumers into a renewable energy plan) reduces support for more substantive policies (such as a carbon tax).[22] The research not only documented the "crowding out" phenomenon but also revealed how it works: The green-energy nudge gives people the false hope that the problem of climate change can be addressed without imposing costlier, but immeasurably more effective, policies. Interestingly, this effect can be counteracted with information. When research participants were informed of how small an overall impact the green-energy nudge was likely to have, the crowd-out effect disappeared.

In a separate line of work, social scientist Seth Werfel provides powerful evidence that these effects apply in the real world. Households in Japan that were randomly selected to report the actions they took to save energy were less supportive of a carbon tax, and those who reported being particularly conscientious about energy saving became especially unsupportive.[23] The paper concluded that the effect is "driven by an increase in the perceived importance of individual actions relative to government regulation." When people take individual responsibility for a problem, it seems, they are ironically less likely to support the kind of systemic change that could actually solve it.

The idea that potentially well-meaning, but ineffective, initiatives can crowd out more substantive interventions is also well illustrated by the enormous growth in "ESG investing" (in companies that meet Environmental, Social, and Governance criteria, aiming for strong financial returns while promoting sustainability and ethical practices). Perhaps the most forceful takedown of ESG as currently practiced by large financial institutions was provided by Tariq Fancy, the former chief investment officer for sustainable investing at BlackRock, who left the company in 2019 and uploaded his explosive story *The Secret Diary of a Sustainable Investor* to the internet two years later.[24] Fancy argues convincingly that ESG investing has little to no direct impact—just shuffling who owns which assets, rather than actually making businesses greener.[25] But, he argues, it plays a crucial role in distracting attention away from the sweeping systemic changes that governments need to enact. And it gives the spurious impression that businesses—or individual investors, through their impact on businesses—can handle environmental challenges and that government action is less urgent or perhaps even largely unnecessary.

In a comment that echoes the themes of this book, Fancy notes, "Many business leaders would no doubt respond that regulation is the correct answer in theory, but it's not possible in the real world. Why? Because it's politically impossible to get anything done right now, especially in the US." So, the suggestion goes, we should look to business to lead the way, if politics is deadlocked. Fancy continues, "While it seems like a fair point on the surface, it's disingenuous for business leaders to argue that they're the best option available today if the ideal method, recommended by the experts, is actively being blocked by those same business leaders through misleading marketing campaigns and political spending and lobbying behind the scenes." This is the sleight of hand in action—focusing our attention on the i-frame (purportedly helping individual investors wanting to invest sustainably) while lobbying at the s-frame to ensure that real progress toward sustainability remains logjammed.[26]

The main problem Fancy identifies is, in our terms, "crowding out" the political pressure and policymaker time that could, in theory, be spent pursuing systemic changes.[27] Fancy also reports an experiment he conducted in which three thousand people from the US and Canada were asked whether government or business should lead the way on sustainability. In one experimental condition, they were first shown headlines about corporate environmental and social initiatives; in the other, they were asked the question without first looking at any headlines. Canadians, perhaps already accustomed to the benefit of greater regulations, chose the government option in both conditions. But, Fancy reports, "there was a large and statistically significant difference in the US. Exposure to the headlines made people 17 percent more likely to say that business, not government, will lead the way in building a more sustainable economy."[28]

The impact of such framing effects on individual citizens may not be the most important type of crowding out. Potentially more important is that politicians, government policymakers, campaigners, journalists, and academic researchers focus their limited time and attention on ineffective i-frame measures at the expense of s-frame policy changes that could really help address social ills. These s-frame policies need as much focus from all sides as possible because the changes required are often large, and choosing the right ones, and implementing them successfully, is enormously difficult. While changing the system, if done correctly, can make a huge positive impact, it could also be ineffective or even counterproductive if done incorrectly. Implementing, monitoring, and adjusting systemic changes so they work as designed requires careful analysis. Building a coalition of support that can make change politically possible itself is a major challenge. So we need to focus as much as possible on getting s-frame change right, and distractions that focus our collective attention and resources on ineffective "alternatives" need to be avoided. Certainly, as academic researchers, we have found our own attention on public policy issues substantially "crowded out" by a focus on diagnosing and correcting individual behavior, and we, Nick and George, are hardly alone. Whole swaths of academics, policy researchers, funders, journalists, politicians, and more have been focusing on finding i-frame solutions to problems that, we would argue, can only be solved by s-frame reform.

Not all our colleagues are convinced that prompting people to think about the i-frame actually does undercut support for s-frame measures. One paper that seemed to argue the opposite point— "Moderating Spillover: Focusing on Personal Sustainable Behavior Rarely Hinders and Can Boost Climate Policy Support"—was written by Gregg Sparkman and his colleagues. In that study, the researchers encouraged some participants to think through their own pro-environmental behaviors—and in some cases also asked them to think about how these behaviors related to their values— while gauging their support for a state-level carbon tax (which was framed as imposing costs either on individuals or on industry). Strikingly, echoing the finding of Werfel and contradicting the paper's title, when the carbon tax was framed as costly to individuals, the authors observed "crowding out": "Participants who reflected on their sustainable actions and were shown a tax framed as having costs fall on the individual had lower support for the carbon tax as compared to participants in the no reflection control."

A second point made by our critics is the correct observation that if you look across people at their support for different policies, those supporting nudges targeting climate change also tend to support *more* substantive policies, such as a carbon tax; in academic parlance, there is a positive correlation between supporting climate-targeting nudges and substantive policies. It is surprising that critics who have made this observation, most of whom are behavioral or social scientists, seem to be ignoring perhaps the single most common correction that social scientists make to lay (commonplace) beliefs: *Correlation does not equal causation.* This applies to the positive relationship between support for nudges on the one hand, and taxes and regulations aimed at mitigating climate change on the other. People who believe in climate change and think it poses a major threat are most likely to support *any* intervention targeting the problem, including both nudges and substantive policies.[29] However, when you assess causality by *manipulating* people's awareness of the potential to nudge climate-related behavior in a rigorous randomized experiment, the most consistent finding is that awareness of nudges actually tends to *reduce* support for the more substantive policies.

So there is a real danger that merely *entertaining* the possibility of i-frame interventions can weaken the impetus behind s-frame change. As usual in the behavioral sciences, where iron laws are vanishingly rare, there will no doubt be nuances and exceptions. Indeed, it is entirely possible that there are some circumstances in which i-frame interventions to, for example, encourage people to make small actions to help reduce climate change (e.g., improving their home insulation, buying an electric car, and so on) might actually *increase* their support for wider policy changes. According to many influential theories in social psychology, for example, people might reason something like this: "Here I am buying an electric car (perhaps actually caused by some imagined, but unusually effective, nudge). So I guess I must be the kind of person who cares about the environment. If so, I must (for consistency) be the kind of person who supports tough government action on climate. OK then—I'm all in favor of a carbon tax."

This might seem fanciful (and indeed, it has not, to our knowledge, been demonstrated in any domain related to climate policy), but psychologists have created many ingenious experiments showing that people use their choices to infer their own beliefs or attitudes according to this kind of logic. Nonetheless, the current state of the evidence strongly suggests that the opposite pattern is far more common: The main impact of highlighting the i-frame is obscuring the s-frame.[30]

In any case, highlighting the i-frame doesn't just divert attention away from the s-frame in the mind of the individual. As noted above, the more pressing issue is the huge diversion of time and attention on the part of academics, journalists, and policymakers. Social and behavioral scientists trying to understand and address society's problems have finite time and grant funding; journalists focusing on social problems have a fairly fixed budget of column inches; and space on political and policymakers' agendas is hotly contested. In all these areas, focusing on i-frame solutions almost inevitably squeezes out consideration of the s-frame. And that is surely what the corporations promoting the i-frame to the public and politicians are hoping to achieve.[31]

The trick of shifting the public's attention from the system to the individual can seem subtle in the case of BP's "Beyond Petroleum" campaign. But other industry-led efforts, such as the "wedge campaigns" that pit individual action against collective action, are far cruder. As Mann writes, "Dividers have sought to target influential experts and public figures in the climate arena as 'hypocrites' by accusing them of hedonistic lifestyles entailing huge carbon footprints."[32] For instance, a subset of attendees of the COP26 summit in Glasgow were attacked in the media for arriving in private jets and producing "over 1,000 tons of CO^2."[33]

One thousand tons is, of course, a drop in the ocean compared to the billions of tons of carbon dioxide emitted each year worldwide. Linking climate advocates with their carbon footprints uses an individualistic focus to discredit those advocating for systemic reform, branding them as "climate hypocrites"—a powerful tactic.[34] As Amy Westervelt, a climate writer, comments, "The strategy of shifting responsibility to the public . . . provides a purity test that no climate activist can possibly pass."[35]

The people with the power and influence to change the system are unlikely to be living entirely sustainable lifestyles on remote islands—so almost everyone pushing for reform can be summarily dismissed, or at least tainted with hypocrisy. Indeed, fossil fuel industry allies have actively backed efforts to "carbon shame" climate scientists and activists for driving, flying, or eating meat.[36]

Not only that: Even if we successfully motivate many individuals to make supposedly climate-friendly choices, market-level effects often undercut well-intentioned individual action. To take a simple illustration, let's return to the green-energy nudge discussed earlier and raise a further problem with it. Suppose that a person or company switches to a green-energy supplier. This marginally increases the demand for green energy and thus slightly pushes up its market price, while at the same time reducing (equally slightly) the demand for so-called brown energy (generated by fossil fuels), the price of which falls. But now that brown energy is cheaper, those who *are* happy to use polluting energy are likely to use more of it—so the use of brown energy remains largely unaffected. Thus, the impact of an individual's green choice is "dampened" by the operation of the market.

Just how powerful these dampening effects can be is illustrated in important recent theoretical work by economists Marc Kaufmann, Peter Andre, and Botond Kőszegi.[37] Their analysis shows that consumers who want to further prosocial ends—e.g., by not eating meat, by reducing flying, or by buying secondhand clothing—may have little to no effect *when they are part of a market*. Suppose, to take an extreme example, that *all* consumers care about the harm they do to the environment (what, in economics, is called fully "internalizing" the costs of their actions on society). One of those consumers choosing to do the "right thing," for example by not flying, doesn't just reduce carbon emissions directly. It also *reduces the cost of flying*. And this in turn will change the equilibrium behavior of other socially conscious consumers. Now that flying is cheaper, consumers (whether socially conscious or not) will fly slightly more than they would have done (everyone is sensitive to price to some degree, after all). Worse, to the extent that they understand this, a fully rational consumer would be less liable to "do the right thing" in the first place, since they would take account of the fact that their own restraint will duly be dampened. Dispiritingly, the dampening effect still applies even if everyone wants to be green.[38] While these extreme conclusions are undeniably dependent on the specific assumptions the authors incorporate into their model, at a minimum this theoretical exercise highlights the importance of taking account of market-level effects when predicting the impact of individual actions.

On the positive side, Kaufmann, Andre, and Kőszegi show that traditional s-frame policies such as carbon taxes and cap-and-trade schemes can effectively accomplish the goals that individual action cannot (indeed, their analysis helps to clarify how to design these schemes). Their conclusion is that old-fashioned "social planning" approaches to externalities, such as regulating pollution emissions, are, at least in these contexts, more effective than relying on an individualistic approach.

The very effectiveness of carbon tax and cap-and-trade schemes (which discourage hydrocarbon extraction by increasing the cost of carbon-intensive goods and services) is, of course, why the fossil fuel industry wants to distract us from supporting such interventions.[39] For fossil fuel producers, having their opponents distracted by unworkable solutions while fossil fuel extraction continues as usual is the desired (and, so far, largely realized) outcome.

———

By focusing on the individual, we are thinking of the problem in entirely the wrong way—indeed, just as the architects of BP's marketing campaign wanted us to. Individual behavior matters, of course, and we should each seek to play our part in solving the global challenge of averting irreversible climate change. But cajoling, informing, or nudging the players will be hopelessly ineffectual unless we radically change the rules of the game—and the rules of the game that govern climate change are dysfunctional in ways that by now we understand quite well. The rules are not dysfunctional by accident; they have been shaped by the relentless political campaign funding, lobbying, and misinformation from the companies whose profits, and indeed long-term future, depend on this dysfunction.

There is a scientific and policy consensus concerning what needs to change. A series of global agreements, from the 1997 Kyoto Protocol to the 2016 Paris Agreement and beyond, have set out a road map for change—though admittedly one that is persistently too vague and that lacks "teeth." And individual nations and blocs have also set more aggressive targets, now including the UK, the EU, and, briefly under President Biden, the US, pledging to get to net zero greenhouse gas emissions by 2050. With the right regulations and political will, this is entirely possible.

To succeed, governments will need to be extremely active; leaving progress "to the market" alone will be hopelessly inadequate. Key measures will surely include (among many others): massive subsidies for renewable sources of energy; tightening regulatory standards on products and manufacturing; subsidizing insulation and tightening building standards; "carbon border adjustments" (to avoid nations merely driving carbon emissions overseas, with no net overall effect); a shift away from heavily meat-based diets; preserving and extending forests; large government investments (alongside private money) in research and development of green technologies; and large cross-national subsidies so that developing nations benefit, rather than lose, by adopting these policies.[40] Extending carbon cap-and-trade schemes, or imposing a sufficient carbon tax to force polluters to pay for the damage their products cause, is likely to be an important part of the mix (though politically challenging).

Governments also have to *reverse* lots of current policies: They need to eliminate subsidies for fossil fuel exploration, extraction, and use across the world; stop issuing licenses for new exploration and drilling; and eliminate the plethora of perverse incentives rife throughout the energy system. Let's take just two well-known examples. In the US, there is a long history of subsidies for light trucks (and SUVs, crossovers, and vans) that have led them to dominate US roads.[41] In the UK, the costs of decarbonizing the energy network are loaded onto electricity bills (which are increasingly green), but not onto the bill for carbon-burning gas, thereby creating a huge obstacle for the vital rollout of heat pumps. And not only that: To achieve all this, governments will need to restrict the lobbying power of commercial and national interests (most obviously fossil fuel companies and oil-exporting countries) that benefit from slowing the green transition.

Many economic, technological, and financial indicators are starting to move in the right direction. Solar, wind, and battery technologies are growing on a steep exponential curve, and their costs are falling. Entrepreneurial opportunities are emerging across sectors, from the "circular economy" (which minimizes waste by keeping products, materials, and energy in use for as long as possible) to switching to more plant-based diets and finding a range of alternatives to meat, to negative-emissions technologies (whether simply increasing forest cover or the more speculative chemistry of direct air capture and storage), and many more.

Dispiritingly, lobbying power and other distortions of democratic processes (more on this in Part Two) have already proved all too powerful, especially in the US. Indeed, in the second Trump administration the fossil fuel industries and their allies have already begun to decisively shift the rules back in their favor, both domestically (following the ominous slogan "Drill, baby, drill") and internationally (by withdrawing from, and actively undermining, international climate agreements).[42]

It may turn out that our effort to combat climate change will be too little, too late; or against the odds, perhaps we may avoid disaster just in time.[43] It is clear that human ingenuity and cooperation have made astonishing progress in collectively addressing the problem of climate change. But there are powerful interests working hard to frustrate these efforts, and these may be gaining the upper hand. If we collectively fail to address the problem of climate change, human nature won't be to blame; blaming human nature would be like blaming a death by drowning on the human body's reliance on oxygen, while ignoring the role of the concrete shoes affixed to the victim's feet.

Chapter 2

OBESITY: BLAMING THE VICTIM

Americans need to be more active and take greater responsibility for their diets.

—Muhtar Kent, former CEO of Coca-Cola

In the spring of 2012, Michelle Obama appeared on the popular American reality television show *The Biggest Loser.* The show's contestants, who had struggled with obesity for years, managed over the course of a single television season to lose up to two hundred pounds by isolating themselves from their families, jobs, and routines and engaging in an unbelievably intense regimen of diet and exercise, competing to see which of them could shed the most weight. In one episode, the First Lady invited the show's remaining six contestants to come to the White House and work out with her, showing, in the words of *Forbes* magazine, "millions how they could not only improve their own lives, but those of their families and fellow Americans." At the time, such a can-do message fit in nicely with Mrs. Obama's "Let's Move!" initiative, an ambitious program that sought to reduce childhood obesity through a mix of educational efforts, behavioral interventions, and voluntary actions by food producers and retailers. Celebrity endorsements included a segment with Big Bird on *Sesame Street* and a song by Beyoncé called "Move Your Body." As viewers watched clips of the Biggest Losers doing squats and pushups alongside the First Lady, Mrs. Obama made her case for healthy lifestyle choices.

"The most important thing I can say to viewers out there is that no matter what age, size, gender, everyone can find a little bit of time to incorporate fitness and nutrition into their lives," said the First Lady, punctuating her message by repeating the catchphrase of *The Biggest Loser*: "No excuses!"

Alas, the sobering fact is that while "Let's Move!" may have inspired many families to exercise together and improve access to healthier foods, it does not look like it will come close to achieving its rather modest goal of reducing childhood obesity rates by 5 percent by 2030. The percentage of US children and adolescents who are obese has doubled since 1994 and has not, in fact, declined since Michelle Obama's campaign.[1] Today one in five American kids suffer from obesity, which is now the leading cause of preventable death worldwide. It's worth wondering, given the amount of attention and resources paid to the problem of obesity, why, exactly, the trend lines are still going in the wrong direction.

———

Every human act is a product of an individual—their physical and psychological makeup—and their circumstances. Yet individuals are usually easy to isolate and identify, while the circumstances they are embedded in are often shadowy, sprawling, and ill-defined. It is not surprising, then, that we tend primarily to see people as the authors of their own destinies, and to downplay the intangible forces of circumstance. This ubiquitous overweighting of character and underweighting of context in explaining behavior is probably the best-known phenomenon, and one of the most intensively studied phenomena, in social psychology—so much so that it is commonly referred to as the "fundamental attribution error."

Gustav Ichheiser, the social psychologist who first identified this tendency in 1949, wrote that "it is hardly possible to exaggerate the importance of this type of social blindness in the crisis of our age." Rather than appreciating the overwhelming and well-documented impact of people's circumstances on their wealth, health, and education, we tend to see these as stemming from individual traits, such as intelligence, morality, self-discipline, prudence, and resilience.

The fundamental attribution error is, in fact, fundamental to this book. It explains *why* we often incorrectly view complex s-frame problems through the i-frame: why we talk about the climate crisis as a failure of individual willpower, an inability "to curb our addiction" to fossil fuels; and, to turn back to the subject of this chapter, why we blame the obesity crisis on the eating and exercise habits of individuals. Taken to an extreme, the fundamental attribution error can lead us to blame the victim, and can lead victims to blame themselves. In one study that makes this point, research participants read a news story about a seven-year-old obese boy suffering either from severe (a heart attack) or mild (asthma) obesity-related health conditions. The child's obesity was framed as either highly or minimally preventable. Framing the obesity as preventable led to increased blame of the parents, both in terms of attributing the boy's obesity to the parents' behavior and in terms of increasing disgust, indignation, and contempt. This increased blame, in turn, led to more punitive attitudes toward the parents and greater support for public policies focusing on parental behavior.[2]

The rise in obesity has not been associated with a commensurate increase in social acceptance of the condition; "weight stigma" continues to be a significant cause of discrimination in employment, education, relationships, and medical care.[3] At a personal level, many people struggling with their weight suffer deep feelings of personal failure and guilt—blaming themselves for a problem largely outside their control. Indeed, misplaced blame, whether from society or from within, may be as destructive to human well-being as the health consequences of obesity itself.[4] In a cruel irony, the presence of "weight stigma" seems to amplify (rather than, as "common sense" might suggest, reduce) the prevalence of obesity itself.[5]

The result of focusing on individuals rather than on the food system is that citizens and governments focus their energies on trying to tweak individual behavior instead of targeting the food conglomerates and agricultural policies that have, in just a few generations, radically changed the way people eat—or, more accurately, the way people in some countries eat.

While obesity is a major public health concern worldwide, it is a particularly urgent problem in the United States, which ranks first in obesity among countries with populations greater than five million. In 2020, 42 percent of US adults met the criteria for obesity, and 74 percent were either overweight or obese. The obesity rate in the UK, while lower than that in the US, is still an alarming 28 percent, which puts it in third place in Europe, after Turkey and Malta.[6] Across Europe as a whole, 59 percent of the population is overweight, and, according to a 2022 World Health Organization study, obesity is causing 1.2 million deaths annually.[7]

Some countries have managed to escape this epidemic: Japan has an obesity rate of 4 percent, South Korea 5 percent, and China 6 percent.[8] France and Italy—two countries famous for their rich diets and food cultures—have obesity rates around 20 percent, high enough to be problematic, yet half that of the US.

The United States wasn't always an outlier. Through the 1960s and 1970s, obesity rates in the US were no different from those in other countries—around 12 percent. But in the 1980s they began a precipitous rise.

Almost as striking as the differences in obesity rates from one country to the next is the relationship between education and income levels and obesity *within* individual countries. In the US, for example, the obesity rate is close to 40 percent among those without a college degree, compared with 28 percent among those with a degree; similarly, the obesity rate is approximately 40 percent among those in the lower two-thirds of the income distribution and 32 percent among those in the highest third. While these differences are substantial, the high rates even among the educated and affluent attest to the difficulty of maintaining a healthy diet for just about everyone. This is at odds with the pattern in many other parts of the world. Usually, obesity tends to be concentrated among the poor in rich countries, and among the rich in poor countries.[9] When countries transition from poor to rich, the concentration of obesity tends to shift from the "relatively rich" to the "relatively poor" in line with this pattern.

Corporations tend to attribute obesity to individual limitations, as Muhtar Kent, the former CEO of Coca-Cola, did when he said people needed to "take more responsibility" for their diet and exercise choices. Many politicians sound the same note. As George W. Bush announced in a speech to the Dallas YMCA in 2003, "We have a problem when people don't exercise and eat bad food. Obesity can cause serious health problems, like heart disease and diabetes. . . . We must reverse the trend, and we know how to do it. It's exercise and good dieting."[10]

Behavioral economists, too, have tended to attribute obesity to individual factors, and specifically to a tendency called *present bias*, whereby people make decisions that are inherently shortsighted, focusing on short-term gains and downplaying long-term costs. According to the present-bias account of obesity, the problem arises because the pleasures of eating are immediate, while the costs (in terms of, say, ill health) are delayed. Present bias similarly deters those who find exercise unpleasant from doing it in the present; many of us feel we'd rather work out later, which effectively means that we never or rarely get around to it. Present bias provides a neat, simple—individualistic—explanation for why we overeat, underexercise, and are obese.

The behavioral economist's perspective on obesity is understandable: The problem of obesity can seem, at first glance, a particularly clear-cut case in which individuals should be held responsible for their own behavior and its consequences. Each of us is, after all, faced with a continual stream of "choices" about our own actions—how much, and what, to eat; how long and strenuously to exercise. It is tempting to conclude that tackling obesity should focus primarily on helping individuals make better choices, or on helping them follow through on resolutions to change their behavior, whether through better education or nudges. Certainly, for anyone attempting to control their weight, the challenge feels like a deeply personal, and often daunting, individual struggle. Myriad self-help books, a multibillion-dollar diet and slimming industry, and government health campaigns have all focused on helping the individual; yet the problem continues to grow.

But variations in obesity over time, across socio-demographic groups, and across counties and cultures reveal the limitations of an individualistic perspective. For example, there is no evidence that our susceptibility to present bias has changed over time, or for that matter that present bias varies across countries in ways that explain variations in obesity over time and across different locations. Indeed, we are not aware of *any* empirical evidence causally connecting obesity to present bias.

There is, by contrast, very good evidence that people who relocate are powerfully influenced by the obesity characteristics of the locality and culture to which they move. In one of the most careful studies addressing the issue, researchers at RAND and the University of Southern California examined obesity trends for military personnel assigned to different locations (military personnel largely cannot choose where to live, reducing the threat of self-selection effects—e.g., that people who are, or expect to be, obese move to places where they will feel comfortable because there are other obese people there).[11] The researchers found that moving to a county with a high obesity rate (e.g., Vernon County in Louisiana, where 38 percent of adults are obese) increased the parent's chance of being obese by 25 percent and the child's chance of being overweight or obese by 19 percent. By contrast, moving to a low obesity county, such as El Paso County in Colorado, where about 21 percent of adults are obese, decreased the parent's chances of being obese by 29 percent and the child's chances of being overweight or obese by 23 percent. This study and other research show that the likelihood of being obese is also associated with the prevalence of obesity in an individual's social network. In the study of military personnel movers, for example, the effects of a move on adolescents' likelihood of being obese or overweight were substantially greater for those who lived in the local community rather than on the military installation, where one would expect social contagion effects to be greater.[12]

Differences in obesity rates across time, place, and social connections do not, of course, correspond to differences in present bias (nor of genetics); they are differences in *circumstances*. Yet instead of blaming those circumstances, we all too readily blame the individual. Human vulnerability to obesity is a constant factor, like our vulnerability to cold, contaminated water, or infectious disease. This implies that the rapid rise in obesity demands explanation in terms of a change in circumstances, not in human nature.

———

Why are obesity rates rising worldwide, and why is the US so much worse off than other developed countries? This is, admittedly, somewhat of a mystery, but certainly agribusiness as well as the corporations selling processed and fast food play a central role.

After remaining relatively constant for several decades, both calorie consumption (much of it in the form of carbohydrates) and obesity started to climb in the US around 1980. Beverages, and especially fruit juices and soft drinks, were responsible for a large part of the increase: In 1997, the average American consumed fifty-three gallons of soft drinks over the year, a 51 percent increase since 1980. Snacking—food consumed outside of mealtimes—also increased markedly during the same period.[13]

What accounts for these trends? According to one analysis, an important factor was a change in relative prices.[14] Between 1985 and 2000, the nominal (not inflation-adjusted) price of fresh fruits and vegetables, fish, and dairy products increased by 118 percent, 77 percent, and 56 percent, respectively, whereas the price of sugar and sweets, fats and oils, and carbonated beverages increased by just 46 percent, 35 percent, and 20 percent. Indeed, adjusting for inflation, food prices in general started to fall around 1980—by approximately 14 percent from around 1980 through 2000; and the inflation-adjusted price of calorie-dense foods and beverages decreased even more sharply.[15]

This drop in inflation-adjusted prices was driven, at least in part, by innovations in production technologies in the very energy-dense, unhealthy foods that are particularly likely to lead to obesity: processed foods and so-called fast food. Consumption of both grew dramatically during the period when obesity mushroomed, and came to be the dominant sources of calories for most individuals in the US. In a recent study published in the *American Journal of Clinical Nutrition*, for example, public health researcher Filippa Juul and her colleagues analyzed dietary data from nearly forty-one thousand adults who took part in the Centers for Disease Control and Prevention's National Health and Nutrition Examination Survey from 2001 through 2018, and found that ultraprocessed food consumption grew from 53.5 percent of calorie intake at the beginning of the period studied (2001–2002) to 57 percent at the end (2017–2018).[16] It is difficult to know for sure how much this increase contributed to rising obesity, of course, but the authors note that over a roughly similar period (1999 to 2018) obesity in the US rose substantially, from 27.5 percent to 43.0 percent in males and from 33.4 percent to 41.9 percent in females.

Governments have not been a passive player in these developments. Rather than truly combating the obesity crisis, government subsidies have made it much worse. As documented in Grant Ennis's eye-opening book *Dark PR*, government policies favor the ultraprocessed food and sugary-drink industries, and subsidize the production and sales of unhealthy products.[17] According to diverse economic analyses, the biggest factor in consumption is price, and the hundreds of billions of dollars that governments spend on subsidies lower the price and raise the consumption of sugar and ultraprocessed foods.[18] Ennis observes that "we tend to focus on the cost of fighting this pandemic [of obesity], but we would save money and lives by not paying for it in the first place."[19] According to a report by Mike Russo of the US Public Interest Group Education Fund— *Apples to Twinkies: Comparing Federal Subsidies of Fresh Produce and Junk Food*—subsidies of the ingredients of junk food swamp those going to fresh produce.[20] The report concludes that "taxpayers are paying for the privilege of making our country sick."[21]

Referring to the even larger subsidies on meat, as compared with corn and sugar, Christina Sewell notes in the *Journal of International Affairs* that although meat production and consumption contribute to such diverse ills as climate change (through emissions of methane gas, mostly from cattle), deforestation (and hence mass extinctions), water shortages, and poor health, subsidies to meat are over a hundred times greater than those to the production of fruits and vegetables.[22] Sewell cites estimates from sustainable-consumption advocate David Simon in his book *Meatonomics* that externalities produced by meat in the form of health care costs and climate disruption average approximately two dollars for every one dollar of meat (and dairy) sold. Critiquing proposals to introduce a tax on meat, "for which history proves there will always be objections," Sewell proposes that "we are in luck, because no tax is necessary, only a removal of the billions of dollars in subsidies Americans already provide animal agriculture every year."

As the prices of grain and other commodity foods have fallen, the food industry has not been a passive player, simply passing its savings on to hungry consumers and innovating to provide new calorie-rich foods that busy families are demanding.

On the contrary, companies such as Coca-Cola, PepsiCo, Kraft, and Nestlé have worked diligently to get Americans to consume far more calories than they need, and to make sure that an ever-greater share of those calories comes from highly processed foods. Michael Moss, author of *Hooked: Food, Free Will, and How the Food Giants Exploit Our Addictions*, explains that the food industry uses the physiology and psychology of food consumption to "engineer" offerings that contain exactly the right amounts of salt, sugar, and fat to reach consumers' "bliss point," maximizing cravings and in some cases suppressing cues of satiation.[23] And public health researchers Marion Nestle and Michael Jacobson note that "changes in the food environment help explain why it requires more and more willpower for Americans to maintain an appropriate intake of energy."[24]

Processed and fast foods are priced to encourage all consumers—but particularly low-income consumers—to eat more. A key feature of many processed and fast food items is that the cost of the ingredients is a small fraction of the costs of bringing them to market; the main costs are marketing and (for fast food) the cost of labor. Both of these are barely affected by the size of the serving. So, radically different portion sizes are often priced surprisingly similarly (see Figure 2.1). As we write, McDonald's takes this to the extreme; they charge the same price—$1—for a soda of any size: an extra-small Coke with 110 calories or a large one with 290 calories. Likewise, a small portion of french fries at McDonald's costs $1.99 and has 220 calories, and a large serving has 130 percent more calories (490) but costs only 60 percent more. At one large movie chain in the US, a small popcorn, with 225 calories and 11 grams of fat, costs $6.09, and a large, with 1,030 calories and 41 grams of fat, costs $8.10—360 percent more calories for 33 percent more money (see Figure 2.1 for a similar pattern across a range of product categories). And these numbers don't include the added calories from the complimentary "butter," which is actually partially hydrogenated soybean oil. The marginal cost (ignoring the health costs) of providing

POPCORN		FOUNTAIN DRINKS	
Large Tub	6.50	Large	4.25
Large	6.00	Medium	4.00
Medium	5.50	Small	3.50
Small	4.75	**BOTTLED DRINKS**	
Junior	4.00	Water	3.75/4.25
SNACKS		Lemonade	3.25
		Ginger Ale	4.25 20 oz.
Hot Dog	3.75	20 oz. Sodas	3.75
Nachos	4.50		
Extra Cheese	1.50	**CANDY**	
Snack Pack	4.75		
Pickles	2.25	3.50	3.00

Figure 2.1. The less-than-healthy range of food and drink options available at a well-known US cinema chain (redrawn for clarity). Note that larger sizes cost only a little more—creating a powerful pull toward attempting to work one's way through a "Large Tub" of popcorn, the $3.50 portion of candy, or a "Large" fountain drink.

large quantities of additional calories for these products is incredibly low—and they are priced accordingly.

Along with pricing schemes that powerfully encourage over-consumption, cheap raw ingredients have also played a role in a dramatic increase in portion sizes over time (see Figure 2.2). The original fountain drink at McDonald's, in 1955, measured 7 ounces. By 2012, the "Kid's Size" drink at McDonald's was almost twice that: 12 ounces, and a large soda at McDonald's was 42 ounces—six times the size of the original serving (a large at KFC is 64 ounces).[25] But even these mega-quantities are dwarfed by the fountain drinks available at franchises like 7-Eleven (128 ounces) and the unfortunately named Midwestern chain Kum & Go (100 ounces).

Beverage portions have not been the only items that have increased in size; the size of almost all food items—including bagels, sandwiches, hamburgers, and fries—has increased, and indeed most have more than doubled over the past twenty or so years. Overall, food portions at supermarkets and fast-food outlets began to grow in the 1970s, rose sharply in the 1980s, and have continued to expand in parallel with increasing body weights.[26]

	1989	**2009**
Bagel	 140 calories 3-inch diameter	 350 calories 6-inch diameter
Cheeseburger	 333 calories	 590 calories
French fries	 210 calories 2.4 ounces	 610 calories 6.9 ounces

Figure 2.2. How fast-food portions in the US increased over a twenty-year period. (Data from the National Heart, Lung, and Blood Institute, *Portion Distortion Quiz*, US Department of Health and Human Services, 2009.)

The attractions of fast, and processed, foods go beyond their low prices. Fast food is, of course, delivered quickly, and highly processed foods typically require less home preparation both in terms of culinary skill and time. The shrinking time spent on preparing food partly reflects the market's response to the rising costs that people place on time. Many families, and especially lower-income families, with wage earners often working multiple jobs, have increased their work hours, reducing the time for food preparation. The growth of female employment (between 1960 and 2000, the portion of women in the workforce increased from less than 35 percent to around 60 percent) likewise radically reduced the amount of time available to women (the traditional "homemakers") to prepare meals. And the gradual dissolution of traditional two-parent families (putting enormous time pressure on single parents) has also contributed to the intense time crunch that so many families experience. In 1970, approximately 12 percent of children were living in single-parent households; by 2016, that number had increased to over 30 percent. As a result of these developments, an increasing fraction of consumers are dining out, ordering in, eating in their cars, and, when eating at home, eating foods that require little preparation.[27] These options tend to be higher in calories and lower in nutrition than foods cooked from raw ingredients. Numerous studies have shown a strong correlation between consumption of fast food and obesity, and between the geographic proximity of fast food and obesity.[28]

———

Consistent with our central story, concentrated agribusiness interests have worked hard to shift public attention away from obesity-fighting legislative and policy reforms that might threaten their bottom line, while lobbying assiduously to maintain the status quo. A 2016 *New York Times* article, "Coke and Pepsi Give Millions to Public Health, Then Lobby Against It," showed that these companies donated millions of dollars to influential health and non-health groups, which, in several cases, switched the positions they publicly supported in favor of those benefiting the beverage industry.[29] The charity Save the Children, for example, received a $5 million grant from Pepsi for its health and education programs for children, and around the same time withdrew its support for its campaigns for soda taxes (a levy on sugary drinks aimed to reduce consumption) in several states. (Save the Children maintained there was no connection between the donations and its decision.[30]) The Academy of Nutrition and Dietetics accepted almost $1 million from Coke in 2012 and 2013 and, again perhaps coincidentally, opposed New York's ban on extra-large sodas, citing "conflicting research." And the NAACP and the Hispanic Federation jointly received over a million and a half dollars in contributions from 2010 to 2015 and publicly opposed antisoda initiatives despite high rates of obesity in Black and Hispanic communities. Both organizations argued that the initiatives they opposed would disproportionately harm small, minority owned businesses.[31]

Researchers have recently used machine-learning methods to analyze some of the vast swaths of commentary, by businesses and nonprofits alike, that shape US government policy. This work provides powerful evidence that corporate lobbyists are able to use financial contributions to influence the supposedly independent viewpoints of nonprofit groups across many sectors of the economy. The research, published in the prestigious *Quarterly Journal of Economics*, found that

> shortly after a firm donates to a non-profit, that non-profit is more likely to comment on rules on which the firm has also commented. Second, when a firm comments on a rule, the comments by non-profits that recently received grants from the firm's foundation are systematically closer in content to the firm's own comments, relative to comments submitted by other non-profits. Third (and suggesting that these purchased positions make a difference), the final rule's discussion by a regulator is more similar to the firm's comments on that rule when the firm's recent grantees also commented on it.[32]

In response to the introduction of soda taxes in many localities in the US, as well as in many countries across the world (Hungary, France, and Tonga being among the first), the beverage industry has also employed a different line of defense: obfuscation. The food conglomerates know that when voters have been presented with the option of introducing soda taxes, they tend to approve these taxes, despite advertising campaigns funded largely by the beverage industry that have misleadingly presented soda taxes as a broader tax on "affordable groceries." Taking their tactics to a new level of craftiness, the industry has begun to sponsor its own ballot measures, with the (veiled) goal of preemptively ruling out local soda taxes.

In an article tellingly titled "Coca-Cola and Pepsi Have a Strategy to Beat Soda Taxes: Confuse as Many Voters as Possible," food journalist and commentator Chase Purdy notes that the soda industry has initiated a series of ballot initiatives that are quite obviously designed to bamboozle voters.[33] In 2018 in Washington state, for example, an industry-backed measure, Initiative 1634, billed as "Yes! to Affordable Groceries," was enacted to prohibit cities and towns from imposing any new taxes or fees on any grocery items. "Any grocery items," of course, includes soda. Initiative 1634, which was passed with 55 percent voter support, after campaigns with $20.3 million in financial backing from industry (in contrast to $100,000 spent by the less well-funded advocates of public health), was designed to confuse voters into approving regulations that prohibit measures they would typically favor.[34] A 2017 article in the *American Journal of Preventive Medicine* reported that Coke spent an average of more than $6 million per year lobbying against public health measures aimed at curbing soda consumption.[35] Pepsi spent about $3 million per year during that period, and the American Beverage Association spent more than $1 million each year.[36]

The efforts by these companies go beyond attempts to pass referenda and shift the support of influential organizations and legislators away from soda taxes and the like. They also include attempts to portray the obesity epidemic to the public as a problem of inadequate exercise rather than the excessive intake of unhealthy foods and drinks. An investigation by *The New York Times* revealed how Coca-Cola, the world's largest producer of sugary beverages, provided financial support to academics to promote a new "science-based" solution to the obesity crisis that identified individuals' failure to exercise, and not their intake of sugar and processed foods, as the real culprit for the obesity epidemic (Coke disputed the discussion of their motives in the *New York Times* story).[37] Coke and its industrial partners financed academics to publish articles, give public talks, and establish ostensibly impartial nonprofit scientific organizations to promote the view that Americans are focusing too much on how much they eat and drink, and too little on how much (or little) they exercise. For example, Coke gave many millions of dollars to scientists at the University of Colorado and West Virginia University, some of whom later established the Coke-funded *Global Energy Balance Network* (GEBN), which focused on lack of exercise as the root cause of obesity.[38] In the launch video for GEBN, Steven N. Blair, an exercise scientist, said, "Most of the focus in the popular media and in the scientific press is, 'Oh they're eating too much, eating too much, eating too much'—blaming fast food, blaming sugary drinks and so on. . . . And there's really virtually no compelling evidence that that, in fact, is the cause."[39] This is a viewpoint that is definitely out of alignment with the consensus in public health research—but is, of course, well aligned with Coke's aim of avoiding restrictions on its activities.

The full extent of Coke's influence on GEBN and affiliated academics was uncovered by exhaustive analysis of email correspondence obtained through Freedom of Information Act requests by academics and campaigners, who found that Coke aimed both to shift the focus of obesity-related research away from diet and toward exercise, and to establish an international network of academics friendly to this viewpoint.[40] GEBN was closed down in 2015 as controversy around it began to swirl. But Coke attempted to replicate the same strategy elsewhere, including through the International Life Sciences Institute (ILSI), funded by Coca-Cola and other multinational companies.[41] A *British Medical Journal* investigation showed that ILSI's arm in China had helped shape public health policy in China in ways predictably friendly to Coke's commercial aims.[42]

The influence of commercial interests on academics across all policy areas has a long and sordid history. Going back at least as far as the cigarette industry's co-opting of academics who claimed that there was no evidence of a causal link between smoking and cancer, businesses never seem to have much trouble identifying academics ready to sell themselves (out) for the right price. Although our focus is not on industry's direct attempts to co-opt science, these efforts provide "smoking gun" evidence of the readiness of some of the most powerful private sector players to attempt to shape academic and public debate for their own commercial interests, as well as the ineluctable allure of the huge rewards that are on offer. For many academics, and especially those located in business schools or economics departments, salary is a safe but relatively small fraction of their overall remuneration, with much of the remainder coming from industry entanglements. For example, in a *New York Times* opinion piece titled "For Economists, Defending Big Business Can Be Big Business," Peter Coy highlights the huge fees garnered by economists with academic affiliations, who serve as paid expert witnesses in high stakes cases. But these rather extreme cases are really just the tip of a much larger iceberg. The influence of industry in shaping the direction of academic research and policy debates is substantial and ubiquitous, including in the area of food policy.

So, as well intentioned as Michelle Obama's "Let's Move!" initiative may have been, it is noteworthy that it wasn't labeled "Let's Eat Less!" or, indeed, "Let's eat less ultraprocessed, energy-dense food!" And it certainly was not billed as "Let's campaign to change the food industry!" Indeed, rather than standing against the industry, Obama instead partnered with it. The focus on individual exercise rather than diet was likely no coincidence.[43]

While academics who take positions supporting the food industry are well funded, those who criticize the industry are often undermined, either by the industry's enlisting the support of other industry-aligned academics or by more direct means. For example, let us start with a 2020 article in *The Guardian* in which food journalist Bee Wilson summarized much of the well-established research showing that ultraprocessed food is a major contributor to world obesity.[44] Wilson's article highlighted the work of Brazilian epidemiologist Carlos Monteiro, who proposed the highly influential NOVA classification of foods by purpose and degree of processing, and who has also conducted one of the most rigorous experimental studies to document the causal impact of ultraprocessed food on caloric input. Needless to say, the food industry has not been happy with Monteiro's work, and many industry supporters inside academia came to the industry's defense by writing articles disparaging his research. French public health researcher Mélissa Mialon and her colleagues found that, out of thirty-eight academic authors who wrote pieces critical of NOVA, thirty-three had apparent ties to the ultraprocessed food industry.[45] Coincidence?

Worse, perhaps, some academics critical of the food industry have been subjected to concerted personal attacks in an apparent attempt to discredit their work. Consider, for example, clinical psychologist and public health professor Kelly Brownell, who coauthored the book *Food Fight*, which blames the food industry, in large part, for the obesity epidemic.[46] Brownell has been consistently targeted by the Center for Consumer Freedom, which according to its website is supported by restaurants and food companies (the website also notes that many of these "have indicated that they want anonymity as contributors").[47] A search of the website yields 275 results for "Kelly Brownell," many taunting him for his physical girth, as if being overweight renders him unqualified to criticize the food industry.

———

Thaler and Sunstein's now-classic book *Nudge* presents healthy food choices as the "poster child" for nudging; they open their book with a discussion of an imagined benevolent cafeteria manager wondering where in the lineup of food options at a cafeteria to position healthy and unhealthy items. Since people tend to load up on the items they first encounter, Thaler and Sunstein argue, the benevolent cafeteria manager should position healthy items so that diners encounter them first. As noted at the outset of this chapter, obesity—supposedly caused by shortsighted food and exercise choices—has been seen by behavioral economists as one of the canonical illustrations of present bias. Ideas for overcoming present bias include (in addition to Thaler and Sunstein's cafeteria idea) modifying the placement of high-calorie foods in supermarkets, changing the layout of menus, shrinking default portion sizes, and even using smaller plates or serving bowls.

Inspired by this line of argument, behavioral scientists have proposed and tested a wide variety of possible individual-level interventions to attack the problem of obesity.[48] Large bodies of research, including many papers coauthored by George, have explored (1) changing people's interactions with food, including introducing trayless cafeterias, smaller portions, and advanced ordering of meals; (2) financially incentivizing weight loss; (3) diverse forms of calorie labeling, including, for example, showing people how long they would have to run on a treadmill to burn a specific number of calories; and (4) promoting exercise, most commonly by paying people to go to the gym.[49]

These diverse i-frame interventions have proved almost uniformly ineffective. Revisiting the three main bodies of i-frame research, it has turned out that (1) changing the food ordering process (e.g., having people put in a lunch order right after they eat breakfast) produces statistically reliable but small effects;[50] (2) paying people to lose weight does lead them to lose weight, but not only do they not continue to lose weight when incentives are removed, they regain most or all of the weight that they lost;[51] and (3) calorie labeling has minimal, or null, effects in diverse studies.[52] Another line of research, which has examined the impact of providing incentives to visit the gym, has found that such incentives do increase gym attendance (almost entirely by people who, in the absence of incentives, would not have visited the gym), but benefits taper off once incentives are removed.[53] Why do these individual-based interventions have such small effects, despite the ingenuity and commitment of their implementers? Because, in short, they are trying to fix the players, instead of changing the "game."

Thaler and Sunstein didn't claim that nudges alone could solve the problem of obesity. But their work started a small industry of "healthy nudge" research, generating hundreds of papers finding small-to-medium-size effects on individual behavior. Reviewing the range of different nudges applied to diet, a not unrepresentative passage from one paper stated that "nudge holds promise as a public health strategy to combat obesity."[54] The empirical literature examining the efficacy of such nudges has not, however, actually supported this optimistic conclusion. Focusing purely on obesity itself, the i-frame perspective both misdiagnoses the problem and misdirects the search for solutions. People may be present biased, but surely they are no more or less present biased than they were a few decades ago. But the "food landscape" and our everyday pattern of physical activity have changed dramatically. This is the change we need to understand—and reverse—through systemic reform of the economics and regulation of the food industry, to prioritize human health.

———

In a pattern that should by now be familiar—and will become even more so in the remainder of this book—the food industry has sought to focus public attention on the i-frame and to distract attention from the systemic forces that created the epidemic of obesity and that would need to change if this problem is to be successfully tackled. As Kelly Brownell and his colleague Kenneth Warner point out, the industry has consistently aimed to persuade voters and policymakers to "focus on personal responsibility as the cause of the nation's un-healthy diet," *taking the food system as a given.*[55] Indeed, many corporate efforts to undermine support for public health initiatives are framed as attempts to enhance individual freedom, as exemplified by the food industry's aforementioned "Center for Consumer Freedom."

The combination of viewing the problem through an i-frame lens while at the same time resisting s-frame interventions can be seen in the statement of Ric Keller, a Florida Republican congressman who sponsored an ultimately unsuccessful bill to ban lawsuits against food companies similar to lawsuits that have been successfully executed against tobacco companies (this "cheeseburger bill" nearly succeeded; it passed in the US House of Representatives in March 2005 but never received the Senate vote required for it to become law). In a CNN interview, Keller stated that "we've got to get back to those old-fashioned principles of personal responsibility, of common sense, and get away from this new culture where everybody plays the victim and blames other people for their problems."[56] Supporting Keller's position, the then House majority leader, Tom DeLay, said, "It's hard to believe that trial lawyers want to make the claim that 'Ronald McDonald made me do it.' The point of this debate [is] all about personal responsibility. If you eat too much, you will gain weight."[57]

The food industry itself is, however, all too aware that the s-frame is where the real leverage lies. We've discussed only a few of the industry's lobbying efforts; considered overall, it devotes a staggering amount of resources to maintaining political influence and shaping debate around public health. In 2022, agribusiness employed more than twelve hundred lobbyists in the US, with a budget of $165 million.[58] Meanwhile, food and beverage conglomerates in Brazil have, according to a *New York Times* investigation, made payments totaling $158 million to Brazilian legislators with the aim of opposing potential interventions such as government promotion of breastfeeding, bans on junk food advertising to children, and sugar taxes.[59] So the industry quietly works to manipulate the rules governing the food system to enhance its sales and profits, even as it loudly and publicly proclaims the primacy of individual responsibility.

Having our attention misdirected to the i-frame has another unfortunate consequence: As we noted above, it contributes to a

propensity to "blame the victim"—to hold individuals accountable for outcomes and patterns of behavior that are beyond their
control. This individualistic perspective also encourages victims to
blame themselves, which, it has been argued, not only contributes
to low levels of well-being and mental health disorders, but may
contribute to the obesity problem itself.[60] Indeed, self-blame may
contribute to an increase in eating disorders of all kinds, which
have been rising in tandem with increasing rates of obesity.[61]

As for all the problems discussed in this book, individual consumers are no match for firms united by industry associations and
armed with lobbyists—the concentrated forces of Mancur Olson's
"collective action." Individual consumers often care desperately
about their waistlines and their health, and devote huge amounts
of time and money to (usually unsuccessful) efforts to get, and
stay, thin through weight-loss programs, special diets, gym memberships and equipment, and the like. It is not, however, in any
individual's interest to expend time or money in a likely futile
attempt to change the system. But it is very much in the interests of the concentrated, well-funded, and highly organized food
industry to spend large sums in a coordinated attempt to maintain
a food system that is advantageous to its interests.

The situation has become so dire that some health advocacy
groups have begun to call for extreme measures. As we were
writing this chapter, the American Academy of Pediatrics (AAP)
released new guidance about how to treat children who are overweight or obese. The document does recognize that "it is difficult
to make or sustain healthy behavior changes in an obesogenic
environment that promotes high-energy intake, unhealthy dietary
choices, and sedentary behavior." However, the report contains no
proposal for the AAP to use its influence to promote policies that
might change this macro-environment. Instead the seventy-three-
page document's policy prescriptions focus almost exclusively on
the i-frame, including a controversial recommendation that children ages twelve and older be prescribed weight-loss medications,

and that bariatric surgery be considered for those over the age of thirteen with severe obesity.

———

The viewpoint from biologists and public health researchers could not be more different from the i-frame perspective beloved of business and politics, and it fits much better with the data. Reporting on a meeting in 2022 at the UK's Royal Society about the causes of obesity, the journalist Julia Belluz wrote that the discussion

> was infused with an implicit understanding of what obesity is not: a personal failing. No presenter argued that humans collectively lost willpower around the 1980s, when obesity rates took off, first in high-income countries, then in much of the rest of the world. . . . Laziness, gluttony and sloth were not referred to as obesity's helpers. In stark contrast to a prevailing societal view of obesity, which assumes people have full control over their body size, they didn't blame individuals for their condition, the same way we don't blame people suffering from the effects of undernutrition, like stunting and wasting.[62]

Yet i-frame approaches continue to dominate the policy landscape. One high-profile example is the recent US "food is medicine" initiative, in which food-challenged individuals receive "prescriptions" for free, nutritious food. The program has attracted more than $350 million in research funding from the Rockefeller Foundation, the National Institutes of Health, and the Patient-Centered Outcomes Research Institute. Yet in a 2023 *Journal of the American Medical Association* editorial questioning the wisdom of this strategy, Dr. Alyssa J. Moran and Dr. Christina A. Roberto identify a number of weaknesses in the approach, including that (1) people can only enroll in the "food is medicine" programs via the health care system, introducing all the problems of that system, including difficulty of access (see Chapter 4); and (2) adherence to even cheap or free medications with tremendous

proven benefits is abysmally low, suggesting that radical and difficult changes in diet are likely to be even more problematic.[63] The
authors conclude that "food is medicine" programs are unlikely to
lead to long-term improvements in diet or health, and also stress
the "crowd-out" concern that we have highlighted for i-frame
interventions more broadly: "We agree that some well conducted
randomized controlled trials could be useful. But, should so much
of our intellectual talent and resources be directed toward these
research questions when there are other strategies that are far
more likely to improve dietary habits?" They provide examples of
interventions that, they argue, are much more likely to produce
substantial benefits in diet, including improving food served in
public institutions, reformulating foods to be lower in sugar and
salt, as well as taxes on unhealthy food and beverages. Moran and
Roberto note that

> we should not overlook that this shift in attention [seeing obesity as an
> individualized medical problem] is a boon to the food industry, which
> has historically avoided regulation by shaping public narratives about
> the causes of, and responses to, public health problems. Throughout the
> 20th century, the food industry has perpetuated a personal responsibility
> narrative, reducing the social causes of diet-related diseases to unhealthy
> "lifestyle" factors such as poor dietary choices and too little exercise. . . .
> The food is medicine movement risks . . . casting a social problem as a
> medical one and further shifting public discourse away from [the influ-
> ence of] commercial interests as major drivers of disease. It is no surprise
> that many large, influential food companies such as Amazon, Instacart,
> and Kroger have loudly touted their support for food is medicine by
> joining task forces, supporting pilot programs, and integrating program-
> ming into corporate social responsibility campaigns.[64]

If systemic changes in the food industry have led to the problem of rising obesity, then the natural policy response should be
to identify the key changes and reverse them, or at least otherwise

neutralize their impact, just as in any other aspect of public health. What might this mean in practice? Systemic changes would likely include dramatically restricting the marketing and advertising of unhealthy foods; requiring the reformulation of many staple "fast" foods, with lower fat, sugar, and salt content; and radically reducing, or banning, the highly processed ingredients "hiding" in foods ranging from ostensibly healthy breakfast cereals to ready-meals that are known to be metabolically damaging and to lead to obesity and related chronic diseases such as diabetes and heart disease. Perhaps there may be a role for "consumer duty" requirements in the food industry, similar to those starting to be introduced in the financial sector in some countries, requiring the industry to justify how its products are in the best interests of consumers (and removing those products, in cases where they are not). Currently, food producers operate in an environment in which they pay no penalty for—and hence, in the language of economics, "fail to internalize"—the vast costs they impose on their customers and on society as a whole, which foots a large fraction of the bill for expanded obesity-related health care costs, as well as lost productivity.

Probably the single most fundamental change needed is in price: Taxes and subsidies need to favor healthy—and disfavor unhealthy—food options rather than, as now, too often the reverse (and to do so in a way that is, as far as possible, cost-neutral for the poorest in society). The prospect of legal redress for those harmed by foodstuffs may also play a role. Lobbying by the food industry needs to be shrunk to a manageable size, if not quite to zero, and its influence on politics (e.g., through campaign donations) fought at every turn. These points apply also to Western food and beverage companies that have lobbied and marketed their way into developing markets, often with dire health consequences.

Food-related harms, mostly via obesity and associated chronic diseases, are comparable to the toll on human health caused by tobacco. Yet while tobacco regulation has tightened substantially, despite fierce industry opposition every step of the way, the regulation of unhealthy foods remains astonishingly lax. At the beginning of the twentieth century, there was a dramatic overhaul of food regulation to counter mislabeling, to eliminate chemical poisons from food, and to drastically clean up the food chain and improve microbiological contamination. The current challenge—foodstuffs causing chronic rather than acute harm—calls for a similarly vigorous overhaul of food regulation.[65] Many of the major players in the food industry have fought, and will continue to fight, against such reforms, which threaten their business models because they are actually likely to reduce the consumption of unhealthy foods.

There are a few encouraging recent signs. In contrast to the perspective of President George W. Bush's 2003 Dallas speech and the FDA's Obesity Working Group in the early 2000s (which encouraged daily physical exercise, nutritious eating, and preventive screenings as a means of tackling obesity), some contemporary politicians (albeit almost exclusively on the left of the political spectrum) have been taking a systemic approach to the problem. At a hearing of the Senate Health, Education, Labor and Pensions Committee in December 2023, for example, chairman Senator Bernie Sanders noted that "ultra-processed foods, which make up an incredible 73 percent of our nation's food supply, can be as addictive as alcohol and nearly as addictive as cigarettes."[66] Sanders stated that "while we spend hundreds of billions to treat diabetes, the food and beverage industry spent $14 billion last year on advertising to make many of their unhealthy products appealing to the American consumer," and that "$2 billion of this money is used to directly market food predominantly high in sugar, salt and saturated fat to our children in order to get them hooked on these products at an early age." Sanders cited research from the Rudd Center for Food Policy and Obesity showing that children and teens view about four thousand food and beverage ads on television every year, an average of ten advertisements each day. He also cited research showing that "children who watch Nickelodeon and Nicktoons are exposed to over ten unhealthy food and beverage ads every hour." Sanders called for policy interventions that mirror past efforts against smoking:

> Nearly 30 years ago, Congress had the courage to take on the tobacco industry whose products killed over 400,000 Americans every year. Congress did that then. Now is the time for us to seriously combat the type-2 diabetes and obesity epidemic in America. In order to do that, we must have the courage to take on the greed of the food and beverage industry which, every day, is undermining the health and well-being of our children, focusing on reducing the impact of processed foods on youth and tackling food industry influence on dietary habits.

———

There is a final update worth noting in the development of individualized medical approaches to the problem of obesity: the arrival of expensive but incredibly effective antiobesity drugs. These may be an important breakthrough for some patients and may also change the overall "obesity game" in unexpected ways. Will the high cost of these drugs exacerbate income disparities in obesity and health? Might they initiate a new parade of over-prescription and overuse leading to unforeseen crises, as opioids did before them? A particular concern is that obesity is only part of a larger problem of poor nutrition, a problem that these medications not only do not target but may actually exacerbate by redirecting individuals' attention away from the crucial importance of a varied and balanced diet. Most importantly, from the vantage point of the central argument of this book, there is a risk that the availability of this option for weight loss will further—on top of the industry moves we have focused on in this chapter—reduce public pressure for reforms in the agriculture and food sectors that would address the obesity crisis at its source.

Instead of making people fat and then providing them with expensive drugs to curb their appetites, clearly our first collective priority should be to tackle the root cause of obesity—and this means a radical overhaul of how the food industry is regulated, taxed, and subsidized, and reversing the trend toward energy-dense, highly processed foods and drinks deliberately engineered to be as difficult to stop consuming as possible. This means forcing the food industry, through regulations or financial incentives, to create and market products that promote, rather than damage, human health.

A superb model for systemic evidence-based food policy, albeit aimed specifically at coronary heart disease rather than obesity, can be seen in the US ban on trans fats. In 2015, the FDA concluded that partially hydrogenated oils (PHOs)—the primary source of artificial trans fats—were not safe for use in food, finalized its determination to ban PHOs, and gave manufacturers three years to reformulate products without PHOs.[67] The ban went into effect in 2018, though limited extensions through 2021 were granted.[68] The decision to ban trans fats was based on extensive scientific research linking artificial trans fats to health issues such as coronary heart disease, increases in LDL ("bad") cholesterol levels and lowering of HDL ("good") cholesterol levels, insulin resistance, and type 2 diabetes.[69] For example, one study looked at hospitalization rates for heart attack and stroke in urban counties in the state of New York, comparing counties that implemented restrictions on trans fats early on with those that had not. The results showed the restrictions reduced heart attack and stroke events by (a statistically significant) 6.2 percent.[70]

The US ban inspired other countries to follow suit. By 2023, fifty-three countries had implemented restrictions or bans on trans fats, showing that evidence-based s-frame policies can help address challenging health issues and can spread rapidly across the world.[71]

The trans fat ban may have been successful in part because food tastes essentially the same whether or not it includes trans fats, and in part because the added cost to manufacturers (likely passed on to consumers) was relatively marginal. Nevertheless, it shows that change is possible. Admittedly, similar policies aimed at obesity, such as mandating decreases in sugar for sodas and other products, may be met with greater resistance from consumers. But we suspect that, once implemented, they will likely be broadly accepted and even popularly supported—a topic we'll pick up in Chapter 11.

Chapter 3

WHY WE ARE UNPREPARED FOR RETIREMENT

The nudge is really a fudge—a way of avoiding the thornier issues at stake in retirement security. The most worrisome unexpected costs of old age . . . should be addressed by politicians via programs such as Medicare and Medicaid. But by focusing on individuals' decisions to save up for retirement, they can shift responsibility.

—Frank Pasquale, "Why 'Nudges' Hardly Help," *The Atlantic*

George has neighbors who are retirees, about the same age as George and his wife, and both are from modest backgrounds. They don't have much in the way of investments, and they can't count on an inheritance from rich relatives. Still, when George is at his condo, they are seldom at theirs (which is good, because he doesn't have to step softly to avoid disturbing them). Where are they?

Well, they may be at their time-share in Hawaii, where they spend long stretches of the dreary Washington winter, or living it up in New York City, or vacationing in Greece. You get the picture. What is their secret? Other than enjoying each other's company, smart investing, and frugal spending, it's simple: Both worked for the government. He was an agent in the federal Bureau of Alcohol, Tobacco, Firearms and Explosives; she was a social worker who worked for the State of Washington. Their "secret" is, in short, that they both have pensions. They are, alas, a dwindling, endangered species: Good pensions are already largely, and increasingly, a legacy from the past in the US, the UK, and across much of the rich world.

Over the last couple of decades there has been continual talk of a retirement "crisis" facing large swaths of the population in many countries. In the US, the problem is particularly acute—nearly half of households with people ages 55–64 have no savings at all and will have to rely on Social Security payments to fund their retirement, which will almost certainly fall short of their basic needs.[1]

It wasn't always like this. Until the 1980s, most American companies offered pensions, which paid a predictable amount when a worker retired. These pensions amount to a substantial fraction of an employee's earnings each year, and in return pay out fixed benefits on retirement. In some cases, the pension is funded entirely by the employer, but in other cases contributions are made by both the employer and the employee. The specific rules differ from one plan and employer to the next, but typically the payout is some fraction of the employee's final salary (or average salary), weighted by years of contribution. The employer typically hands over the contributions to a pension plan manager, who invests the funds in long-term investments that should earn sufficient returns to cover the future payouts.

For many years, this looked like a winning formula—stock returns were sufficiently high that pension funds could easily pay out the required benefits, sometimes running almost embarrassingly large surpluses. But starting around 1980, things started to go wrong: Investment expectations started to dip, and life expectancies grew more rapidly than pension administrators had forecast. Creating a growing sense of panic, several large employers went bankrupt—albeit in some cases strategically—precisely to avoid their pension obligations. These very real problems came to appear even more daunting with the introduction of "market-based" valuations of pension liabilities, which forced companies to be realistic in putting aside the amount required to fund their workers' retirements. A popular refrain in the financial services industry and the media was that existing "gold-plated" pensions were simply "unaffordable." Another problem was that workers began to change employers more often, and, under some pension schemes, they would lose some or all of their benefits when they changed employers.

How to deal with this problematic situation? Various modifications of existing approaches were—and still remain—possible: raising the retirement age, reducing payouts, increasing employer and/or employee contributions, making "pension pots" portable from one employer to another, and combinations of these approaches. But rather than confronting the problem directly and accepting the unpopular reality that we collectively need to pay more and/or get less, corporations, with the backing of the financial industry, took a different route—one that dramatically increased the scale of the problem. They discovered that, by shifting responsibility for retirement planning onto individual employees, they could entirely abandon their previously assumed responsibility to provide a dependable income stream for retirement.

———

The "solution" to the difficulties of defined benefit pensions was the emergence of "defined contribution" retirement plans—a euphemism for "save for your own retirement." In the face of financial uncertainty that was proving too challenging even for huge financial services companies with their armies of actuaries and economists, the answer was, bizarrely, to pass the problem on to individual workers far less equipped to manage it.

Defined contribution pension schemes emerged gradually. Originally, they were envisioned as supplements to conventional pensions.[2] But in the 1980s, companies began to realize that they could drastically reduce not only the cost of funding their workers' retirements, but also the administrative burden of, and potential liability associated with, managing investments in pension funds by offloading onto their employees not only the complexities of making investment decisions but, in fact, most of the funding of retirement. And once some employers ceased to fund pensions, their competitors were forced to follow suit to remain competitive. The transition from old-fashioned pensions to defined contribution retirement schemes is, at this point, almost complete; at present, final salary pensions are largely confined to public-sector workers, and even in the public sector many such schemes are being gradually eliminated. Moreover, traditional pensions are now commonly referred to as "defined benefit retirement plans," a term that seems calculated to frame its counterpart, "defined contribution plans," more positively by giving two radically different approaches nearly identical labels.

The typical defined contribution (or save-for-your-own-retirement) approach is a complete disaster on many dimensions. The first dimension, which is illustrated in Figure 3.1, is that most people—literally *most*—can't afford to put *any* money aside every month into retirement savings, let alone the 10 to 20 percent of income that would be required to fund a comfortable retirement given current life expectancies (the average retirees can expect to live after retirement for half as long as they worked). Astonishingly, median real (inflation-adjusted) family income rose by only about 37 percent over the forty years between 1984 and 2023, while the incomes of those in the top fifth of the income distribution increased by 144 percent (those in even higher income categories rose even more).[3] How is this possible? Virtually all the gains in real income have gone to the wealthiest (we discuss inequality more broadly in Chapter 5). Stagnating incomes for the average family make dire savings numbers inevitable. So we have an immediate, and fatal, problem with people being forced to fund their own retirement—most of them simply can't afford to do so.

Retirement account savings of families age 32–61 by savings percentile, 1989–2016 (2016 dollars)

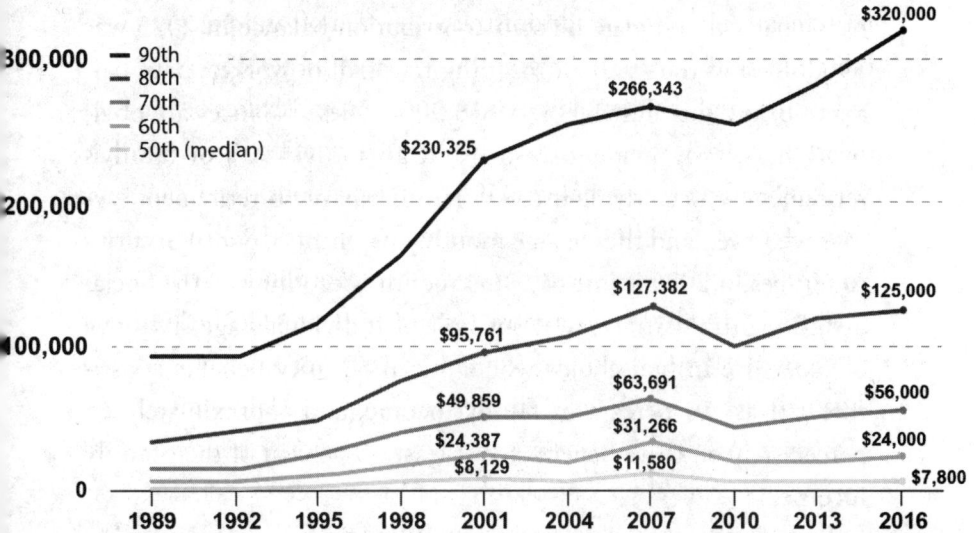

Note: Retirement account savings include funds in 401(k)-style define contribution plans and in IRAs. Scale changed to accommodate larger values.
Source: EPI analysis of Survey of Consumer Finance data, 2016.

Figure 3.1. The woefully skewed distribution of retirement saving in the US.

Compounding the problem, many people (33 percent of US workers in 2020) work at companies that either don't offer retirement plans or offer plans with no matching contributions alongside what workers themselves pay in, rendering such plans of dubious value.[4] Adding to the problem is the rapidly increasing number of so-called gig workers, such as those who drive for Uber or Lyft or who work as independent contractors (as do most truck drivers, for example) and hence do not receive retirement benefits.

In the US, the Pension Protection Act of 2006 gave companies incentives to automatically enroll their workers in retirement plans, and enrollment in retirement plans did rise substantially at those firms that offered their workers defined contribution plans (such as the so-called 401(k) schemes, of which more shortly). Yet nearly two decades later, only 66 percent of workers are even offered defined contribution retirement plans, and only 70 to 75 percent of these participate. Among those offered a plan who do participate, the average defined contribution balance in 2023 was $90,000, and the median (meaning that half of workers have balances below this number) was $18,000.[5] These balances are obviously hopelessly inadequate to fund an individual's or family's retirement. Currently, half of US families have no retirement savings whatever, and the average monthly payment of Social Security to retirees in 2025 is just $1,976 a month. According to the Social Security Administration, about half of individuals age sixty-five or older live in households where Social Security benefits constitute at least 50 percent of family income, and approximately 25 percent rely on these benefits for at least 90 percent of their family income.[6]

Even for those who are lucky enough to have an employer that offers a traditional defined benefit plan, match rates for paying in and formulas for paying out benefits are at the discretion of individual companies, and vary widely. In the US, data on match rates offered by different companies are sparse. But a survey of Vanguard retirement plans found that many plans only match employee pension contributions up to a few percentage points of a worker's salary.[7] Indeed, some only match fifty cents to the dollar even for those few percent (e.g., a common formula is to match fifty cents to the dollar for only the first 6 percent of salary, limiting the employer's contribution to a maximum of just 3 percent of salary).[8]

What about the tax savings offered to those who have retirement savings accounts? Understanding how these tax savings work is a bit complicated: First, income put into a 401(k) isn't taxed; nor are matches offered by employers. Effectively, this means that workers get a tax deduction for both, or, stated differently, that contributions are in "pretax" dollars. Second, earnings on investments in a 401(k) are not subject to taxes on dividends or capital gains. Both of these breaks dramatically favor the affluent, because they tend to be in a higher tax bracket (which makes tax deductions more lucrative), tend to have much larger 401(k) balances (the top 20 percent of Americans by income hold approximately 83 percent of funds in all retirement accounts, while the bottom 60 percent hold just 8 percent), and because they are more likely to work for companies that offer matching 401(k) contributions.[9] Admittedly, the picture is a bit more nuanced because retirees *do* pay income taxes on withdrawals when they receive the income from their investments following retirement (though they are likely to be in a lower tax bracket than they were in while they were working).

All in all, however, these tax breaks favor the wealthy: An analysis by the Congressional Budget Office found that about 70 percent of the benefits from tax breaks on retirement savings accrue to households in the top 20 percent of the income distribution.[10] This astounding inequity is perverse not only because it favors the affluent, who—unlike those with low incomes—are perfectly able to save for retirement in the absence of this huge giveaway, but also because there is no evidence that tax benefits actually serve their ostensible purpose: to increase saving.[11] Like many of the existing policies we discuss in this book, which are widely recognized as unfair or dysfunctional (or in this case, both), this bizarre feature of the current system in the US persists despite widespread criticism by economists and policymakers. But, dysfunctional as it is, this policy does have powerful beneficiaries—and hence supporters: the affluent, and corporations that are "off the hook" from having to provide for their employees' retirements.

The problems with the current defined contribution approach to retirement go far beyond the fundamental flaw that people can't afford to save for their own retirement. Recall that a feature of defined contribution plans is that individuals are required to make their own decisions about how to invest their retirement "nest egg." Each of us is now, in effect, supposed to be our own financial guru. But, not surprisingly, few of us are in a position to play that role effectively. So, for example, a 2010 study found that workers made poor investment choices that reduced their lifetime saving by 20 percent compared with a baseline that would be achieved with sensible investment decisions.[12] Similarly, a 2016 University of California at Berkeley study of the state's public school teachers concluded that six out of seven would have less money for retirement if they switched their defined benefit scheme (known as CalSTRS) for the supposed flexibility of the defined contributions, self-investment 401(k) scheme.[13]

Moreover, the very people who most need a retirement nest egg—those at the lower end of the income spectrum—are likely to be the least capable of making savvy investment decisions, the least able to access advice, and under the greatest short-term financial pressures.[14] Passing the buck to each individual member of the public can be attractive to corporations, regulators, and even politicians: If people make the wrong calls and leave themselves destitute, it can conveniently be argued that they only have themselves to blame. But for workers, the bewildering array of investment options is a recipe for an all-too-predictable disaster.

Beyond the rather unreasonable demands on each citizen's actuarial abilities and financial knowledge, not to mention lack of time and lack of interest, there is also a fundamental economic problem with this approach—that by failing to pool our risks (both regarding exposure to investments and likely longevity) as in a traditional pension plan, we are no longer insured against bad outcomes. So each person has to save substantially more than would be necessary in a collective system because each of us is acting not only as our own financial guru but also as our own insurer. Throwing this hugely complex decision back to each individual, moreover, invites new and unscrupulous players to join the game, leading both to outright fraud and a great variety of investment mis-selling.[15] Dependable financial advice would help—but is too costly for anyone but the wealthy.[16] The charlatans, however, are more than willing to step in with "help," often using very intrusive selling methods.[17]

The conventional narrative around the transition from pensions to defined contribution schemes has often been that defined benefit schemes, however appealing in principle, are simply unaffordable given lower investment returns and longer life expectancies. But what is expensive is not defined contribution schemes per se, but funding retirement adequately by any means whatever. Indeed, throwing the problem back to the individual makes it even *more* expensive, not less, by removing the crucial risk-sharing benefits of pension schemes and passing investment decisions to countless individuals with no relevant training.

———

How have behavioral economists responded to this calamitous situation? Most have enthusiastically embraced the view that the solution lies with the i-frame, generating a large literature proposing and testing different mechanisms to help people make the right choices when it comes to retirement savings. Much of this work assumes that the psychological root cause of the retirement savings crisis is the very same human tendency that was presumed to underlie rising obesity: *present bias*, our tendency to overvalue an immediate reward (such as an impulsive purchase) and undervalue the future consequences (a comfortable retirement). But again this explanation doesn't survive scrutiny. First off, if present bias is a hard-wired feature of human nature, then how could it be the cause of the retirement crisis, which was far less severe only a generation or two ago? Second, present bias itself is hardly a ubiquitous feature of human behavior. True, people are sometimes shortsighted, but just as often they are preoccupied with the future—think of people studying for exams, building careers, learning the violin, training for a marathon, or starting a business.[18] People are perfectly able to put in lots of effort now, with the prospect of long-term gain, and frequently do so. Indeed, government payouts designed to help American families weather the COVID pandemic illustrate the point in the case of personal finance. If people were exhibiting present bias, they should have frittered all that money away on short-lived pleasures; yet most Americans with limited means used the extra cash to build a small nest egg. According to an estimate by the Federal Reserve, families in the bottom half of the income distribution saved, on average, about $5,500 each.[19]

When *does* present bias strike? Often when we are in the grip of some powerful emotion or drive, like lust or hunger, that makes us focus on satisfying that craving.[20] Present bias can sometimes also catch us out when a very tangible present reward must be balanced against a very uncertain future goal.[21] But the ongoing challenge of balancing earnings, spending, and saving over a lifetime has a rather different character.

For all these reasons, targeting present bias through behavioral nudges has sadly produced very poor results when it comes to helping people save more for retirement. This was not for lack of trying, or lack of ingenuity. Indeed, some of the smartest people in the field of behavioral economics devised the remedies, with every reason (at the time) to believe that they could have a dramatic impact.

Certainly the most significant intervention proposed by behavioral economists to help people save for their own retirement was to harness the power of defaults, as we saw with green energy in Chapter 1. Across the US, the UK, and many other nations, people have been *auto-enrolled* into pension plans, albeit with the possibility of opting out. Defaults get them to start saving for retirement in the first place, but getting them to the point where they are saving *enough* requires an additional behavioral trick: a mechanism called *auto-escalation*, whereby people's contributions—the amount of their paycheck going toward retirement—increases automatically over time, ideally as their income grows.[22]

Auto-enrollment and auto-escalation have been broadly seen as *the* most successful nudges; and, in "elevator pitches," they are almost invariably the interventions used to illustrate just how powerful nudges can be. Thus, in a 2019 roundtable discussion with many of the leading lights in behavioral economics and public policy, Stephen Dubner, the coauthor of the popular Freakonomics book series, congratulated Richard Thaler for the role he had played in advancing auto-enrollment and auto-escalation, which Dubner cited as "the most successful nudge, and the greatest triumph to date of behavioral economics."[23]

But only a year after Dubner's enthusiastic remarks, in a prestigious keynote talk delivered to a joint session of the American Economic and American Finance Associations, David Laibson, perhaps the economist most closely associated with these interventions, presented a much less optimistic perspective.[24] After taking a close look at empirical data on the two key nudges seen as solving the retirement financing problem—auto-enrollment and auto-escalation—Laibson concluded that neither intervention had, in fact, moved the needle on actual retirement saving.

Many nudges produced large "short-term effects," Laibson explained, which led researchers to conclude that they were dramatically successful. But a longer-term analysis revealed that these effects evaporate quickly. For example, Laibson reported the results of studies that followed employees at four firms that had implemented auto-enrollment, three of which also implemented auto-escalation. One of these firms was, in fact, the very company discussed in the 2001 paper that first drew attention to the apparent success of auto-enrollment.[25] Tracking workers at these companies, Laibson and his colleagues found that aggregate retirement savings did not end up measurably higher for employees who had been auto-enrolled or auto-escalated than for those who had not.

Why? Laibson first noted that, even in the absence of auto-enrollment, a large fraction of employees at all four companies ended up enrolling in the firms' retirement plans; auto-enrollment did accelerate the process, but not to a very meaningful extent. Second, and even more significantly, there was a problem of "leakage":

Employees took advantage of opportunities to remove funds from retirement savings accounts when they changed jobs, and to borrow at relatively low interest rates using their "pension pots" as collateral for the loans (a particularly unhelpful feature of the design of US retirement plans).[26] Recent research suggests that leakage rates are on average about 40 percent—i.e., non-retirement outflows from retirement funds average about 40 percent of inflows.[27] Leakage rates are especially high for lower-income employees—averaging a staggering 70 to 80 percent—and were, tellingly, higher for people who had been auto-enrolled (suggesting that perhaps they perceived themselves as having more pressing needs than saving for retirement but were, in effect, nudged into saving against their will).[28] Probably most of these "outflows" were ill-advised from the point of view of the person's long-term financial future. But many of these workers had no access to good advice, and no way of estimating the long-term impact on their retirement. They probably also had good reasons to prioritize immediate financial objectives, like obtaining further education for themselves or their children, or purchasing a house.

Inadequate saving vies with obesity, the topic of the last chapter, for the number one spot among problems that behavioral scientists use to illustrate present bias, the presumed human tendency to focus excessively on present needs at the expense of the future. Much as with obesity, however, this story doesn't make much sense when evaluated in a historical and cross-national context. Many other countries are not suffering from retirement shortfalls; nor were the US and the UK, at least to the same extent, in the past. Such an analysis makes it obvious that the problem is not one of individual limitations, but of a system that renders it close to impossible for low- and moderate-income individuals, no matter how farsighted, to fund a comfortable retirement.

Laibson and a team of colleagues later did a much deeper dive into the data—an analysis of saving over time of 118,367 employees at nine firms that incorporated a mix of auto-enrollment, auto-escalation, or both.[29] Fortuitously (at least for research purposes), the policies applied only to employees hired from a certain date onward, so the researchers were able to compare the savings over time of the 62,430 employees hired in the years *after* the policies were introduced with the savings of the 55,937 employees hired in the years *before*. The study incorporated several innovations that, in combination, were a huge improvement over prior research on the topic: (1) It followed up the large numbers of workers who left their firms; (2) it better captured "leakage" (as discussed above) than did most earlier investigations; and (3) it captured *actual* pension contributions (prior studies had often made strong assumptions based on planned rather than actual contributions).

The results were almost uniformly disappointing. Auto-enrollment increased so-called steady-state savings rates (i.e., the stable long-term savings rate) by 0.6 percent of income, auto-escalation by 0.3 percent of income, and the combined impact of both together was still less than 1 percent of income. Only 40 percent of people with an auto-escalation default actually ended up escalating on their first escalation date, and still more opted out later. The increased savings rates were less than one-quarter of the optimistic earlier estimates that had led Dubner to herald auto-enrollment and auto-escalation the "greatest triumph of behavioral economics."[30]

The UK experience may appear to offer some comfort, but appearances are misleading. The UK system, known as NEST, is better designed—there is much less room for leakage. But, in truth, the virtues of the UK system are that it is very close to a fairly inflexible mandate requiring employers to set up pension plans and pay a (small) amount into them (in addition to the employee's contribution). The only nudge-like aspect of the scheme is the possibility that people can opt out; around one in ten do this, and it is almost certainly financially disadvantageous for the great majority of them to do so, primarily because they lose the employer's matching contribution.[31] Ironically, then, the only behavioral aspect of the UK scheme is arguably its weakest point.

In parallel with the high-profile proposals—auto-enrollment and auto-escalation—that had been seen as the big "success stories" of behavioral economics, other more speculative approaches have been explored. For example, one study found that showing people an artificially "aged" photo of themselves increased self-reported intentions to save for retirement, though it did not measure actual behavior.[32] In public presentations, George used to joke that seeing a morphed photo of himself in old age might well cause him to save *less* for that alien guy in the photo rather than to save more—until it occurred to him that he already *was* the age of the oldest morphed photo used in the study. In any case, there is currently no evidence that nudge-like i-frame strategies, whether conventional or more inventive, have the power to make inroads into the pension crisis.

Other than auto-enrollment and auto-escalation, almost certainly the most widespread and touted i-frame interventions involve attempts to improve customer understanding of pensions—or to increase "financial literacy."[33] While it might seem difficult to argue against attempts to enhance financial literacy, Lauren Willis does exactly that—and quite compellingly—in a law review paper provocatively titled "Against Financial-Literacy Education."[34] Specifically critiquing i-frame interventions involving disclosure, Willis writes, "The dominant model of regulation in the United States for consumer credit, insurance, and investment products is disclosure and unfettered choice. As these products have become more complex, consumers' inability to understand them has become increasingly apparent, and the consequences of this inability more dire. In response, policymakers have embraced financial-literacy education as a necessary corollary to the disclosure model of regulation." Willis goes on to question whether such education makes much difference, and concludes with an argument much like our own: "When consumers find themselves in dire financial straits, the regulation through education model blames them for their plight, shaming them and deflecting calls for effective market regulation. . . . The search for effective financial literacy education should be replaced by a search for policies more conducive to good consumer financial outcomes."

Trying to solve the problem of financial insecurity in retirement is like building bridges with no guardrails, and then trying to figure out how to stop people from toppling off; or licensing poisonous foods and drugs but trying to encourage people to avoid them, perhaps through education programs and helpful labeling. As Robert Kuttner wrote in an article in the progressive publication *The American Prospect* (in 2009, when auto-enrollment still appeared to be a magic bullet), "To pursue the example of the employees helpfully 'nudged' into joining savings plans, the deeper problem today is that fewer companies offer pensions at all, and tax-deferred savings schemes such as 401(k)s (which aren't real pensions) are taking a beating from the stock-market collapse. Systemic reform requires more than a nudge; it may even require dreaded commands and controls like the expansion of Social Security."[35]

A decades-long shift in the pensions industry has forced people to play a bafflingly complex investment game in a fog of genuine uncertainty and sometimes active misinformation. Once upon a time, pensions were "easy" and people managed pretty well. Now the game has changed into one of fiendish complexity, sometimes with actively malevolent adversaries offering bogus or biased propositions and advice. No amount of clever behavioral design is likely to help substantially. We need radical s-frame reform: to reverse the destructive trends of the past few decades and revert to a pensions "game" that is simple, where people know what they are supposed to do (and don't need to do very much, if anything) and also have a clear sense of what they will get in return.

How did the current, flawed US system come into existence? Initially, by accident, as documented by Michael Steinberger in a 2024 article in *The New York Times Magazine* titled "Was the 401(k) a Mistake?"[36] The article details how the Revenue Act passed by Congress in 1978 included an obscure provision, Section 401(k), which clarified a tax benefit that, at the time, applied almost exclusively to top executives. The benefit, which the congressional aides who drafted it viewed as "a minor regulatory tweak, of no particular consequence," allowed companies to set up supplementary retirement plans that enabled employees to defer taxes on limited amounts of income and to invest the money tax-free, only paying taxes on the accrued values of the accounts when the money was deducted (typically following retirement, when the employee's income would be predictably lower).

An obscure retirement-benefits consultant named Ted Benna, tasked with figuring out how to provide retirement benefits for executives that could help them to avoid taxes, implemented these accounts at his own company, initially calling it "cash-op," though it ultimately came to be known by the number—401(k)—of the tax loophole that spawned the approach. Seeing the success of the approach at Benna's firm, more and more companies started to offer 401(k)s, and gradually these came to be viewed not as pension supplements but as pension substitutes—an irresistible attraction to firms whereby they could reduce or altogether avoid paying for their employees' pensions, as well as skirt responsibility for making pension investment fund decisions. According to Steinberger's article, the finance industry, "eyeing a lucrative new revenue stream, threw its lobbying muscle behind these investment plans."

Consider, for example, TIAA (Teachers Insurance and Annuity Association), one of the largest administrators of defined contribution plans, which, ironically, peppered the online version of the *New York Times Magazine* article just discussed with its ads—"ironically" because the article called for an end to the very retirement approach that is TIAA's lifeblood. The advertisements featured photos of happy-looking retirees and slogans such as "TIAA's Promises Pay Off," "Building a Retirement That Lasts," "Understanding the Importance of a Safety Net," and "Long-Term Strategies for Investing and Saving."

TIAA runs the TIAA Institute, which has as one of its objectives to "assemble leading thinkers with diverse views to explore key topics from multiple angles." Perhaps not surprisingly, given the interest of the parent organization, very few of these "leading thinkers" conduct research questioning the defined contribution retirement system that TIAA operates under; rather, they presuppose that the problem is to help the individual somehow deal with the chaotic pension system as it is. TIAA is by no means alone in adhering to, and perhaps advancing, this i-frame perspective. At present, it seems to be widely accepted that defined contribution plans, for all their problems, are the only viable option. Indeed, Congress has reinforced the defined contribution approach in a variety of ways, including expanding the amount of money that people can contribute, delaying the age by which they must start withdrawing money, and introducing legislation aimed at encouraging auto-enrollment and auto-escalation.

It could, of course, be argued that auto-enrollment and auto-escalation are, if not solutions to the problem of undersaving, at least improvements on an imperfect system. This indeed has been the focus of heated arguments between George and his fellow behavioral economists. Given the system we have now, what's the harm in promoting ways to "help people help themselves"? As we saw with climate change, however, there is a real danger that the promise of individually focused solutions can draw attention away from, and reduce support for, the systemic changes that are required to fix the problem: returning to collective pension solutions, sharing risk across people, and giving predictable benefits.

Indeed, in another experiment from the "crowding out" study discussed in Chapter 1, people evaluated two policies to increase retirement savings.[37] They were asked to think about how effective the policies would be if they were implemented, and how painful they would be for someone like them. One group first evaluated an expansion of the Social Security system, and then evaluated an auto-enrollment intervention added to a defined contribution savings plan; a second group was asked about the two programs in reverse order; and a third group evaluated both programs side by side. The main finding of this study was that support for the expansion of Social Security decreased when people either were first exposed to the auto-enrollment nudge or were exposed to the two policies simultaneously. The mere existence of the Band-Aids of auto-enrollment and auto-escalation, the study suggested, decreases support for the types of policy changes that could really turn around the problem. The very possibility of nudging the players makes us forget that we need to fundamentally change the game.

If the shift to defined contribution retirement plans is such a disaster, then, asks *Atlantic* author Frank Pasquale, "why are policy makers so enamored of it?"[38] Pasquale lays part of the blame at the feet of academics, for framing retirement savings as a problem of individual behavior and responsibility. He notes that the emphasis on helping individuals save "is not surprising given that nudging comes out of microeconomics and psychology, [which focus on] isolated individuals and firms. A sociological or political perspective, on the other hand, points to the real roots of retirement insecurity: a great shifting of risk from corporations to individuals." Pasquale points out, moreover, that exhortations that people take personal responsibility for saving for their futures are bound to fail, after decades of stagnant wages for low- and middle-income workers.

A skeptic might respond: But surely making retirement savings affordable through some kind of mandatory collective pension scheme will just mean workers get a better pension in the future at the expense of lower wages now. Or, if pensions are restored without a sharp cut in wages—a charming prospect in theory—won't the costs drive companies out of business? More pay for all surely can't be a serious solution, can it?

Well yes, we would argue, it absolutely can; perhaps not more pay for all, but more evenly distributed pay across the economy. Properly taxing the spiraling wealth and incomes of the top earners, who have taken almost all the benefits of economic growth over the past several decades, could easily address the problem. And, as we will discuss later in this book, this dramatic increase in inequality has by no means arisen spontaneously, but is itself the product of systemic policies benefiting the rich and powerful, and politically supported (of course) by the rich and powerful.

―――――

Is there a sensible and politically feasible replacement for a retirement system that amounts to little more than "save for your own retirement" and that, worse, disproportionately subsidizes savings by the affluent (who for the most part already save enough)? The obvious solution is to shift back to the defined benefit pension plans that are known to work. This would be a pretty seismic shift, though probably a welcome one for most of us. But less radical changes can be made—and indeed have successfully been made. Focusing on the US, where the pension system is especially badly broken, there is a good model to draw on: Australia.

Middle-income Americans and Australians seem to be in the same boat with regard to their savings rates: They save very little, and some even go into debt for several decades. But when it comes to their retirement balances, Australians are far better off. Currently, Australia boasts the second-highest ratio of pension assets to gross domestic product (151 percent; only the Netherlands is higher, with 187 percent). The US's ratio isn't all that low (68 percent), but the number hides the deep problem of inequality that we have already touched on: In the US the vast bulk of both discretionary and retirement saving is done by those in the very highest income groups.[39]

Australia, like the US, has a retirement system that relies on two components. The first (somewhat similar to Social Security in the US) is the Age Pension, a benefit targeted at lower-income and less wealthy individuals that is funded out of general taxation.[40] The second, far more significant pillar of the Australian system is the mandatory retirement saving program known as "the Super" (short for Superannuation Guarantee). Unlike the US system, which is voluntary on the employer side, the Super requires employers to contribute 12 percent of regular salary for all employees ages eighteen to seventy into a personal, portable pension fund. On the employee side, the key feature of the Australian system that differentiates it from the US system is that loans and preretirement withdrawals are generally forbidden. Australians can, however, begin taking the money as early as age fifty-five, if they're retired.

There are downsides to the Australian system, of course. One is unavoidable: The money devoted to retirement savings has to come from somewhere, and there seems to be a broad agreement among economists that workers are paying for it in the form of reduced wage rates. This makes sense: Traditional pensions may be affordable, but they are still expensive, and the money to pay for them does not come out of thin air.

An avoidable weakness of the Australian system, at least in our view, is that individuals are required to make decisions about how to invest their pension pots.[41] If there are good political reasons why Australian citizens must be given a choice of how to invest their own retirement funds, at least the Super scheme employs good behavioral economics principles—yes, nudge-style!—to maximize the chance that these decisions are made wisely. Super participants are given three broad approaches to investing that vary in how hands-on they wish to be. Listed first, and easiest to invest in, is a default option titled "PreMixed." Described as "Hands-on level: low," the plan offers "different combinations of assets like shares, property and cash. Simply choose an option and leave the rest to us." According to the Super website, more than 90 percent of members are investing at least part of their pension pots (and close to 70 percent of total contributions) in the PreMixed option, which offers a nice combination of diversified investments and low fees.

More broadly, there are plenty of other viable options for retirement savings systems that successfully ensure financial security in retirement. Rather than copying success, however, many nations seem intent on replicating failure—the UK, for example, has increasingly followed the US in "liberalizing" its pension arrangements, giving individuals greater flexibility in using their pension pots early, switching to nonstandard investment schemes, and the like. But this is a triumph of ideologically driven hope over experience (the idea that liberalizing *anything* just must be a good thing has a strangely powerful grip for many on the right), and it is an ideological trend that has enthusiastic support from a finance and business sector that benefits from such trends.

As a model for the US, the beauty of the Australian approach to retirement saving is that it has been tried and it works, and in a country that is not all that dissimilar to the US. There is no need to take a plunge into the unknown. However, it must be acknowledged that there is one big difference between the US and Australia that might weigh against the success of such a system in America: Health care is universal and free in Australia, but not in the US, where it is provided in large part by employers. And because health care in the US is so costly (about twice as costly as in comparable countries), providing these benefits imposes a crushing burden on employers, reducing their ability to also provide a pension.[42] High health care costs are also the cause of much of the "leakage" from the current US retirement system, which happens when people cash in their 401(k) to pay for uncovered medical expenses. This points to the urgent need to address the malfunctioning US health care system. We cross that bridge in the next chapter.

Chapter 4

FLAWED INCENTIVES:
THE OUTSIZE COST OF
US HEALTH CARE

Health care in the United States is astronomically expensive, and the quality of care Americans get in return for their lavish spending is remarkably poor, especially when compared to other affluent countries. Health care costs eat up about 18–20 percent of America's GDP. That works out to about $13,000 per person per year—42 percent of the median American income. This figure dwarfs the 3 percent of GDP America spends on defense, or the 4.8 percent of GDP that goes to Social Security. Other rich countries spend only about 12 percent ($6,000 per person) of their GDPs on health care (see Figure 4.1).

Yet the US ranks last in health care quality and access, according to one widely publicized metric, in comparison to its natural comparators such as France, Germany, the UK, Australia, and Japan.[1] For example, the maternal death rate—the number of women who die each year as a result of complications from childbirth—is on average 4.5 per 100,000 live births in comparable countries, but it is 23.8 per 100,000 live births in the US—over five times higher. The US is also a grim outlier for

Health care spending as a percentage of GDP, 1980–2023

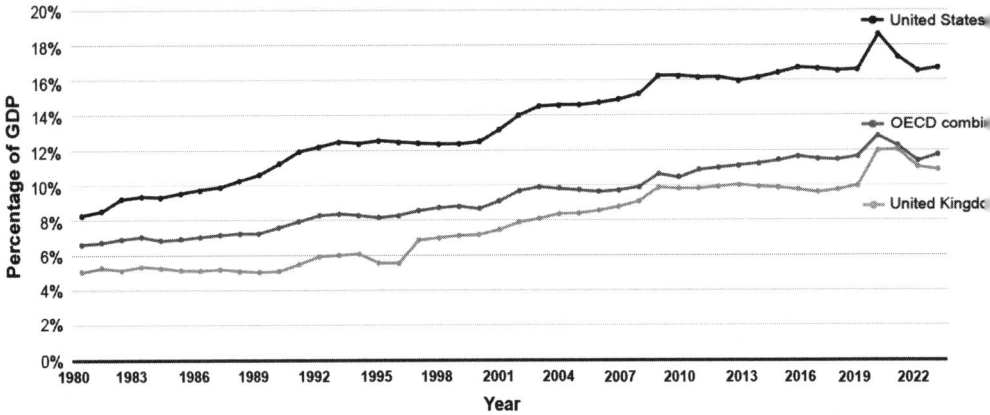

OECD combined includes France, Sweden, Germany, Netherlands, Switzerland, Denmark, New Zealand, Canada, Japan, Norway, and Australia.

Note: GDP refers to gross domestic product. Dutch and Swiss data are for current spending only and exclude spending on capital formation of health care providers. Source: OECD health data.

Figure 4.1. Health spending has grown over time across the OECD countries. But costs in the US have steadily pulled away from the pack. (Chart redrawn and reanalyzed based on David Squires and Chloe Anderson, *U.S. Health Care from a Global Perspective: Spending, Use of Services, Prices, and Health in 13 Countries*, Commonwealth Fund, October 2015.)

rates of childhood mortality (see Figure 4.2); and Americans live substantially shorter lives, on average, than their counterparts in comparable countries (Figure 4.3).

These statistics are shameful and upsetting—which is why they are often cited by politicians and pundits lamenting the state of American health care. What is discussed far less often is *how* the American health care system became so expensive and dysfunctional in the first place. In this chapter, we show that the high cost and low quality of US health care can largely be traced to a single cause: an almost unfathomable variety of conflicts of interest, arising from a vast array of deeply flawed incentives. These arrangements benefit a wide range of concentrated interests—doctors, hospitals, and other health care providers,

Infant mortality rate
Estimated share of newborn deaths before the age of one year

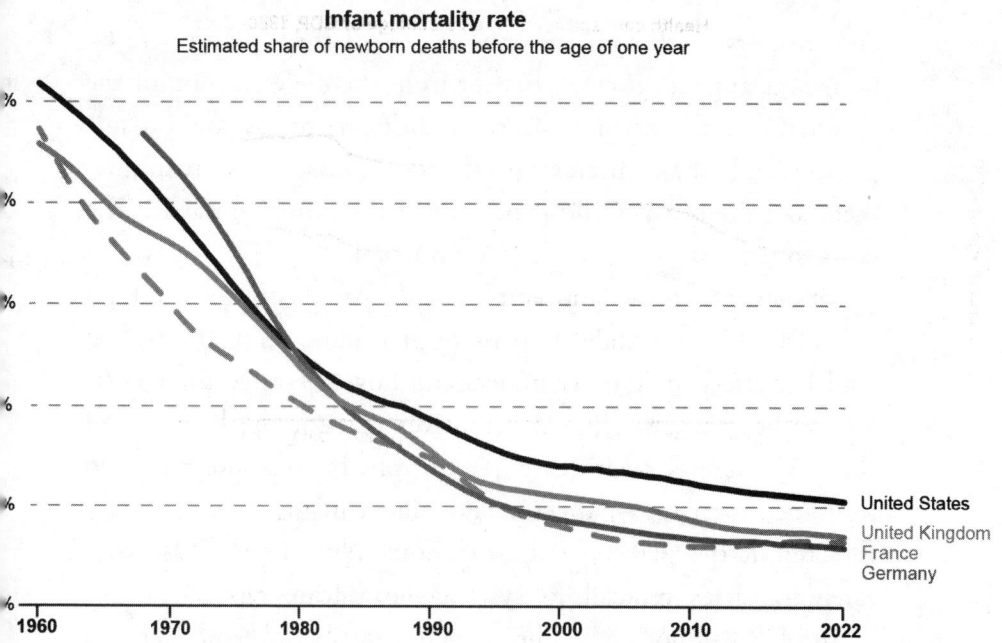

United States
United Kingdom
France
Germany

1960   1970   1980   1990   2000   2010   2022

Data source: United Nations Inter-agency Group for Child Mortality Estimation (2024).

Figure 4.2. Childhood deaths in the US have been falling, but much more slowly than in comparable countries.

Life expectancy at birth in years, 1980–2022

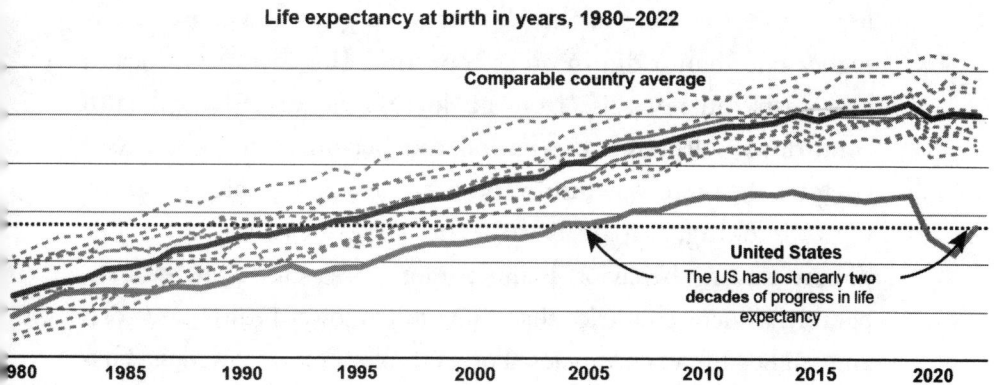

Comparable country average

United States
The US has lost nearly two decades of progress in life expectancy

1980   1985   1990   1995   2000   2005   2010   2015   2020

Figure 4.3. Life expectancy in the US is substantially below that in comparable countries. The average of a range of comparable countries is shown in dark gray (and the underlying countries in dotted light gray to give a sense of the degree of variability). As so often, the US is a striking outlier, especially hard-hit recently in the wake of COVID-19 and the opioid crisis. Note that US life expectancy has not increased in the last two decades, in contrast to comparable countries. (Chart redrawn from analysis by the Peterson-KFF Health System Tracker.)

and insurers. Although the interests of all these players are by no means aligned, they all benefit from the huge fraction of the national income that flows to the health care sector. So, not surprisingly, all these interest groups lobby assiduously to implement and retain rules and regulations that favor themselves. The costs to the rest of society are monumental.

Patients, taxpayers, and employers all pay dearly for the high cost of health care, indeed far more than most people recognize. And because people don't understand how pervasive these costs are, or how far misaligned incentives corrupt the behavior of those who deliver health care (the doctors, but also hospitals and insurance companies), anger at the failures of the system is often directed at the players—e.g., insurance company CEOs—and rarely translates into calls for systemic health care reform.

The US has not always been such a terrible overspender and underperformer when it comes to health care costs and outcomes. In the 1970s, the US spent about 7 percent of its GDP on health, which was higher, but not much higher, than the approximately 5 percent spent by other wealthy countries.[2] However, in the 1980s, health care spending in the US started to grow at a substantially higher rate than it did in other countries. This increase in health care costs did not arise from an increase in underlying health conditions. Although the nation did become more obese (see Chapter 2), there was also a dramatic decline in rates of smoking.[3] Smoking, which is still the largest easily preventable disease-causing behavior, is much more prevalent in many comparably affluent countries that enjoy much lower health care costs and higher life expectancies. For example, France, Sweden, Germany, and Spain all had smoking rates higher than 25 percent in 2021, in contrast with a US rate of around 14 percent.[4]

So if the ballooning costs of American health care had little to do with the underlying health of Americans, what was the cause? As it turned out, in a curious parallel with the inadvertent creation of the 401(k) pension "revolution" we discussed in the last chapter, a seemingly inconsequential policy rule and a fluke of history had drastic, dire, and completely unpredictable consequences.

———

During World War II, the Internal Revenue Service made two seemingly innocuous policy changes designed to benefit both employers and employees. The first was that employees would no longer be taxed on the health insurance benefits they received from their employer. The second was that employers could deduct the cost of providing health insurance for employees from their taxable income. In an accident of history that spawned the current system of employer-provided health care benefits, this favorable tax treatment coincided with a war-induced labor shortage and a wage freeze designed to prevent the runaway inflation that was feared as a result of high wartime government spending. Employers, who couldn't attract workers by raising wages directly, realized they could effectively offer higher salaries by providing health care benefits and, under the new rules, receive a tax break for doing so. Even better, their employees would not be taxed on this valuable new benefit. This combination of changed tax regulations and historical circumstances led to the expansion of employer-based health insurance in the US, a setup quite different from that in other affluent countries. Summarizing these and other developments, Troyen Brennan, the former chief medical officer of CVS Health (which during his tenure acquired the health insurer Aetna), writes, "If this evolution of health policy seems haphazard, it should. When these legal interventions took place, no one saw the impact they would have. There was no comprehensive rationality applied to the problems of American health care."[5]

Employers, in turn, outsourced this highly specialized benefit to a growing number of health insurance providers. Some of these companies were for-profit (like Aetna), while others were at least nominally not-for-profit (like Blue Cross / Blue Shield). Some dealt only with the financial side of the equation (and faced incentives to lower costs, while providers want to keep costs high), while other, "vertically integrated" providers, such as Kaiser, provided not only insurance but medical care as well.

There is nothing inherently expensive about a system that operates through employers; employers will be motivated to reduce all costs, including those associated with providing health care to their employees. However, the decentralized system that emerged does tend to proliferate costly administrative functions, and their associated costs, across health insurers. With its fragmented private insurance market, the US spends more than three times as much on administrative costs as does Germany, the next highest spender.

But the real problem with the US health care system is its layer upon layer of perverse incentives—such a rich compost that it is almost impossible to describe in full. One particular feature, however, stands out above all the others in the steaming pile of misaligned incentives: America's fee-for-service approach to compensating providers.

Whereas most countries with public health services, such as the UK, pay physicians a fixed salary, in the US if you go to an orthopedist, for example, it is entirely possible that the person diagnosing your condition and (likely) recommending surgery is the same individual who will perform the surgery and who stands to financially gain from it. The same is true for myriad other tests and procedures. Gastroenterologists tend to perform far more colonoscopies than clinical guidelines call for because they get paid for each one they do (and they use anesthetics—despite the fact that many other countries perform the procedure without them— because that entails an additional profitable charge).[6] Oncologists who get a commission for the chemotherapy they administer tend to give their patients a substantially higher volume of chemotherapy solution.[7] Fee-for-service arrangements encourage overprovision of health care services—a pattern that diverse studies have documented.[8]

"The overwhelming problem with American health care is its deep dependence on a fee-for-service financial system," notes Brennan (the health care executive heard from earlier). In the US health care system, "all the key players a patient encounters—doctors, nurses, hospitals, medical device manufacturers, pharmaceutical manufacturers, pharmacies and pharmacists, employers' health benefit staff, and insurers—are profit seekers driving toward a profit margin."[9] Alas, as he notes, "the profit motive in fee-for-service is indifferent to value."[10] Brennan concludes that "the best way to understand any issue in health care is to discover who profits, and how they do so."[11]

Although the conflicts that arise from fee-for-service arrangements are almost certainly the greatest contributors to overpriced health care, conflicts of different kinds are everywhere in the US health care system. For decades pharmaceutical companies have given enormous rewards to doctors who prescribe their name-brand (i.e., nongeneric) drugs. Although these practices have gradually been reduced by the introduction of ever more stringent guidelines, such grift remains a persistent problem. Surgeons often receive payments from the companies whose medical devices they use. Some, although by no means all, of these payments are disguised—e.g., taking the form of "consulting fees" when no real consulting services occur, or "educational" trips to luxurious vacation spots (often with expenses paid for family members), or lavish meals. These practices create obvious incentives for doctors to prescribe not the best (or in some cases the cheapest) drugs, nor to use the best medical devices, but instead to prescribe, use, and implant those that are personally more profitable.

Conflicts of interest are also rife among regulators, who often cycle back and forth between regulatory roles in government and—when they behave as companies desire—highly paid positions in industry. A particularly egregious, though by no means nonrepresentative, case of a conflict of interest involving regulators was that of Dr. Jeffrey Suren, who presided over the medical device division of the Food and Drug Administration for fifteen years while his wife represented the interests of device makers as the coleader of a team of lawyers at one of Washington's most powerful law firms (both Jeffrey and Allison Suren have argued that they complied with all relevant ethical standards).[12] Similar conflicts of interest also played a key role in the opioid crisis (see Chapter 6).

Such conflicts pose a problem even if most doctors are honorable people (although, as in any profession, there will be dishonorable exceptions) trying to do the right thing by their patients. Conflicts of interest often operate at the margins, the gray areas where a judgment could go either way. And where this is so, doctors, like all of us, will find themselves erring imperceptibly on the side of the choice that aligns best with their own interests. Of course, doctors are able to convince themselves that the surgery, drugs, and devices they will profit from are also best for their patients. The human brain is remarkably adept at convincing itself that the moral course of action is the one that will most benefit oneself.[13]

Life continually presents us with difficult choices that we are ill-equipped to make. Most of us don't know much about cars, for example, but we have to buy them anyway. Few of us are equipped to value real estate or to appraise the quality of contracting work, but we launch into house purchases and renovation projects nonetheless. And who is really able to figure out with any certainty whether, or whom, to marry, whether to have children, or which career to pursue? Mostly, though, we somehow muddle through, though each of us with our share of mishaps.

But sometimes help, or what looks like help, is at hand. Journalists, product reviewers, financial advisers, forecasters, life coaches, self-help gurus, religious leaders, and—particularly relevant to this chapter—doctors and other medical providers are all too willing to tell us how they think we should manage different aspects of our lives.

Whom should we trust? Here, the deep psychological bias toward the i-frame can badly mislead us—we tend to focus on the individual giving us advice. Do they seem knowledgeable about the topic and well qualified? Do they seem intelligent, warm, and perhaps even smartly dressed? Do they have an "honest look"? Some of these characteristics may be useful; many are not. But to frame the problem of whom to trust in terms of individual traits at all is to miss a more fundamental, s-frame, question: What incentives does my adviser face? What does my adviser stand to gain (if anything) from advising me to do X, not Y? How is my adviser's performance being measured or overseen, if at all? How do they build a reputation in their profession? How are they regulated? Even to entertain such questions seems cynical; to ask them explicitly seems downright impertinent or even insulting. Indeed, social etiquette requires that we treat our adviser as "above" any such s-frame forces, and instead as a benevolent and dispassionate oracle. That's the pretense, whether or not we entirely believe it.

It should come as no surprise that incentives can and do dramatically shape pronouncements from expert sources of all kinds. It is a familiar story (and one to which we shall return) that scientists and executives paid by big tobacco, many of whom were doubtless highly intelligent and knowledgeable—and who had honest, kind faces—denied the link between smoking and cancer for decades; and, in a repeat performance, as we've seen, scientists and executives paid by the fossil fuel industry, and who were equally intelligent, expert, and honest-looking, denied the link between CO_2 emissions and climate change.

But what if people are transparent about their interests? Surely, if we know that an adviser benefits from providing biased advice, we will ignore that adviser's recommendation—or at least take it with a grain of salt? Unfortunately, the fundamental attribution error—our psychological tendency to focus on the person rather than the situation—leads us to underestimate the impact of incentives on the advice we receive. We focus on the intelligence, expertise, and honest face of the advice-giver and largely forget that they are playing a game, and that what really matters (at least to them) is what it takes to get ahead in that game. Disclosure—fessing up to conflicts of interest—is no panacea; indeed, as we'll see, it is more than likely to backfire, leading to more biased advice and worse decisions by advice recipients.

An extensive and varied series of experiments has shown that people are indeed remarkably trusting of advisers who have conflicts of interest—who are, in essence, incentivized to give poor advice. This research shows not only that people are not as skeptical as they should be when they learn their adviser has a conflict of interest, but, worse, the advisers give even more misleading advice when advisees are informed about their conflict.[14]

Why would advisers give *more* biased advice after disclosing a conflict of interest? George's research has shown that when advisers disclose their conflicts, they expect their clients to take the advice with a grain of salt, so they compensate by being even more biased. George and his coauthors called this "strategic exaggeration." And another perverse factor—called "moral licensing"—makes a bad situation worse: Once the advisers had disclosed their conflicting incentive, they became unmoored from ethical concerns that might have, in the absence of disclosure, led them to rein in their tendency to favor their own interests; since the clients had been warned about the conflict, advisers no longer felt it was their responsibility to give impartial advice.

Doctors are susceptible to all these effects, but patients also respond in unexpected ways to the disclosure of a conflict of interest. In a separate project, George and coauthors Daylian Cain and Sunita Sah found that when a physician reveals a conflict of interest—such as saying, after recommending an expensive test, "I should tell you that I own an interest in the facility"—it does decrease trust in that physician and their recommendation.[15]

However, despite this loss of trust, and because of an effect George and his colleagues dub "insinuation anxiety," the patient unexpectedly feels more pressure after such a disclosure to follow the biased advice. To understand how it works, imagine that you go to your physician, who recommends a test or procedure without any disclosure, and you decide not to get it. In this situation, there are any number of innocuous reasons why you might choose not to follow the doctor's advice. But what if that advice did come with a conflict-of-interest disclosure? Now there is a new, highly salient reason why you may not have followed this advice: because you don't trust your physician's ability to transcend the conflict and offer you advice that's in your best interest. Most patients will not want to risk conveying such distrust to a physician, which ironically increases the pressure to comply with the distrusted advice.

————

Just how easy it is for the most respected of professionals to be lured into rigging the game—or more specifically, deliberately ensuring that the game can be rigged—was brought home forcibly to George back in 2007, when he received a phone call out of the blue from his friend Robert ("Rocky") Schoen, a gastroenterologist at the University of Pittsburgh Medical Center (UPMC). Rocky was excited and perplexed.

"You'll never believe what's happening, George. There's a firestorm over here."

The firestorm was ignited by what might have seemed like uncontroversial guidelines that UPMC had floated with its faculty to help avoid conflicts of interest. Rocky knew George would be interested because they had been discussing the problem of conflicts of interest in medicine for years. The proposed guidelines were pretty innocuous, including provisions that would, for example, limit the value of gifts that UPMC physicians could receive from pharmaceutical companies and medical device manufacturers. It barred altogether visits to physician offices by so-called drug "detailers"—almost invariably attractive young men and women who are expert in using their charm (as well, often, as material rewards) to persuade doctors to prescribe their company's drugs—a practice widely agreed to be unhelpful to achieving the best choices for patients. One might expect UPMC physicians to warmly (or at worst slightly grudgingly) agree that these guidelines were "doing the right thing" by patients.

Not at all! Several physicians sent outraged emails to pretty much all their colleagues. These doctors were fighting against "changing the game" and saw themselves as backed by reason, not mere self-interest—even if their arguments seemed highly questionable, at least to an outsider.

George wondered how the doctors writing such emails would view the same arguments if they were themselves outsiders: i.e., if the topic were an area of work other than their own. So, he set out to answer the question.[16]

Teaming up with Rocky and graduate student Zack Sharek, George created two distilled versions of a conflict-of-interest policy, one dealing with physicians and the other—almost identical except for changing a small number of words—dealing with financial advisers. From the emails that Rocky had forwarded to George, the team distilled six objections to UPMC's policies. For different groups of respondents (including physicians; more on that in a moment), participants in the research were first shown, and asked to evaluate their support for, one of the two conflict-of-interest policies (the one aimed at physicians or the one aimed at financial advisers). Then they were shown the six objections to the policy and asked how reasonable they found each of them. Finally, they were shown the original policy again and were asked to reevaluate their support for it in light of the objections they had been exposed to.

The researchers' first step was to run the study both on doctors at UPMC (an administrator who favored the policy was accommodating in giving access to an email list of physicians) and on readers of *The New York Times* (thanks to the generosity of *Times* columnist John Tierney, who put a link to our survey on his online blog at the *Times*). The *New York Times* readers were an ideal comparison sample because they had almost as much education and income, on average, as the doctors. But, of course, they did not have the doctors' special perspective on matters relating to medicine.

The two groups had similarly positive views on the policies aimed at avoiding conflicts of interest among financial planners. As expected, however, the physicians hated the policy proposals aimed at avoiding conflicts of interests for doctors; the *Times* readers had a much more positive view toward the policy. Not only that: The physicians rated every *objection* to the policy as more reasonable than did the *Times* readers.

Initially, George and his coauthors found it impossible to get the paper published in a medical journal. One journal after another rejected the paper with the general, quite possibly valid (at least in George's case), objection that the authors seemed to be on a kind of "witch hunt" against doctors. To protect themselves from this charge, they decided to collect more data. Recalling that an old friend worked at a trade journal for financial advisers, George persuaded her to send an email to subscribers to the journal asking them to participate in the study. Now the researchers also had financial advisers evaluating a conflict-of-interest policy that applied to their profession (or to doctors), evaluating objections to it, then reevaluating the policy. Perhaps not surprisingly, the financial analysts had, compared with the doctors, almost the mirror-image response to the policies: They hated the policies aimed at them and thought the objections to those policies were much more reasonable than those aimed at the medical conflict-of-interest policy.

So, in the end, there were three samples—doctors, financial advisers, and *New York Times* readers—and the very consistent finding was that people objected to policies if those policies adversely affected *them*. Interestingly, after reading the objections to the policies, the *Times* readers *increased* their level of endorsement for the anticonflict policies. They seemed to reason that "if these rather feeble objections are the strongest you can come up with, it must be a good policy." But when physicians read the very same set of objections they became even more convinced that medical conflict-of-interest policies were a bad thing; and, in mirror image, the financial planners became even more convinced that the financial conflict-of-interest policies were ill-advised. Most doctors and financial advisers aren't knaves. They just exhibit a universal human tendency: to find it all too easy to be convinced by arguments that happen to align with their interests. This tendency has a name: the self-serving bias.[17]

The self-serving bias kicks in when there are multiple interpretations of what is "fair." In such situations, people tend to choose whatever interpretation best suits their own interests. A slew of experiments has not only established the existence of this bias but also shown that people who exhibit it are not conscious that they're stacking the deck in their own favor. Not only that: Research has found that people are unable to resist the self-serving bias even in cases when they are motivated (through the offer of some reward) to be impartial. Furthermore, when you explain to practitioners how the self-serving bias works—in the hope that they might be able to combat the problem in their own thinking—they believe that others may be affected by the bias but that their own judgment is unaffected.[18] This was nicely illustrated by a study of medical residents, 61 percent of whom said that promotions from drug companies "don't influence my practice." Only 16 percent of the residents believed the same thing was true about other physicians' practices.[19]

———

Conflicts of interest in the American health care system are by no means limited to health care providers such as doctors. One might think that professional medical societies would try to rein in this perverse incentive structure, but nothing could be further from the truth. American medical societies not only tolerate these practices, but they play an essential role in enabling and perpetuating them. For example, the American Medical Association has long and successfully opposed many of the reforms that could have had a chance of reining in costs and broadening access to health care. The pejorative term "socialized medicine," for example, was first used by the AMA to attack health care reforms backed by the Truman administration.[20] Then there are the severe conflicts that arise when physicians own, or have an interest in, specific testing (e.g., MRI) or treatment facilities. In 1989, the Office of Inspector General of the US Department of Health and Human Services conducted a study on physician ownership of clinical laboratories, which found that Medicare patients of referring physicians who own or invest in clinical laboratories received 45 percent more clinical laboratory services than the Medicare patients of physicians without such ownership conflicts.[21] Likewise, a study by the US Government Accountability Office found that providers' referrals of MRI and CT services substantially increased the year after they purchased or leased imaging equipment, or joined a group practice that already self-referred.[22]

Incentives are flawed at many other levels. Pharmaceutical companies often conduct their own clinical trials, or hire (and can fire or subsequently not rehire) companies to perform those trials on their behalf. So it's no mystery why trials performed or funded by these companies are far more likely to yield results favorable to the drugs than are trials performed by independent entities.[23]

But perhaps the worst offenders when it comes to stacking the deck are the insurance companies. In their brilliant recent book, *We've Got You Covered: Rebooting American Health Care*, economists Liran Einav and Amy Finkelstein document the myriad, mind-boggling ills of the US health care system—which Walter Cronkite, they remind us, described as "neither healthy, caring, nor a system."[24] They catalog the absurd cost of insurance coverage; the overwhelming paperwork required to obtain and retain coverage (far beyond the capabilities of many disadvantaged individuals who need it most); the arbitrary factors such as age, income, and medical conditions that limit eligibility and often cause people to lose coverage (sometimes without notification, so they don't realize they have become uninsured); and the limits on reimbursements, which leave even insured individuals facing crushing medical bills. Einav and Finkelstein conclude—consistent with the central theme of this book—that the current health insurance system is so broken that "incremental reform is not the answer. We can't rely on yet more Band-Aids and partial patches."[25]

The bewildering complexity of private insurance products is another major problem with medical insurance. In their research on the health insurance market, George, the Harvard economist David Laibson (whose work on retirement savings we discussed in the last chapter), and several other economists found that the average individual can't make sense of even the most basic elements of a health insurance plan, even though they are required to choose a plan from a dizzying array of choices.[26] The research was conducted with the participation of executives from a large medical insurance company that was initially skeptical of George and his team's claim that their customers didn't understand their products. An amusing incident occurred during the research when the academic researchers came up with what they thought were some very simple questions to gauge laypeople's understanding of basic elements of medical insurance and, at an in-person meeting, asked the executives for the correct answer to each question so that the research team could be sure they would be marking the test accurately. Despite the fact that the insurance executives on the team were among those responsible for designing the company's insurance products, they themselves were unsure of how their own policy worked and asked for a day to get back to George and his fellow researchers with correct answers.

In another study, titled "Choose to Lose," George and two colleagues, Saurabh Bhargava and Justin Sydnor, documented the experience of a large (Fortune 25) US company that gave its employees a choice among forty-eight insurance plans that differed in deductibles, co-pays, coinsurance rates, and out-of-pocket spending limits—a scheme the company called "Choose Your Own Plan."[27] Although executives at the company were unaware of it, Saurabh glanced at the huge matrix of plans and had a brilliant and shocking insight. A majority of the plans from which employees could choose were what economists call "dominated"— they would result in higher spending under any possible circumstance, and thus made no sense for anyone. With the generous provision of the enrollment and claims data by the company to the team, it emerged that a majority of employees—and an especially high number of low-earning employees—choose such dominated plans (and end up paying, on average, an extra $500 yearly for their mistakes). Follow-up studies reported in the same paper showed that the main cause of these bad decisions was a failure to understand health insurance; when the consequences of choices were made much more transparent, then people made sensible choices.

Seniors insured under Medicare Part D or in Medicare Advantage plans select from numerous plan options that differ on multiple dimensions, and individuals who enroll in medical insurance under the Affordable Care Act (ACA, popularly known as Obamacare) choose from large numbers of plans. In theory, such choice should improve the position of insured individuals, both by allowing them to sort through competing plans and by encouraging cost-reducing and quality-improving competition among providers of insurance. As Kathleen Sebelius, the US secretary of health and human services from 2009 to 2014, stated during the rollout of the ACA exchanges, "Exchanges offer Americans competition, choice, and clout. Insurance companies will compete for business on a transparent, level playing field, driving down costs, and Exchanges will give individuals . . . a choice of plans to fit their needs."[28] But if consumers fail to understand the most basic elements of medical insurance, how can they possibly choose a plan to "fit their needs"? And if consumers don't have a clue when choosing among plans, what is the chance that their decisions will drive insurance companies to provide better, and lower-cost, options?

Clearly, the key to reducing health care costs (and using some of the savings to actually improve health and health care) is to enact s-frame reforms, and another finding from George's "Choose to Lose" paper has important implications for what form such s-frame reform efforts could take. Further analysis of the data revealed that almost all employees would have been better off if they had been offered a single plan—the same one for all employees. Moreover, given the health care they in fact obtained, there was almost no difference between what they would have paid in such a single-plan setup and what would have been the cheapest of any of the available plans for them, personally (which they couldn't have known, in any case, at the start of the year before they actually received health care). This strongly suggests that giving people choices among alternative plans to "fit their needs" is an absurd idea, and is even worse when people can't make sense of those plans and don't know what their health care needs will be in the upcoming year. If almost all consumers would benefit from being in the same plan, why give them a choice of alternative plans? And assigning everyone to the same plan would have an additional benefit: Health insurers could no longer compete by obscuring the reality of the plans they offer via small print and confusing features. Instead, they would be forced to compete on price and quality.

Not surprisingly, such s-frame reforms, and especially those that eliminate the role of private insurers altogether (e.g., so-called single-payer plans) are vigorously resisted by the army of businesses and professional groups—pharmaceutical companies, device manufacturers, health insurers, and physician groups—whose bottom line would be hurt. Insurance companies' public relations departments have framed efforts to reduce costs as "death panels" (mentioned in the Introduction), and funded the masterfully effective "Harry and Louise" advertising campaign—portraying a middle-age suburban couple drowning in bureaucratic red tape—that helped to turn public opinion against the 1993 Clinton Health Care Plan, a health care reform initiative led by Hillary Clinton during Bill Clinton's first term in office. These PR and political lobbying campaigns were sufficiently effective that what had started as a flagship initiative for the new administration was effectively dead by the very next year, after losing a key Senate vote.[29]

A huge backlash against reform in health care is, of course, to be expected. In the UK, the founding of the National Health Service (NHS) by Prime Minister Clement Attlee's government in 1948—a free-at-the-point-of-use, state-funded health care system that, despite recent underfunding and consequent travails, remains extremely popular—was opposed relentlessly by the medical establishment, and especially by general practitioners.[30] This opposition was in part pitched as stemming from a concern for patients.[31] But in reality the new system was a vast step forward for patients, and a loss of autonomy and income-generating opportunities for many doctors. These tensions have a lasting legacy today—the government was forced to concede to senior doctors' demands to continue lucrative private work alongside publicly funded activities, resulting in a tangled mix of private and public health care, in which the very same doctor and patient can have parallel, but intertwined, interactions (effectively allowing wealthier patients to jump ahead in line for treatment). Eliminating these conflicts has been seen as too challenging for successive governments to even contemplate.

Health care is yet another example of the phenomenon discussed by Mancur Olson in which concentrated economic interests triumph over those of atomistic individuals. As President Obama wrote in a *New Yorker* article detailing the pains of enacting his watered-down version of health reform, "Unlike the insurance companies or Big Pharma, whose shareholders expected them to be on guard against any change that might cost them a dime, most of the potential beneficiaries of reform—the waitress, the family farmer, the independent contractor, the cancer survivor—didn't have gaggles of well-paid and experienced lobbyists roaming the halls of Congress."[32]

As is true of the other problems we discuss in this book, the interests that are opposed to change have often cast the health care crisis as the product of flawed individuals rather than flawed incentives. The message is conveyed through actions such as the provision of rewards for exercise or subsidization of fees at fitness clubs. Although there is strong evidence that employers believe that these programs reduce health care costs, and also evidence that employees also believe they are helpful, there is an almost complete lack of evidence that such incentives have any impact on health, and let alone health care costs.[33] One study found that among employers who offer such programs, only half had tried to evaluate their efficacy, and only 2 percent reported having achieved savings. More rigorously, another study randomly assigned close to thirty-three thousand workers at a large firm to either receive or not receive a wellness program that emphasized nutrition, exercise, and stress reduction.[34] There were no significant differences between the two groups on health, health care spending, or absenteeism, either shortly after their implementation or three years later.[35] Another study employing a similar methodology reached the same conclusion.[36] Similarly dispiriting conclusions have been reached in research testing more targeted disease management programs. As summarized in health care executive Troyen Brennan's book *The Transformation of American Health Insurance*:

Medicare conducted six demonstration projects involving nearly thirty-four disease management programs. The Congressional Budget Office coldly summarized the results in a definitive publication: "All of the programs in those demonstrations sought to reduce hospital admission by maintaining or improving beneficiaries' health, and that reduction was the key mechanism through which they expected to reduce Medicare expenditures. On average, the 34 programs had no effect on hospital admissions or regular Medicare expenditures. . . . After accounting for the fees that Medicare paid to the program . . . Medicare spending was unchanged or increased in nearly all the programs.[37]

The "Safeway Amendment" of the ACA enables employers offering health insurance to employees to adjust the health insurance premiums by up to 30 percent (and possibly up to as much as 50 percent, at the discretion of the secretary of health and human services) based on the health behaviors of their employees (such as smoking) and on outcomes seen to be the result of behaviors (such as obesity). The premise of such measures is that employees will respond to these incentives by losing weight and quitting smoking, thus improving their own health and reducing costs for themselves and their employer.

It is clear that such measures mean that individuals with lower levels of education and income, who tend to smoke more and be heavier, pay more for their health insurance. It is also clear that successful implementation of these measures infringes on privacy by subjecting employees to a new range of tests—such as cotinine tests to determine if they are eligible for the lower rates received by nonsmokers (cotinine is produced when nicotine is broken down in the liver). These measures may also help employers and insurers to "cherry pick" low-cost customers by deterring, with high premiums, the sickest patients from enrolling in their plans.

What is far less clear is whether these schemes actually promote good health. The Safeway Amendment got its name from comments by the CEO of the Safeway supermarkets chain that his company had kept health care costs from rising at all from 2005 to 2009 by tying health insurance premiums for its employees to outcome-based wellness incentives.[38] But these claims of flattened health care costs through changing employee health-related behavior were later called into question (although not the Safeway claims specifically).[39] Indeed, careful randomized studies of health care schemes at a university found no evidence that financial incentives for members of these plans affect health outcomes and costs.[40] In short, such schemes, however well-intentioned, functioned in practice primarily as a tax on the unhealthy, who are also disproportionately poor.

———

Behavioral economists with a focus on health have unwittingly helped fuel the perception that measures targeting individual behavior could help improve overall health and lower health care costs. In a typical passage from one of many papers proposing behavioral interventions for health problems, George and his coauthors wrote that "individual behavior plays a central role in the disease burden faced by society. Many major health problems in the United States and other developed nations, such as lung cancer, hypertension, and diabetes, are exacerbated by unhealthy behaviors. Modifiable behaviors such as tobacco use, overeating, and alcohol abuse account for nearly one-third of all deaths in the United States."[41] While such statistics are, to the best of our knowledge, accurate, they effectively, and mistakenly, point the finger at patients as the major cause (or at least *a* major cause) of the high-cost, low-quality health care received by the average American.

A huge variety of behavioral interventions have been proposed to make people healthier. In parallel, information programs (e.g., alcohol labeling), injunctions on products (e.g., "please drink responsibly"), and industry-funded wellness programs attempt to provide i-frame solutions.[42] However, the results have been very similar to those of i-frame interventions to combat obesity: Attempts to improve health behaviors through i-frame interventions such as cleverly crafted incentives and reminders and apps have largely been shown to be ineffective in changing those behaviors, and are almost never found to improve health outcomes.[43]

Despite periodic crises in its National Health Service, the UK has been much more successful than the US in providing public health care at a manageable cost. One factor keeping costs under control is a powerful s-frame innovation: The government has empowered an agency—the National Institute for Health and Care Excellence (known as NICE)—to make the difficult decision about what drugs and services will be covered by the National Health Service. The closest analog that the United States had to NICE was called the Agency for Health Care Policy and Research (AHCPR). While it did not determine which procedures would be covered by public health programs such as Medicare and Medicaid, the AHCPR played the important regulatory role of evaluating which procedures were effective and issuing guidelines that helped insurers and patients. Or at least the AHCPR *did* play that role until the mid-1990s, when it had the audacity to publish strong evidence that most back surgeries were unnecessary and in many cases subjected patients to additional harm. Outraged by this threat to their livelihoods, a coalition of back surgeons banded together to lobby Congress, which, in turn, effectively neutered the agency. This is to be expected: The special interests that benefit from a rigged system will typically fight reform at every turn, even where this is clearly to the detriment of the rest of us.

The costs of America's extravagantly expensive health care system go far beyond dollars and cents. We've already shown how life expectancy and maternal mortality rates in the US are no better (and in some cases far worse) than in other developed countries that pay far less per person for health care. But to illustrate how such an inefficient system hurts its patients, consider the case of the so-called doughnut hole in the Medicare Part D prescription drug coverage benefit. The "hole" here refers to a gap in coverage that occurs after you and your plan pay a certain amount of money to cover the costs of prescription drugs. Once patients reach that limit—which was a bit over $4,000 for 2024—they must pay 25 percent of the costs of their medications out of pocket, up to $8,000, after which their coverage resumes. Many people on Medicare can't afford additional out-of-pocket expenses and can't reduce or simply stop taking their medications during this period—many are taking drugs for serious medical conditions, like heart disease. In a paper published in the *Quarterly Journal of Economics*, Harvard's Amitabh Chandra and his colleagues calculated that, when their out-of-pocket drug expenses increase due to falling into the doughnut hole, people consume fewer drugs and die earlier.[44] High-risk patients (those most likely to have a heart attack) cut back more than low-risk patients, and they do so on exactly the drugs from which they would benefit the most. In a happy development, one of the many features of the Biden administration's Inflation Reduction Act is to enhance Part D drug coverage in a way that eliminates the doughnut hole in 2025.[45] Despite this one encouraging development, however, the broad conclusion from this research is that America's expensive health care system isn't a coherent "system" at all.

———

The systemic failures of US health care are, as we've seen, numerous, and, not surprisingly, they have generated widespread public anger. The anger is justified—but should be directed to wresting control of the rules of the health care system from the powerful interests that benefit from the status quo, and remaking those rules for the benefit of patients rather than health care providers. There are many ways of funding health care, many of which are running successfully on a large scale in developed economies across the world, at lower cost and with better results than the woeful US model.

Yet public anger can so easily become misdirected at specific individuals in the health care sector, rather than toward reform of the system itself. This is simply the fundamental attribution error in action again—the human tendency to see "bad people" rather than flawed systems as the problem. As we complete this book, this has been illustrated by public reactions to the tragic killing of Brian Thompson, CEO of UnitedHealthcare, in midtown Manhattan on December 4, 2024—reactions ranging from a simple lack of empathy to outbursts of grimly dark humor.[46] Public anger at denials and delays in health insurance claims is surely a justified response to a broken health care system. But to rail against particular individuals is to keep on the very i-frame blinders that make building a coalition of support for systemic change so difficult.[47]

Chapter 5

INEQUALITY BY DESIGN

In a classic 1960s study, the psychologist Melvin Lerner analyzed how people responded when they watched someone receive electric shocks for poor performance on a learning task. In one condition, the observers could intervene to stop the shocks, and most did so to the best of their abilities. In another condition, however, participants were powerless to alleviate the person's apparent suffering, and here an interesting pattern emerged: Observers developed a more negative judgment of the "victim" in order to reduce, Lerner concluded, what would otherwise be an intolerable sense of injustice.[1] According to Lerner's "just world" hypothesis, human beings find injustice emotionally painful and difficult to tolerate. When a situation seems *unfair*, we first try to take actions to restore fairness. But if and when these actions fail, or when there is simply no action we can take, we try to reduce the painful sense of unfairness. And an effective way to do this is to find a way to rationalize that the victim of the injustice *deserves* the apparent injustice.

Applying Lerner's "just world" hypothesis to the issue of income and wealth inequality suggests that people are motivated to believe, despite evidence to the contrary, that the game of life more or less fairly rewards people according to their talents and hard work. Even if we observe dramatic differences in life trajectories for different people, we assume that the *playing field* must be level. Not everyone can win Wimbledon, but anyone can pick up a tennis racquet. In a just world, it is only the most dedicated, talented, and *deserving* who triumph.[2] This intuition is everywhere, from clichés ("you reap what you sow" and "what goes around comes around") to cosmic notions of karma, or of heaven and hell, which balance out any apparent inequities in our current lives with payback in lives to come. When we imagine that everyone has a "fair shot" in the game of life, then the inequalities we experience can seem perfectly reasonable. We can come to feel that they are merely a natural by-product of competition between individuals with different levels of skills, talent, and motivation. Inevitably, some will come out on top.

As the original research on the "just world" hypothesis suggests, when we see no way of restoring justice we trick ourselves into believing that what seems unfair is actually inevitable and natural, that this is just *the way things are*. And so we unwittingly accept the cost of economic globalization, even though it shifts manufacturing and other jobs overseas and pulls down wages.[3] We allow a few powerful technology companies to disrupt entire industries, creating a small number of global "winners" in entertainment, news, sports, software, or technology itself, that displace patchworks of local providers and take their revenues.[4] And we tolerate a mushrooming financial services industry that has become increasingly divorced from, and parasitic on, the real economy. In relation to the scale of the problem of growing inequality, public disquiet, though very real, is strangely muted. An individualist conception of society, it turns out, can be compelling, even to those people most disadvantaged by rising inequality. The fundamental attribution error blinds us to the decisive power of the s-frame—and can leave voters backing policies that directly work against their interests.

Far from attempting to counter these forces, to ensure that wealth is spread across society so that the proverbial rising tide raises all boats, government policy, at least in the United States and Britain, has done practically nothing.[5] And in some cases, policy has actually *driven* inequality, making it easier than ever for the 1 percent, the 0.1 percent, and the 0.01 percent to grow their incomes and increase their wealth. As noted by former *New York Times* columnist Anand Giridharadas in his insightful book *Winners Take All*, "the system—in America and around the world—has been organized to siphon the gains from innovation upward, such that the fortunes of the world's billionaires now grow at more than double the pace of everyone else's."[6] Some of these developments have been aided by misconceptions about economic policies. Because of factors such as misinformation, partisan loyalty, and short-term economic concerns, many voters, including members of the working class, support policies that exacerbate inequality.[7]

By now it should hardly surprise you that the world's economic elite, which controls a vastly disproportionate amount of global wealth, has lobbied and campaigned hard to shape government policy, at an s-frame level, in their favor. Whether it be arcane tax breaks and tax loopholes that few people understand, or efforts to gut the US Internal Revenue Service, the rich and powerful are constantly at work to create and administer laws and regulations that will enable them to retain and grow their wealth.[8] At the same time, they promote an i-frame vision of society according to which people are fairly rewarded for their individual contribution, and in which, supposedly, everyone gets a "fair shake." This perspective has consequences when it comes to attributions of blame toward those who end up at the wrong end of the income and wealth spectrum, and also consequences for support of different policies. One paper, for example, presented five studies, both cross-sectional and experimental, showing that attributing poverty to individual as opposed to situational (systemic) forces led to reduced concern about inequality as well as diminished support for policies aimed at combating the problem.[9]

**Cumulative change in real hourly wages of all workers
by wage percentile, 1979–2013**

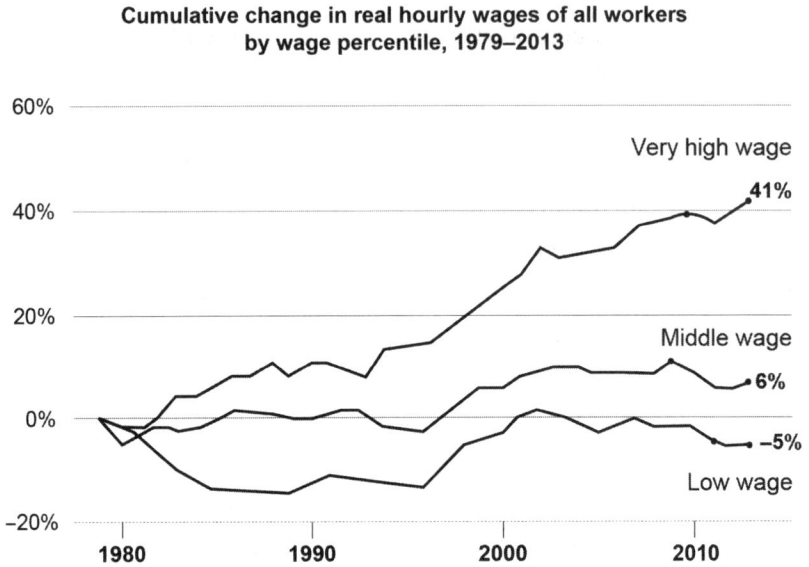

Figure 5.1. How the rich have become richer. While low-wage workers in the US had roughly static real hourly wages from 1979 to 2013, hourly rates for high-paying jobs increased steadily. Low wage is 10th percentile, middle wage is 50th percentile, and very high wage is 95th percentile. (Lawrence Mishel, Elise Gould, and Josh Bivens, "Wage Stagnation in Nine Charts," Economic Policy Institute, January 6, 2015.)

Moreover, whether well-intentioned (as is likely) or not, some prominent members of the economic elite have also, as Giridharadas expresses it, declared themselves "partisans of change," "taking on social change as though it were just another stock in their portfolio or corporation to restructure." Giridharadas shows how these initiatives often adopt market-based perspectives that bypass government and regulation. He notes that "conferences and idea festivals sponsored by plutocrats and big business host panels on injustice and promote 'thought leaders' who are willing to confine their thinking to improving lives *within the faulty system rather than tackling the faults*" (emphasis added). But allowing elites to lead social change can perversely maintain the status quo— reducing public anger, improving the image of the wealthy, and crowding out much-needed systemic changes with market-based half measures.[10]

———

The rise in inequality is recent, and its origin is telling.[11] Income inequality as we know it can be traced back to 1980, when something dramatic happened in the US—or, rather, stopped happening (see Figure 5.1). That year, the incomes of the median earner and those below the median became largely stagnant. Although average per capita family income more than doubled from 1980 to 2021, virtually all those gains went to those at the top; the median income (the income of a person ranked right in the middle of the distribution of earnings) was remarkably stagnant, and this was even more true of those with already abysmally low incomes.[12] Similarly, UK income inequality rose rapidly during the 1980s, when the liberal reforms kicked in, though the picture has been mixed since.[13] As we'll see below, though, the very richest in the UK, as in the US, have continued to become disproportionately even richer, although the extent of this is difficult to quantify. The very wealthy often shroud their wealth in opaque trusts and nests of shell companies, and assets are often hidden offshore in so-called tax havens.

Focusing back on the US, the Nobel Prize–winning MIT economist Daron Acemoglu summarizes the situation in stark terms:

There is no doubt that labor-income inequality has surged at least since 1980, and that the trend has continued since the post-2008 Great Recession. This trend stands in stark contrast to the post-war era, when labor-income inequality was stable or declining. From the 1950s to the early 1970s, workers with a high-school diploma or less enjoyed real wage growth at the same rate as those with a college degree or more. But this pattern of shared prosperity ended sometime in the late 1970s and early 1980s. While the real earnings of workers with college degrees has continued to rise steadily, workers without one now earn less today than they did in 1980.[14]

Let this sink in for a moment: The wages of workers without college degrees have been flat or declining over a period of *more than four decades*. Since 1980, the proverbial rising tide has very much not been raising all boats—quite the opposite.

The statistics on wealth inequality, as opposed to income inequality, tell an even direr story. In the US, for example, the three richest people in 2019—Warren Buffett, Bill Gates, and Jeff Bezos—together owned considerably more wealth than the bottom 50 percent of the US population. The top 1 percent of wealth holders in the US held more than twice as much wealth as the bottom 90 percent.[15] For an indication that the problem is getting dramatically worse, consider that the richest American in 1983 (Sam Walton, founder of the retailer Walmart) had a wealth of $2.15 billion ($5.6 billion in 2020 dollars). By 2020, the combined wealth of Walton's family had grown to $247 billion, an inflation-adjusted fortyfold increase.

At the time of writing, there are no fewer than ten Americans worth more than $100 billion—or roughly twenty times the inflation-adjusted wealth of the very richest American in 1983: Jeff Bezos (Amazon), Elon Musk (Tesla), Mark Zuckerberg (Meta/Facebook), Larry Ellison (Oracle), Larry Page (Google), Warren Buffet (Berkshire Hathaway), Sergey Brin (Google), Bill Gates (Microsoft), Steve Ballmer (Microsoft), and Michael Bloomberg (Bloomberg LP).[16]

Wealth is more unequal than incomes because people with high incomes save much more, proportionately, than people with lower incomes, and hence accumulate more wealth. Wealthier people also earn a higher return on their wealth—consistent with the common saying that "the rich get richer." As the influential French economist Thomas Piketty has argued, this effect is further amplified by the long-term trend that the value of investments increases faster than does the size of the economy, so that the wealthy take an ever-growing slice of the economic pie.[17] Indeed, a substantial fraction of people have almost no wealth (calculated as a person's net total assets, including property, after you deduct their debt). For example, in the UK around a third of households have wealth that is at or close to zero, while half of all wealth is held by roughly 10 percent of the population.[18] In both the US and the UK, around 10 percent of households have *negative* wealth; their debts are greater in value than their assets.[19]

From the perspective of happiness, rising inequality is not only unfair but astoundingly wasteful. It is uncontroversial that the marginal impact of additional money on the welfare of the poor will be greater than its impact on the welfare of the rich.[20] It would be difficult to deny that a shift of resources from the superwealthy, who are almost unaffected at the margin by their level of wealth, to the many people who could benefit from modest material improvements would enhance the overall well-being of the population immeasurably. And further factors compound the damage: One is that the wealthy can outcompete the general population for scarce resources, including health care, educational opportunities for their children, and, perhaps most importantly, housing. Another is that the very wealthy have become increasingly detached from the rest of society—from public services, local schools, and communities— further entrenching their lack of alignment with, and hence motivation to work for, the wider public good.[21]

From our perspective, however, a more important point is that inequality is both a cause and a consequence of many of the other important public policy problems we discuss in this book. In the United States, this fact is particularly stark. Poverty drives poor nutrition and obesity, and poor health, in turn, amplifies poverty. Poverty is a huge cause of low educational outcomes, and low educational outcomes, in turn, contribute to poverty. Poverty fuels addiction, including gambling,[22] and both exacerbate poverty. With causality running in both directions, inequality becomes self-perpetuating: The rich get the nutritious diets, high-quality health care, good education, and retirement security to allow them to prosper further; for the poor, the inverse of the same factors is also (downwardly) self-perpetuating.

Is inequality the by-product of inexorable forces beyond our control? Does its solution mysteriously elude human ingenuity? As is true for carbon footprints, obesity, retirement savings, and health care, there are known solutions to this problem; they are out of reach only because powerful and concentrated forces want them to be. And, as usual, the strategy deployed by these forces involves a sleight of hand—an attempt to frame public debate about the problem in individualist i-frame terms, while behind the scenes the affluent manipulate the rules to benefit themselves.

———

A small number of corporations and wealthy individuals—as well as the "think tanks" funded by these individuals and the corporations they control, such as the Heritage Foundation, the American Enterprise Institute, the Cato Institute, and Americans for Prosperity—have worked hard to propagate an individualist perspective on how the economy works. The superrich want us to see their wealth as no more than the just rewards for their personal innovation and hard work.

With the help of right-wing media outlets, political contributions, and funding of right-leaning universities (such as Pepperdine and George Mason University) and individual academics sympathetic to this perspective, these think tanks have successfully advanced a narrative that emphasizes personal responsibility and self-reliance, and implicitly conveys the message that individuals have the power to overcome poverty through hard work, discipline, and determination. An overlapping group of right-leaning individuals and organizations direct blame toward marginalized groups or immigrants, suggesting that they are the ones responsible for taking jobs or sequestering resources from native-born citizens, fostering feelings of resentment and fear among struggling individuals.[23]

In a pattern that should by this point be familiar, at the same time as the forces of the right devote plentiful resources to advancing an i-frame perspective on equality, when it comes to practical matters such as taxation the same forces have fought equally successfully to tip the scales in favor of those accumulating vast fortunes.

In the US and UK, key choices that have driven inequality include cutting taxes on high incomes, capital gains, inheritances, and corporate profits; creating loopholes through which wealth can be passed down between generations tax-free; and radically reshaping pension provisions (as we saw in Chapter 3).[24] The spectacular scale of tax avoidance in the US by the ultrawealthy has been exposed through investigative journalists' access to, and analysis of, IRS tax records.[25] Likewise, the 2016 leak of 11.5 million documents from a Panamanian law firm (the "Panama Papers") revealed how numerous high-profile individuals—including politicians, celebrities, and business leaders—use offshore tax havens to conceal their wealth, evade taxes, and engage in illicit activities such as money laundering.[26] Yet none of these revelations led to the uproar they merited. In 2020, *The New York Times* gained access to tax records showing that Donald Trump, then president of the United States and a self-professed billionaire, had paid close to zero in taxes over a period of many years. Public outcry was again remarkably muted.[27] The story continues right up to the present, as documented from a UK perspective by a recent anonymous exposé of ongoing tax-dodging tactics widely employed by the wealthy, which generated the usual journalistic outrage and public indifference.[28]

In late 2017, the US Congress passed the Tax Cuts and Jobs Act, a huge tax cut spearheaded by the first Trump administration, with the vast majority of savings going to affluent individuals and corporations. Despite the enormous increase in budget deficits—the policy added between $1 trillion and $2 trillion to the national debt—the tax cuts were positively received by much of the population, and especially by conservatives, many of whom had long claimed to be concerned about the mounting federal debt and budget deficits.[29] To be sure, in some quarters these developments provoked outrage, but their overall political impact was transient and minimal. Indeed, the tiny tax cuts that low-income individuals received seemed to be an effective smokescreen for the huge cuts that high-income individuals and corporations obtained.

Alongside tax changes, there have also been concerted attacks on labor unions, with dramatic downward impacts on wages.[30] And another less obvious factor is the deregulation of financial services, and in particular the creation of opportunities for high-risk, high-return financial speculation in the banking sector—resulting not only in huge transfers of wealth from the "real economy" to the financial sector, but also, notably, in the catastrophic financial crisis of 2007–2008.[31]

A rigged game can all too easily be rationalized as fair, with the "winners" from a profoundly unequal system viewed as deserving their rewards, however extravagant, even by the disadvantaged themselves. So rather than being horrified by the revelation that Donald Trump has gone many years paying almost zero taxes, we see a sense of "that's just the way things are" or, even worse, admiration that he can get ahead by bending the rules.[32]

———

Where inequality has persistently been increasing it has, we suggest, been doing so *by design*. The good news is that inequality can be tackled (or at least drastically reduced) by design, too—if there is the political will to do so. The policies that have driven rising inequality in the US and the UK have not been replicated by all economically successful countries, leading to strikingly different outcomes.

Figures 5.2 and 5.3 show the fraction of income earned by the top 1 percent of earners across different countries. Strikingly, English-speaking countries (the US, UK, Canada, Ireland, and Australia) saw a decline in the share of income taken by the top 1 percent until around 1980, after which the trend made an abrupt reversal, taking levels of inequality back to or near where they stood a century ago. In sharp contrast, other developed economies (France, Japan, Spain, and Denmark) saw little or no upswing in inequality over the last forty years. Note how the increase in inequality is by no means a product of inexorable global forces or the rise of technology, which have affected all the countries.[33] The contrast between Figures 5.2 and 5.3 shows that rising inequality is specific to particular economies—those that have actively

Income share of the richest 1% (before tax), 1900–2023

The share of income received by the richest 1% of the population. Income is measured before taxes and benefits. The dotted lines represent extrapolations due to limited data availability.

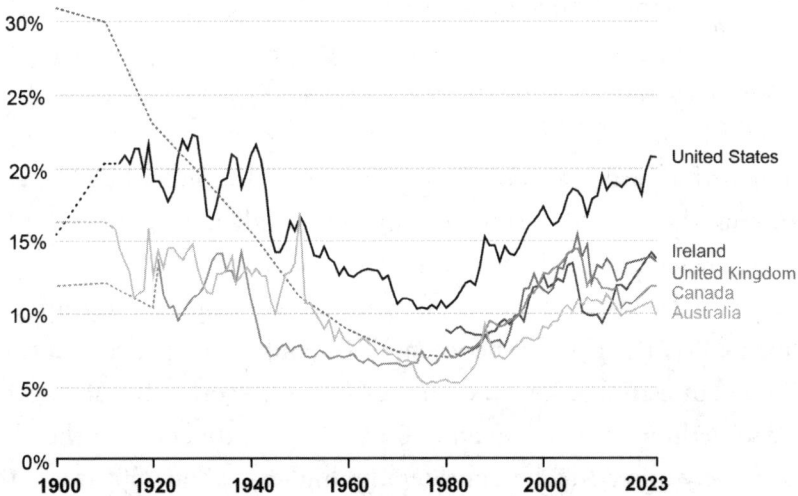

Data source: World Inequality Database (2025).
Note: Income is measured before payment of taxes and non-pension benefits, but after the payment of public and private pensions.

Figure 5.2. Percentage share of total pretax income earned by the top 1 percent of earners in the United States, the United Kingdom, Canada, Ireland, and Australia.

Income share of the richest 1% (before tax), 1900–2023

The share of income received by the richest 1% of the population. Income is measured before taxes and benefits. The dotted lines represent extrapolations due to limited data availability.

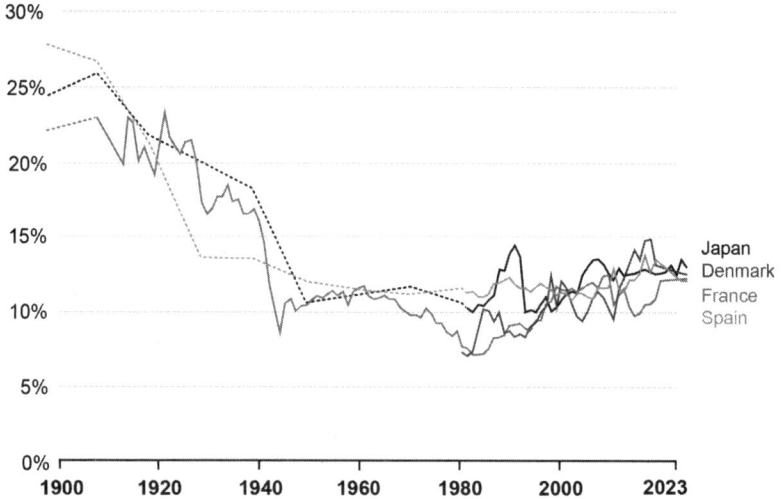

Data source: World Inequality Database (2025).
Note: Income is measured before payment of taxes and non-pension benefits, but after the payment of public and private pensions.

Figure 5.3. Percentage share of total pretax income earned by the top 1 percent of earners in France, Japan, Spain, and Denmark.

pursued a particular policy agenda, starting around 1980. Even among these, the US is something of an outlier, in terms of both the policies and, as the graph shows, their effects.

A similar contrast can be seen in another popular measure of inequality: the pay gap between CEOs and workers in a country. Different estimates put the ratio of CEO-to-worker pay in Japan at something between 15 and 60 to 1.[34] The same ratio in the US is widely agreed to be considerably higher—about 300 to 1 as we write. It was not always so: In 1965, the US chief-executive-to-worker compensation ratio was approximately 20 to 1.[35] Inequality, it seems, is not inevitable but varies dramatically across countries and over time. In other words, inequality is a matter of political choice.

From an i-frame perspective, the problem of inequality is a matter of figuring out how to help individual people, living in precarious circumstances, navigate "the system" better; in a time of political deadlock, this can seem to be the only option available. But inequality arises from the systems that we live within—it cannot be fixed one person at a time. Individualist approaches to inequality, however well-intentioned, are destined to fail.

In an insightful essay on homelessness, the journalist Jerusalem Demsas identifies an essential problem with many attempts to help individuals. Beyond homelessness itself, the homeless manifestly suffer from a range of adversities—poverty, joblessness, lack of education, family breakdown, mental and physical health problems, substance abuse, and many more—problems that homelessness itself only amplifies. So it is all too easy to see the problem of homelessness as one stemming from the broken lives of homeless people, and the solution as involving helping those people find a different path. As Demsas observes, however, "when we have a dire shortage of affordable housing, it's all but guaranteed that a certain number of people will become homeless" in the same way that, in a game of musical chairs, there will always be kids who end up with no chairs.[36] Demsas points out that in musical chairs, it is quite true that the kids who don't get a chair are likely to be different—e.g., slower moving, less attentive—on average, from the kids who do. But no amount of coaching those kids to be more alert or assertive is going to "solve" the problem of musical chairs, though it might shuffle the losers slightly. The only way to solve musical chairs is *more chairs*.

The same logic applies across many aspects of inequality where there is a valuable, but limited, resource at stake—not just housing. Consider education in the UK, where the school one attends correlates strikingly with academic results, places in elite universities, and long-term career success. The supply of places at the most prestigious fee-paying schools is inevitably tiny—but those children who get one have a huge lifelong advantage. A particularly striking illustration of this advantage is the UK Cabinet, which typically derives the majority of members from fee-paying schools, even though these educate just 7 percent of the population.[37] Since the eighteenth century, fully twenty of the fifty-eight UK prime ministers were educated at a *single school* (Eton College), with seven educated at Harrow and six at Westminster (note that these are what Americans would call private high schools, not universities).[38] An individualistic approach to the problem might be to call for more scholarships to, say, Eton for children from less well-off families; but, while this adjusts the mix of people who get through to the "express lane" to a successful political (or indeed finance or business) career, the more fundamental problem is that there is an express lane at all.

Regional and local variations in the funding and quality of schools in the US are a significant contributor to inequality, as is the huge disparity between the quality of the private schools that affluent people can afford to send their children to and the quality of the underfunded public schools that the children of the less affluent are forced to attend. In the US, public (i.e., state-funded) schools are funded in large part by local property taxes, which exacerbates inequality because more affluent localities have a greater tax base and hence, on average, better-funded public schools than poorer localities. The result is that low-income students—who need *more* resources to overcome their disadvantages—end up getting far less.

Inequality also passes from one generation to the next. This is transparently true of wealth via inheritance—indeed, increasingly so according to a recent analysis.[39] But the picture is also true for income. Where you begin in life (the ranking of your family's income relative to the population as a whole) has a huge impact on where you end up. For example, consider the incomes of children whose families had incomes that were in the bottom (or the top) 20 percent of the US income distribution. Of children from the bottom group, 43 percent stayed in that same group, and just 4 percent climbed to join the top group. Conversely, among children from the top group, just 8 percent had dropped to join the bottom group, and 40 percent remained in the top group.[40]

Education *could* be a tremendous economic leveler. If you make it to an elite college, for example, your parents' income matters far less in determining where you will end up. If elite college students have wealthy parents, their income will on average be around the 77th percentile; but even if their parents are at the bottom of the income distribution, they are still likely to make it to the 70th income percentile. And it turns out that the same story applies more broadly—what determines income is mainly educational level: For people with the same educational background, parental income matters relatively little. This sounds reassuring until we realize that *whether* you make it to college depends *very strongly* on family income (Figure 5.4).[41]

Headed to college? Depends on family income

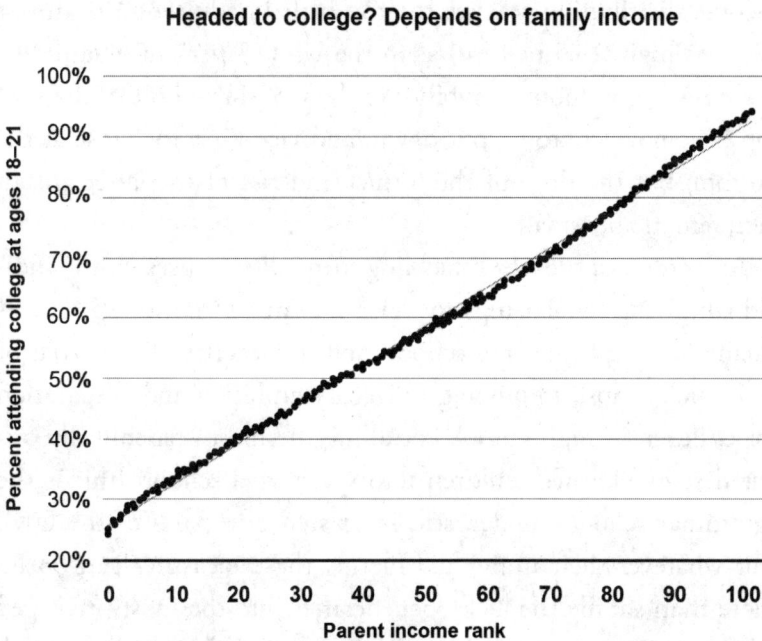

Figure 5.4. College levels the playing field *once you get there*. But as this graph shows, whether you make it to college at all depends all too directly on the wealth of your parents (US data, for people born from 1980 to 1982). (Figure redrawn from Chetty et al., "Income Segregation and Intergenerational Mobility," 2020.)

So, yes, education is a great leveler. But the problem is that how much education you get, and where you get that education, are *hugely* dependent on your family's income rank, and education is the main way that families affect the economic outcomes of their children. Figure 5.4 shows that about 95 percent of children coming from families at the top of the income distribution attend college, but only 25 percent of children coming from the very bottom do.

Parental income impacts not only children's college attendance but also their economic mobility. There are a number of different ways to measure mobility, and all of them point to the same conclusion: The US—the so-called land of opportunity—in which, it is widely believed, anyone can "make it," in fact performs very poorly when it comes to economic mobility. In Canada, for example, the likelihood that a child born in the bottom fifth of the income distribution reaches the top fifth in adulthood is almost twice as high (13.5 percent) as in the US (7.5 percent). Naturally, there is some economic mobility in the US, since those at the very top have nowhere to go but down, and vice versa for those at the bottom; but the drop of the former and rise of the latter are, in fact, remarkably small.

An i-frame approach to tackling inequality focuses on the individual: giving scholarships to clever children to go to top schools (many leading fee-paying schools and universities offer partial or full scholarships); improving university ambition and preparation for children in high school; corralling the most academically oriented state-educated children into specialized schools (this is the "grammar school" model, still in existence in parts of the UK). But whatever their individual merits, these measures can do no more than shuffle the lucky beneficiaries into the most privileged schools at the expense of those shuffled out. What is really needed, of course, is an education that provides at least decently good opportunities for everyone: more chairs, not simply more attention to who gets the chairs.

The coexistence of private and public schools does not only contribute to inequality directly, by exacerbating discrepancies in the quality of schooling received by the poor and by the affluent. It also reduces the incentives for rich and disproportionately influential families—who tend to send their children to private schools—to lobby for improved public education. In fact, these people are incentivized to maintain the status quo, since their tax dollars would have to pay for improvements that they wouldn't personally benefit from.[42]

––––––––

Inequality per se has not been much of a focus of nudge research. But a wide range of work in psychology, as well as some in behavioral economics, has searched for i-frame solutions for some of the diverse social problems associated with inequality. The hope that targeting interventions at the level of the individual might lead to substantive social change is, of course, a noble one. But as we've seen throughout this book, i-frame interventions to help individual players rarely make much impact when the "rules of the game" are rigged to produce socially bad outcomes. The weakness of "psychological" interventions is cataloged in a brilliant and exhaustively researched book, *The Quick Fix: Why Fad Psychology Can't Cure Our Social Ills*, by journalist Jesse Singal.[43]

Some of what Singal labels "fad psychology" is academically flimsy and rather plainly overhyped by its proponents. But much is based on long streams of careful academic work by leading scholars. Yet, Singal argues, attempts to apply the results of even the most serious and careful work typically turn out to be disappointing.

Singal focuses, for example, on the concept of "grit," a much-researched and often-discussed idea advanced by a friend of George's, the University of Pennsylvania psychologist Angela Duckworth. The idea is that grit—the "propensity to tenaciously attack difficult problems," or "perseverance and passion for long-term goals"—is crucial to academic and life success.[44] If so, it is natural to hope that inequality might be reduced through educational interventions to instill the grit required to help disadvantaged children overcome their disadvantages, and hence to enhance both their academic performance and later life-chances.

Can this work? Our reading of the extensive literature on grit is somewhat more optimistic than Singal's, but nonetheless the effect of "grit" interventions is at best mixed. A 2017 meta-analysis of prior studies carried out by psychologists concluded that "interventions designed to enhance grit may only have weak effects on performance and success."[45] More recently and encouragingly, a 2019 randomized controlled trial in Turkish elementary schools published in the prestigious *Quarterly Journal of Economics* found that a program for instilling grit through videos, case studies, and classroom activities did enhance academic performance in math and Turkish.[46] Disappointingly, however, one of the largest field studies of grit, conducted with thirty-three thousand students across 350 schools in North Macedonia, and, notably, coauthored by Duckworth, again found mixed results: positive effects of the intervention on one dimension of grit—perseverance—and positive effects of the intervention on grade point averages for disadvantaged students, but negative effects of the intervention on the other dimension of grit, namely the students' ability to maintain consistent interest for long periods.[47] It is possible that fine-tuning what are complex grit-based educational interventions may generate cost-effective strategies for helping children learn and thrive. But these effects are too modest and fragile to counter the vast systemic forces driving inequality.

Grit is only one among several concepts advanced by psychologists that seem to hold out the promise that short-term and subtle interventions can overcome years of disadvantage. For example, Stanford social psychologist Claude Steele's concept of "stereotype threat" refers to the consequences—mainly anxiety and low performance—of being put in a situation in which one fears confirming negative stereotypes about one's social group. An early and highly influential study by Steele and Joshua Aronson (with over fifteen thousand citations) found that African American students performed worse than white students on standardized tests when the tests were described as a measure of intellectual ability. However, when the same test was described as unrelated to ability, performance differences between the two groups diminished dramatically—hinting, tantalizingly, that such racial differences in educational outcomes could be substantially reduced by interventions that diminish the impact of stereotypes.[48] Alas, later studies with larger samples failed to replicate the strong effects of stereotype threat observed in Steele and Aronson's original work, and meta-analyses reviewing all tests of the idea have yielded mixed results, with some showing small to moderate effects but others suggesting minimal or negligible impacts.[49]

Psychologist Carol Dweck's important research on fixed versus growth mindset is another example of an approach that initially showed great promise but for which claims were ultimately moderated in light of follow-up work (Singal mentions it briefly but critically).[50] A fixed mindset is a belief that abilities and intelligence are static traits. A growth mindset is a belief that abilities and intelligence can be developed with effort, learning, and persistence. Dweck and her collaborators found that people with a fixed mindset often avoid challenges, give up easily, and view effort as fruitless if they believe they lack inherent talent, whereas people with a growth mindset embrace challenges, persist through difficulties, and see effort as a path to mastery. These intriguing findings were taken to suggest that fostering a growth mindset could lead to greater motivation, resilience, and academic success. Once again, however, follow-up research has failed to replicate the original findings, or has obtained effect sizes smaller than were found in the original research. Meta-analyses have generally supported the idea that there is "something there" but qualified the magnitude of the effects as well as the populations who might benefit from interventions to instill a growth mindset.[51]

Interventions of this type (e.g., cultivating grit, combating stereotype threat, or instilling a growth mindset) are often grouped together as "wise" interventions: aiming to help people better manage their lives. Yet these individualistic interventions run the risk of unintended side effects. Specifically, a focus on individual responsibility might lead to greater blame for individual failure and reduced concern for disadvantaged groups. A recent paper documents just such an effect in a series of three studies. In the first, participants read about an educational intervention aimed at reducing the racial achievement gap that was either "wise" (a so-called self-affirmation task) or a substantive intervention (tutoring and curriculum changes). Reading about the wise treatment increased perceptions that minorities could overcome disadvantage on their own. The second and third studies showed that learning about a wise intervention (as compared with more substantive interventions) to promote safe sex (study 2) or to help Black students adjust to college (study 3) increased blame toward those who failed to achieve either goal.[52]

In behavioral economics, perhaps the work most closely related to the problem of inequality is by Chicago economist Sendhil Mullainathan and Princeton psychologist Eldar Shafir, on "scarcity."[53] In their original and highly influential book on the topic, Mullainathan and Shafir propose that scarcity—whether of time, money, or other resources—creates a "scarcity mindset" that focuses attention narrowly on immediate needs, often at the expense of long-term planning and broader goals. This focus can lead to "tunneling," where people prioritize urgent matters but neglect other important tasks or opportunities, creating a vicious cycle of poor decision-making and further scarcity. Although the claims advanced in the scarcity research have received considerable attention, again follow-up research has yielded only limited support for a number of the book's claims, including an extensive empirical replication conducted by the authors themselves.[54]

Research on scarcity led to a variety of public policy proposals aimed at addressing the challenges faced by individuals experiencing resource constraints. These proposals focus on designing interventions and systems that account for the psychological and behavioral effects of scarcity, with the goal of reducing its negative impacts and promoting better outcomes. Many proposals, such as improving access to resources and benefits, framing and presenting information simply and effectively, or addressing poverty traps and investing in early interventions, overlap with proposals for substantive interventions and align with proposals from other theoretical perspectives. Most of these suggestions are not particularly nudge-like, and include both i-frame and s-frame elements.

Finding i-frame interventions that make even a dent in inequality is, in short, extremely difficult—even when driven by the ideas and experiments of some of the best researchers in psychology and behavioral economics. And perhaps this should not be surprising: By focusing on the individual we are looking in the wrong place. As Singal notes, inequality starts early and runs deep:

> By the time a child enters kindergarten . . . he or she has already gone through an absolutely crucial half decade of development. To ask how a five-year-old is likely to do later in life is to be faced with the depressingly unfair fact that the answer has to do with factors well beyond that five-year-old's control—factors that have likely already thumbed the scale quite a bit. At five, a child either has or hasn't had access to sufficient nutrition, to sufficient cognitive stimulation, to sufficient family stability, and to protection from the sorts of adverse childhood events that have now been linked, in later life, to everything from smoking to heart disease.[55]

Inequality arises from social, economic, and educational systems that are *designed* to entrench the advantages of the rich and powerful; and they do so all too effectively.

There is a wide range of well-tested systemic remedies for reducing inequality, including "downstream" policies such as redistributive taxes and welfare benefits, and "upstream" policies that seek to reduce inequalities in wages and income in the first place. Upstream approaches to addressing inequality have been labeled "pre-distribution" by Yale politics professor Jacob Hacker and include, for example, providing free high-quality health care and lifelong education and training across the population.[56] Pre-distribution also involves shifting the bargaining power between employees and employers, whether by strengthening labor rights, allowing workers the right to more flexible employment contracts (e.g., part-time working, flexible hours), increasing parental and sick leave and holiday benefits, or offering greater job security, as well as "softer" measures such as the right to know the pay of fellow workers. Pre-distribution has been influential in British political discourse, particularly regarding the most direct (though controversial) pre-distribution tactic of all: raising the minimum wage.[57]

There has been a monumental decades-long debate in economics about whether raising the minimum wage leads to higher unemployment.[58] A simple application of conventional economics would say that it should: If you make anything more expensive (including workers), that thing should be purchased less (so fewer workers and higher unemployment). But actually, the data are mixed. And people at the bottom of the income distribution tend to spend every penny they make (rather than simply squirreling it away) and do so locally, so that raising their incomes tends to have a disproportionate benefit on the local economy. So the supposed economic downsides of minimum wages may be greatly exaggerated, or nonexistent.

In any case, few people question that raising the minimum wage increases the incomes of the lowest-paid and poorest workers. Indeed, the introduction in the UK of a minimum wage in 1999, and its subsequent fairly rapid rise, have helped lift many Britons out of poverty, seemingly without harming employment levels.

Various types of government transfer programs also raise the incomes of the most disadvantaged and thereby have a beneficial effect on income inequality. In the US, Social Security and Medicare (which target the elderly), and Medicaid, the Earned Income Tax Credit, and Food Stamps (which all target low-income individuals and families), are examples of federal transfer programs that disproportionately benefit the poor. During the COVID pandemic—with the main goal to stave off a recession—government relief to those financially impacted by the pandemic was provided in the form of the Coronavirus Aid, Relief, and Economic Security (CARES) Act. These payments were determined by the declared adjusted gross income of the filing individual. Even though a family of four could only gain up to $3,400 of direct financial relief through this program, the large observed positive impact these minimal funds had on those who received them illustrates just how large an impact transfer programs can have on individuals living near the poverty line.[59]

While increasing the minimum wage and government transfer programs can have an impact on poverty, thereby reducing inequality, *taxes* are really the only mechanism capable of doing the "heavy lifting." Hence, it is not surprising that taxes have been the target of numerous information—and, more significantly, *disinformation*—campaigns (which we'll learn more about in Part Two), including attempts to cast taxes as theft or seizure of rightfully earned income.

There is also a further complication with any strategy that involves taxing the rich: The rich can always relocate to a place where taxes are lower. Indeed, competition among localities and countries to attract corporations, wealthy individuals, and investment funds creates a "race to the bottom" in which all states and countries end up worse off because they lack funds for needed public expenditures. And the fear of tax competition provides a powerful argument against a more equitable tax system: Rather than paying up, the high rollers will simply leave. This is clearly a case of system failure, where the obvious solution is cross-state (ideally federal) or cross-nation agreements. The "Global Tax Agreement," hammered out in negotiations at the Organisation for Economic Co-operation and Development (OECD) and supported in principle by 130 countries in 2021, is just such an agreement.[60] It stipulates that large corporations will pay more taxes in countries where they have customers, and less in countries where they have headquarters, employees, and operations. But the really critical part of the agreement is the establishment of a minimum tax of 15 percent on earnings, which prevents multinational corporations from skirting taxes by locating their headquarters in low- or zero-tax countries. The agreement was supported—and indeed spearheaded—by the Biden administration. Republicans in the US Senate, however, not only failed to endorse it but introduced legislation specifically designed to undermine it, and in January 2025 the Trump administration definitively rejected the agreement.[61] But over the long haul, this agreement, or some successor, may nonetheless make it over the line and perhaps ultimately be strengthened further.

———

A degree—perhaps a considerable degree—of inequality is inevitable in any free society. How much, of course, is a decision for the people of each nation. Reasonable people can differ on the economic and social trade-offs involved (e.g., will dividing the pie more equally tend to make the pie smaller, larger, or make no difference?). Reasonable people can also differ concerning which type of society they would rather live in. But the relentless rise in inequality in the US, the UK, and many other countries is not the result of a spontaneous public demand for a more unequal society. Rather, as we've seen, the shift has been deliberately engineered by the concentrated interests of the powerful and wealthy, who are its main beneficiaries.

Is it possible that there will be a public outcry against inequality that will lead to needed reforms? The prospect may seem distant today, but pent-up public frustration with the status quo is very real. It is a strange irony (though, again, no accident, as we'll see) that in the US, and in many parts of the world, the "populist" agenda appealing to those badly treated by the status quo has been captured by powerful interests seeking to aggressively cut taxes on the rich. But it has not always been so, and it need not be so in the future.

The reformers of laissez-faire Victorian England, and those outraged at the excesses and corruption of America's Gilded Age, did not fight in vain. Indeed, social movements in democratic societies have a long history of overturning the power of the few over the many—from campaigns to widen the franchise; to establish workers' employment rights, holidays, and safety; to advance civil rights. As Mancur Olson noted, the concentrated interests of the few are so powerful because they can most easily be aligned and coordinated to carry through a coherent plan of action. But coordinated action by the many, once achieved, is unstoppable.

Chapter 6

THE PATTERN IS EVERYWHERE!

We have to hammer on the abusers in every way possible. . . .
They are the culprits and the problem. They are reckless
criminals.

—Richard Sackler, chairman and president of Purdue Pharma

The Baader–Meinhof phenomenon, more prosaically known
as the frequency illusion, refers to the strange feeling of learning something new and then suddenly seeing it everywhere. In
the late 1960s, a far-left militant group called the Red Army
Faction—also known, after the name of two of its founders, as
the Baader–Meinhof group—emerged in West Germany with
the goal of overthrowing the government through armed struggle, including bombings, assassinations, and kidnappings.

The term "Baader–Meinhof phenomenon" arose from the mus-
ings of a commentator on a discussion board in the late 1990s who
noticed that, after having just learned about the group, he suddenly started noticing references to it everywhere. He named the
effect the Baader–Meinhof phenomenon, and it quickly became a
widely recognized term.

The Baader–Meinhof phenomenon is rooted in the way our brains process and filter information. Our minds are constantly assailed by far more sensory information than we can consciously process. To manage this influx, our brains have to be selective. Most of this information isn't terribly useful and can safely be ignored; but if a name, say, is familiar, we pay more attention: Perhaps we may learn some important information about a friend or acquaintance. And similarly, if we see what seems to be a familiar pattern, we look more closely. So once we become aware of a name, or a face, or anything else, our limited attentional system is more likely to notice it in the future. With each new observation, the familiar item becomes even more salient and likely to be noticed again.

We've experienced a kind of Baader–Meinhof phenomenon in writing this book. First coming across what we hope is by now a familiar pattern for the reader—attempts by industry to cast problems as the responsibility of individuals, coupled with lobbying to maintain the status quo—we soon began to see the same pattern everywhere. We have so far discussed a range of different policy issues: climate change, obesity, financial provision for retirement, health care, and inequality. Drawing further attention to the ubiquity of the phenomenon, in this chapter we briefly discuss five additional issues where the pattern plays out: plastic waste, privacy, addiction to prescription drugs, gun violence, and automobile deaths and injuries.

———

There's no controversy that the production and disposal of plastic bottles, bags, and containers of all kinds constitute a major environmental problem. While plastics are undeniably useful, the problem of plastic waste is urgent. Plastic bags, for example, clog sewage systems, kill an estimated one hundred thousand marine mammals every year, and degenerate into toxic microplastics that pollute oceans and landfills for up to a thousand years.[1] Shoppers collectively use around five hundred billion single-use plastic bags globally every year. That's more than sixty bags per person.[2] In recent years, microplastics have been discovered in diverse parts of the human body—lungs, maternal and fetal placental tissues, breast milk, and blood (microplastics were found in the blood of seventeen of twenty-two adults tested in the Netherlands).[3] Although health risks have not been proved, there is real concern in the scientific and medical community that they may be substantial.[4] A product of oil, plastics also have a substantial carbon footprint.

Many of us try, in our personal choices, to be mindful of the problem of plastic pollution. We may try to switch to reusable bags when shopping, avoid excessively packaged products, carefully sort plastic waste for recycling (when such schemes are available), and of course avoid littering the natural world. But the sense of personal responsibility for this problem is surely misplaced: The prevalence of plastics, and plastic waste, has not been caused by

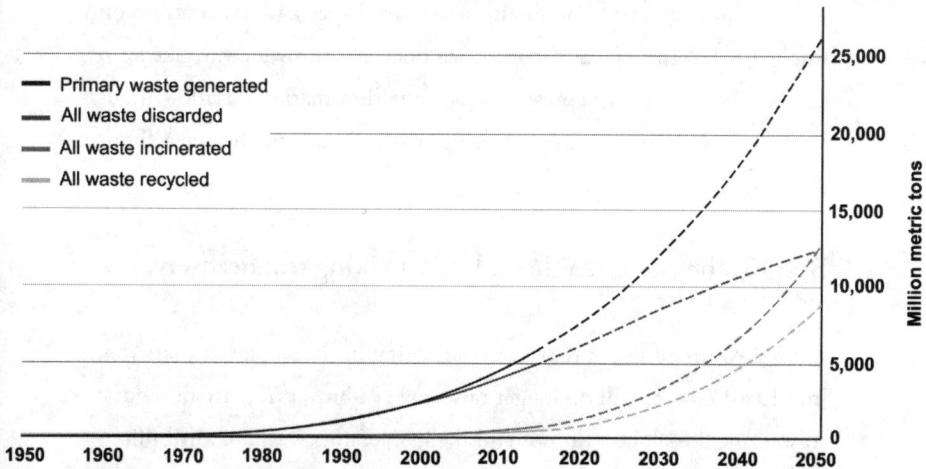

Figure 6.1. Cumulative growth in plastic waste creation and disposal. Solid lines give historical data from 1950 to 2015; dashed lines are projections from 2015 to 2050. (Figure redrawn based on Geyer et al., "Production, Use, and Fate of All Plastics Ever Made," 2017.)

individual careless consumers. It has been caused by the relentless growth of the plastics industry (see Figure 6.1).

Until the 1950s, plastics were used only for highly specialized purposes, especially in the military. Since then, the rate of plastic production has been increasing rapidly, touching almost every consumer product and/or its packaging. Indeed, the global compound annual growth rate of plastic production has been estimated at more than 8 percent, far higher than the rate of global GDP growth (around 3 percent).[5]

In the face of a tsunami of plastic production, and the diffusion of plastics through almost every aspect of the economy, the behavior of the individual consumer can only be of marginal significance. And the tsunami is very much the product of deliberate intent. For example, the explosion of disposable plastic packaging can be traced to the vision of Lloyd Stouffer, the editor of the trade magazine *Modern Packaging*, who at a meeting of the Society of the Plastics Industry in New York in 1956 stated that

the future of plastics is in the trash can. . . . It [is] time for the plastics industry to stop thinking about "reuse" packages and concentrate on single use. For the package that is used once and thrown away, like a tin can or a paper carton, represents not a one-shot market for a few thousand units, but an everyday recurring market measured by the billions of units.[6]

By 1963, he could see the industry making real headway:

It is a measure of your progress in packaging in the last seven years that [my 1956] remark will no longer raise any eye-brows. You are filling the trash cans, the rubbish dumps and the incinerators with literally billions of plastics bottles, plastics jugs, plastics tubes, blisters and skin packs, plastics bags . . . and sheet packages—and now, even plastics cans. The happy day has arrived when nobody any longer considers the plastics package too good to throw away.[7]

Happy days, perhaps, for the plastics and oil industries.

But while those industries created the problem of plastic waste, they have worked hard to encourage individuals to blame themselves for it. Readers who view the problem of plastic pollution as a matter of individual responsibility (and try to reduce it by using reusable bags when shopping, for example) may be surprised to discover that a perspective they have come to embrace can be traced back to the influence of the industry that created the problem in the first place.

Keep America Beautiful—the same industry-funded organization that in the 1970s cynically produced the "crying Indian" ad with which we began this book (telling viewers that "people start pollution—people can stop it")—today counts the Dow Chemical Company, the International Bottled Water Association, and the Plastics Industry Association among its many corporate sponsors.

But advocacy of the i-frame perspective goes far beyond the plastics companies. For example, the L'Oréal Group of beauty products recently "re-upped" their "'One Green Step' Campaign to Promote Greener Living." According to their website, "Standing up for the environment includes small everyday actions. The idea is to encourage people to share the steps they are taking day-to-day to help the environment. Many of us want to do our part for the planet by living and consuming more responsibly."[8]

Behavioral scientists have generated a range of potential interventions focusing on reducing litter, such as the "Keep Britain Tidy" initiative.[9] Pictures of "watching eyes" have been widely deployed in the UK after research suggested that these might encourage good behavior in general and reduce littering in particular.[10] Likewise, an intervention tested in Copenhagen in 2011, which involved painting footprints on the ground leading to brightly colored trash bins, received substantial media coverage.[11] Unfortunately, despite its touted success, the "footprints" strategy was never rigorously tested and, to the best of our knowledge, was only implemented in one other locality: Stirling, Scotland.[12]

When and where interventions do appear to be effective, they are difficult to sustain or scale up, and we are unaware of any proven initiatives operating at scale with a strong evidence base.[13] Putting "watching eyes" on packaging, which seemed to reduce littering of a leaflet in one field study, has been suggested to potentially be scalable—although the costs of this intervention, and the potential diminution in impact if "watching eyes" become ubiquitous— all argue for caution regarding real-world effectiveness.[14]

The problem of plastic waste is one in which s-frame interventions, in contrast to such nudges, can be highly effective. A large number of countries (from the UK to Mexico, Canada, Australia, and South Africa, to name a few) have successfully banned plastic bags, or taxed their use; at the time of writing, eight US states (California, Connecticut, Delaware, Hawaii, Maine, New York, Oregon, and Vermont) have banned single-use plastic bags at a statewide level.[15] This policy has been shown to have dramatic effects; for example, in San Jose, California, a plastic bag ban led to a 60 percent reduction of plastic bags in storm drains, rivers, and residential areas, and the average number of bags used per person per day decreased from 3 to 0.3.[16] Yet the plastics industry is fighting back, with a fair amount of success. By March 2022, seventeen US states (Arizona, Florida, Idaho, Indiana, Iowa, Michigan, Mississippi, Missouri, North Dakota, Ohio, Oklahoma, Pennsylvania, South Carolina, South Dakota, Tennessee, Texas, Wisconsin) had enacted preemptive laws that prevent municipalities from implementing plastic bag bans or regulations.[17] Needless to say, these bans aren't spontaneous expressions of public hostility toward a relatively obscure policy; they arise from lobbying by industry, including the oil industry (which provides the raw materials for plastic bags and bottles). The same pattern of opposition can be seen with respect to statewide "bottle bills," which would require the beverage industry to pay a redemption fee for, and process, used bottles, passage of which has failed in numerous states in large part because of industry-funded marketing.

An environmentally conscious, and conscientious, reader who owns an assortment of reusable bags but has occasionally arrived at a grocery store without one (as the two of us have experienced ourselves) might have concerns about a complete ban on disposable bags. However, it turns out that a less rigid policy—charging consumers a very small amount for each disposable bag they use—is almost as effective as a complete ban, as demonstrated in a series of important studies as well as in real-world test cases. Textbook economics predicts that paying people a five-cent subsidy for each reusable bag they bring to a store would have almost the same impact as charging them five cents for each disposable bag that they use; but behavioral economics—and specifically a well-documented phenomenon called "loss aversion"—predicts that charging five cents should have a much bigger impact than providing a five-cent reward. Confirming the behavioral economics prediction, studies find that charging people a small fee for using disposable bags has a huge effect, reducing their use by between 80 percent and 95 percent (depending on the countries and the policy initiative)—almost the same as with an outright ban. In contrast, paying people a comparable amount for bringing their own bag has a barely discernible effect. Losing five cents is far more potent than gaining five cents; and, perhaps as crucially, the twinge of discomfort we feel from that loss reminds us that we are doing a "bad thing" by taking a new plastic bag. So the framing of the policy is crucial. Indeed, this is a perfect example of how behavioral economics and insights need not necessarily be focused on helping individuals make better choices, but can inform s-frame policies. While behavioral interventions often don't scale, the small disincentives inherent in the "plastic bag tax" scale very well—indeed, such policies have been implemented successfully across the UK and in many US states. But complete bans scale well, too, of course—and have been widely adopted across Europe, Africa, and Asia.

Corporate interests have also actively opposed more sweeping s-frame measures, such as the application of "extended producer responsibility" (EPR) for packaging, cigarettes, bottles, and other waste, according to which producers may potentially bear the full social and environmental cost of the waste they produce and are therefore strongly incentivized to redesign their products to reduce that waste.[18] But where these schemes have been implemented, against industry opposition, they have proved highly effective.[19] For example, pioneering schemes in Spain and Portugal saw amounts of waste per household fall 13 percent and 9 percent faster than the EU average, respectively, from 2008 to 2014: Products and packaging were redesigned, and manufacturers and companies financially supported the sorting and recycling of waste.[20] EPR shifts the challenge of reducing waste "upstream," away from the consumer, driving manufacturers to pay (an approximation) of the full cost of their products, including social and environmental costs, rather than being able to generate vast quantities of nondegradable waste and blaming its pernicious effects on littering individuals. Germany's "end-of-life vehicle" (ELV) regulation mandates environmentally sound disposal of vehicles.[21] It includes regulations that require automakers to take back end-of-life vehicles free of charge; lays down technical requirements for the reuse and recovery of end-of-life vehicles; restricts the use of mercury, cadmium, lead, and hexavalent chrome in cars; and specifies that only companies that have ELV regulation certification can dismantle and scrap cars.

Might recycling be the solution for plastic waste? Currently, at least, it is largely a distraction. In an episode of the NPR series *On Point*, host Meghna Chakrabarti interviewed a number of experts on the environment and on plastics, including Lisa Song, a ProPublica reporter covering the environment, energy, and climate change, and author of an article titled "The Delusion of 'Advanced' Plastic Recycling."[22] In the course of the interview, Song argued that the best way to attack the problems caused by plastics "is to reduce the amount of new plastic that's being made." Song refers to the UN Intergovernmental Negotiating Committee, a group of more than one hundred countries that has gathered yearly since 2021 with the goal of developing an international legally binding instrument on plastic pollution. A key tension-point of the committee is whether there should be a focus on plastic production—an approach that, Song notes, "the plastic and oil and gas companies really don't want to talk about." She adds, "It's in their business interest to keep talking about recycling rather than turn the conversation to reducing the amount of plastic that's made." Another panelist, Anthony Schiavo, a sustainability analyst, picks up on Song's theme: "We're really focusing this whole sustainability question through the lens of consumer choice, right? Through the lens of which product you choose to buy on the shelf. And I don't think that's a really good way to think about this issue at all. We need systemic solutions."[23] Exactly right.

———

The transition to the digital age has been so rapid that adequate systems and regulations for maintaining privacy lag far behind technological and commercial innovation. Currently, even with the protections put in place by the European Union's General Data Protection Regulation (GDPR), a semblance of privacy is an unachievable goal for most individuals who own smartphones, use credit cards, shop at supermarkets (perhaps using their loyalty cards), drive their car on toll roads, or surf the web.[24] We are each leaving a digital trail that is all too easy for companies, governments, or malign individuals to track and exploit.

Following the by-now-familiar pattern, technology companies promote i-frame approaches to the problem of privacy while simultaneously opposing tighter regulatory laws that would restrict their ability to collect or disseminate consumer data, hold them accountable for the damage caused when they do collect and pass on such data, or make them pay for the data they harvest from individuals. The "notice and consent" approach advocated by industry, which requires people who want to access a web service to click on a consent button (which typically gives the company carte blanche to make use of the individual's data as they like), is precisely such an i-frame approach.

The tech industry often says what may sound like the right things. For example, Rachel Welch, the senior vice president of policy and external affairs at Charter Communications, a major broadband company, testifying at a meeting of the Senate Committee on Commerce, Science, and Transportation, expressed Charter's support for a national policy framework that provides consumers with a "meaningful choice for each use of their data. We believe the best way to ensure consumers have control over their data is through opt-in consent."[25] This i-frame approach may sound laudable; yet research has found that when people are given greater control over their privacy settings, they tend to be more trusting and to share more information without actually exercising the control they are given—a phenomenon that public policy and management scholar Laura Brandimarte and colleagues have dubbed the "control paradox."[26]

Welch went on to spell out a "national framework" that would "empower and inform consumers." In this model, all companies doing business online would have to tell consumers about their privacy practices and obtain their affirmative consent before using or sharing consumers' data—a continuation of a status quo that has proved highly beneficial to internet-based businesses.

Such a notice-and-consent approach is widely recognized to be close to useless as a strategy for protecting people's privacy, because few of us will ever read the lengthy and legalistic policies attached to the products, apps, and services that we use.[27] In any case, people lack bargaining power when it comes to the companies that use their data: If one doesn't consent to the company's terms, then access is denied.

What role has academia played in this debate? As elsewhere, well-intentioned behaviorally inspired i-frame interventions have been proposed, such as keeping information private by default, using a warning "red" font to highlight choices that might lead to a privacy violation, telling people when their behavior differs from other people's choices (e.g., "most people withhold their private phone number"), and so on. These typically do have small to medium-size effects.[28] Indeed, in the digital world small tweaks can matter—though those tweaks are often set up to encourage people to disclose their data. But nudging people more benignly can, at best, only make a dent in the problem of privacy. It's a little like helping pedestrians stay away from railway lines with discreet notices ("watch out for high-speed trains"), when what is needed is a high fence that actually keeps people off the tracks. In the real digital world, we are all giving away private information on a vast scale, and nudges will, at best, only modestly reduce this vast flow of personal information. Yet advocates for the tech or e-commerce industry might ask: Does any of this really matter? Sure, people *say* in conversation and surveys that they care about online privacy. But doesn't their actual behavior—their patent willingness to tick boxes, link accounts, fill out personal information, and share personal photos and opinions—indicate that in reality people care very little? This disconnect between apparent concern for privacy and behavior that appears to show a flagrant disregard of privacy has been widely discussed in the academic literature, and has been labeled the "privacy paradox."[29] Actually the privacy paradox label may be a little unfair: Achieving desired levels of privacy is not, in fact, within the power of individuals, however highly motivated they might be. People's online sharing of their personal data isn't mostly a matter of choice; it's simply unavoidable.

Not only that: The implications of sharing information are entirely opaque to users—who have no idea how information can be resold, combined with other sources, used by scammers, and so on. Dealing with privacy concerns by letting people figure out whether or not it is safe to share their personal data is not an approach that we tend to find acceptable elsewhere. We don't, for example, deal with problems of food safety by giving consumers information about toxicology and bacteriology and leaving it to them to determine whether or not a food is safe to eat. Just as we have s-frame food regulations to maintain minimum standards of food safety, we surely need strict s-frame regulation, rather than individual-level prompts, to deal with the problem of maintaining privacy online.[30]

Here, the EU, among others, has been proactive, with both the sweeping General Data Protection Regulation and the e-Privacy Directive. In theory, great: People have the power to "be forgotten" and to have access to data that are held about them. But in practice, not so great (so far, anyway): We citizens typically have no way of knowing who knows what about our lives; and even when we do, the right to "see" often is no more than the right to receive an uninterpretable "data dump" from the tech company. The processes by which data are shared and sold remain utterly opaque, and the "mashing" of our data (whether our pictures or posts or just traces of our searching, browsing, and purchasing patterns) along with everyone else's by AI algorithms compounds the challenge further. And the algorithms by which our data are used to make decisions about our creditworthiness, employability, insurance premiums, and whether and how we may be targeted by ads or political messages, and more, remain shrouded in secrecy.

There is, as with any aspect of regulation, a balance to be struck. So, for example, free availability of our data provides opportunities for commercial gain and potential public benefit from "smarter" algorithms; but it also raises the very real possibility of constructing an Orwellian surveillance state, whether controlled by government or corporations, which can crush opposition by monitoring, influencing, or exploiting us, or threatening us with disclosure.

The tipping point beyond which we can no longer collectively reverse the accumulation of knowledge (and hence, potentially, of power) by corporations and governments over citizens may be close, if it hasn't been reached already. Sweeping regulation and oversight by ethicists, lawyers, computer scientists, and social scientists to change or open up the tech industry to detailed scrutiny are desperately needed—and creators of such regulation should have resources and expertise similar to those of the tech sector itself. Although the details of how such regulation should work are complex and much debated, creating such regulations is, we believe, among the most urgent challenges the world now faces.[31] The tech sector will wish to be unconstrained to be able to "move fast and break things"—once CEO Mark Zuckerberg's motto for Facebook.[32] But if regulation continues to be weak, one of the things that is likely to get broken is a free society.

———

In the early 1990s, the academic literature was replete with articles arguing that pain was undertreated. There was no indication that these articles represented anything other than the disinterested observations of academics trying to rectify a mistaken reluctance on the part of physicians to prescribe painkillers to patients. We now know that many of these ostensibly scholarly articles were written by academics funded by Purdue Pharma, which was paving the way for its promotion of the drug OxyContin. Journalists have now revealed the full scale of corporate greed and government sellout that created a wave of addiction that by 2022 killed more than one hundred thousand Americans in a single year.[33]

Beginning in the mid-1990s, Purdue Pharma funded a multi-faceted campaign to encourage long-term use of prescription opioids for chronic pain.[34] Purdue provided financial support to the American Pain Society, the American Academy of Pain Medicine, the Federation of State Medical Boards, pain patient groups, and other organizations, which in turn all advocated for aggressive identification of pain and treatment of it using opioids. In 1995, the American Pain Society initiated a very successful campaign titled "Pain Is the Fifth Vital Sign," which encouraged health care professionals to assess pain as they do other vital signs, and to treat a broader range of ailments with opioids. Purdue-funded academics also advanced the baseless claims that only 1 percent of patients put on opioids went on to become addicted, and, later, that obvious indications of addiction were really cases of "pseudo-addiction"—a bogus theory according to which people who appeared to be addicted were actually suffering from *under*treatment of their original pain-causing malady.[35]

In Chapter 4, we already saw the lamentable role played by American medical societies in propping up the current disastrous health care system. The American Medical Association played a similarly questionable role in the opioid epidemic.[36] In 2007, a year in which doctors prescribed enough opioid painkillers for every American adult to get a bottle, and in which Purdue Pharma had already pleaded guilty to felony charges for misleading regulators about the dangers of OxyContin, the AMA received a $3 million gift from Purdue and used it to create a twelve-module pain management course for its members.[37] Substantial amounts of content in the course perpetuated the myth that doctors were too reluctant to prescribe opioids, such as the line that "the effectiveness of opioid therapy may be undermined by misconceptions about their risks, particularly risks associated with abuse and addiction." The course also included references to pseudo-addiction, and encouraged doctors to elicit self-reports of pain from young children using a "Poker Chip Tool," which laid out four poker chips in front of a child and asked them to report how many pieces of hurt the child has. Physicians were instructed, "Do not give children an option for zero hurt."

Alongside these immensely successful efforts to buy off academics and ostensible public-interest groups, Purdue also promoted an i-frame perspective on the problem it was playing such a central role in creating. Indeed, a focus on the i-frame was a factor both in the creation of the problem and in proposed solutions. As highlighted in Richard Sackler's quote opening the chapter, as the opioid epidemic started to come into view, Purdue sought to portray its victims as weak-willed, irresponsible drug addicts.[38]

Purdue Pharma was very successful in disseminating such a perspective, one consequence of which was to focus the attention of federal and state policymakers on issues of law enforcement, targeting the illegal use of opioids by individuals (i-frame) instead of regulating the pharmaceutical companies and pill-pushing medical system that led to the opioid crisis in the first place (s-frame).[39] Like so many public policy problems (corruption being another salient example), once the metaphorical genie is out of the bottle, it is extremely hard to get it back in; once a sizable fraction of the population is addicted, the initially sensible policy of massively reducing opioid prescriptions has the unintended consequence of driving addicted individuals away from the comparative safety of prescription opioids to the Wild West of illegal opioids, which are often laced with fentanyl, contributing to the current rash of overdose deaths.

In addition to diverting public policy away from the most productive directions (specifically limiting opioid prescribing), blaming addicts for their addiction had other adverse consequences. Framing addiction as a crime rather than as a disease led addicts to hide their addiction from doctors and other people who could have provided help. As former US Surgeon General Jerome Adams said in a speech about addiction, "Stigma keeps people in the shadows. Stigma keeps people from coming forward and asking for help."[40] It also compounded the misery of the addicts themselves by adding self-blame to the already devastating consequences of addiction.

The scientific and medical community proposed, and offered, a variety of i-frame solutions such as treatment programs. Once a person is addicted, these programs probably provide the best, if disappointingly slim, chance of helping them to overcome their addiction (and we support calls to increase their funding). In addition, and in our view less constructively, researchers focused attention on the characteristics of addicts as the main culprit, as opposed to the environment that vulnerable individuals are placed in.

Just as with obesity and retirement savings, *present bias* was put center stage. It seems to make intuitive sense that addicts care more about the present than the future: They seem clearly to be prioritizing present benefits (e.g., of reducing pain or, more likely, staving off withdrawal symptoms) over long-term health and well-being. This used to seem plausible to us—and indeed it became an influential line of thinking in the academic literature. For example, Warren Bickel, a prominent addiction researcher (and occasional collaborator with George) has written several papers attributing addiction to present bias. A representative passage in his most cited paper states, "Individuals who abuse drugs persistently choose the relatively immediate and short-term rewards of drug use over a variety of delayed larger rewards," and then in the following paragraph, he adds, "A possible explanation for drug users' persistent choices to use drugs despite the long-term consequences is in the degree to which future outcomes impact their current decisions."[41] According to this perspective, people become opioid addicts not because of the ready availability of opioids (and, in fact, their promotion by doctors), but because users prioritize the immediate pleasure of drug use over the delayed and hence discounted consequences, such as dependency, poor health, family estrangement, job loss, and so on. Whether intended or not, focusing on present bias tempts us to see opioid addiction as a problem of individual human frailty, to be countered, perhaps, by moral injunctions and a general focus on prudence and clean living. But human nature is, of course, roughly constant across times and places, while the availability of highly addictive prescription drugs is not. Attributing the dizzying growth of opioid addiction in the US in recent decades to unchanging features of human nature is hardly credible.

While advancing the i-frame perspective to the media and government, when it came to its own efforts Purdue focused on the s-frame relentlessly, lobbying heavily to oppose regulation to limit opioid prescribing. This lobbying was remarkably successful. Successive US administrations, and their regulators, failed to avert a crisis that built up in plain sight over several decades. Purdue and other opioid manufacturers managed to effectively infiltrate the Food and Drug Administration to obtain rulings favorable to their business. When, in 2002, the FDA convened an advisory committee meeting of ten "outside experts" to determine whether opioids should be marketed for common chronic pain conditions, allegedly, many of the experts had financial ties to pharmaceutical companies, including Purdue. Perhaps not surprisingly, therefore, they advised the FDA against narrowing the indications for opioid prescribing.[42] In an even more flagrant example of policy manipulation, two of the principal FDA reviewers who originally approved Purdue's oxycodone application for uses beyond cancer patients took positions at Purdue after leaving the agency—another "revolving door" problem that is largely unregulated (but easily fixed with an s-frame policy change).

Just how effective the right s-frame actions could have been is indicated by international comparisons. For example, Germany, the country second to the US in opioid prescriptions (and hence a conservative point of comparison), resisted efforts by Purdue to foist opioids on patients, and managed to largely avoid both the addiction epidemic and rash of overdose deaths experienced in the US. In 2016, 200 per 100,000 Germans struggled with opioid addiction, while a rough estimate of the corresponding number in the US is 3,000 per 100,000—fifteen times higher.[43] In 2016, 1,333 people died of overdoses in Germany (approximately 1.6 out of 100,000), in comparison to 63,000 in the US in the same year (approximately 20 out of 100,000). Indeed, opioid addiction has significantly contributed to a measurable decrease in life expectancy in the US.[44]

Addiction is, of course, not limited to opioids, or indeed to drugs of any kind.[45] People get addicted to electronic games, gambling, and social media such as TikTok or Instagram, and can even become addicted to attracting attention from others—e.g., keeping track of "followers" and "likes." In each of these domains, the same i-frame arguments against regulation are made by commercial interests who want their products to be as addictive as possible. In the aptly titled book *Addiction by Design*, the anthropologist Natasha Dow Schüll describes how slot machines have been designed to be addictive, and also makes the case that casinos and slot machine manufacturers want policymakers, the public, and even gamblers themselves to adopt the i-frame.[46] Schüll points to a 2010 "white paper" released by the American Gaming Association titled "Demystifying Slot Machines," which asserts that "the problem is not in the products [players] abuse, but within the individuals."[47] And, as with virtually all the problems discussed in this book, the gambling industry has found many behavioral scientists to be willing supporters of this perspective. As Schüll notes, "The preponderance of [academic] research tends to concentrate on gamblers' motivations and psychiatric profiles rather than on the gambling formats in which they engaged," a tendency that was advanced by the American Psychiatric Association's inclusion of "pathological gambling" as an official psychiatric diagnosis in 1980. In a world in which multibillion-dollar gambling companies can actively exploit human weakness on a monumental scale, it will be more effective to rein in the companies rather than take on the hopeless task of changing human nature.

Obviously, many potential s-frame policies to address these problems could be reinforced with i-frame elements. For instance, casinos could be required to offer gamblers "self-precommitment strategies," restricting how much money they could bet on a given day. New AI tools could also help companies to monitor gambling behavior. For example, it should be easy to detect and counteract dangerous gambling patterns, such as "loss chasing" (where gambling rapidly escalates as people attempt to win back their ever-mounting losses). And companies could be held liable—an s-frame policy—when they fail to use such tools to introduce a pause (perhaps just for twenty-four hours, or perhaps much longer) when indicators reveal that individuals are behaving in ways they are likely to end up regretting.

————

Why are there so many mass shootings, gun-related murders, and suicides in the US compared to other similarly prosperous nations? It is unlikely that Americans are just that much more violent by nature. A widespread common (though not universal) view in criminology is that systemic factors are decisive—in particular, the availability of cheap and powerful firearms.[48] Other nations have imposed strict s-frame regulations that restrict the types of weapons that can be owned, rigorously control who can own a gun, and impose strict rules concerning locking guns safely. Such policies have proved remarkably successful. For example, in the UK, since legislation was enacted in the aftermath of the 1996 Dunblane Primary School massacre (in which one individual killed sixteen students and a teacher), public access to firearms has been severely restricted. The results of such regulation were immediate, dramatic, and persistent. At the time of writing, there have been only two mass shootings (defined as a shooting in which at least four people are killed) in Britain since the legislation was enacted, and only three fatal shootings of police. In contrast, mass shootings in the US occur approximately once every single day.[49]

In 2018, it was estimated that there were more than 120 guns per 100 people in the US, compared with, for example, 0.3 per 100 in Japan, 4.9 in the UK, 14.5 in Australia, and 19.6 in France and Germany. And the sheer number of US firearms is compounded by the firepower of many of those weapons.[50] Being awash with guns, including assault rifles, it is hardly surprising that the US has anomalously high levels of gun violence. Of course, "disarming" the US would be a huge undertaking, given current extraordinary levels of gun ownership—but legislating to restrict and regulate gun ownership, reducing the firepower of weapons, requiring safe storage, and perhaps introducing technological innovations such as fingerprint locks all seem like commonsense steps that could save many lives.

The National Rifle Association (NRA), partly funded by the firearms industry, has, of course, fought every attempt to regulate guns.[51] Adopting the ubiquitous catchphrase that "guns don't kill people; people kill people," the NRA has largely succeeded in cloaking the problem of gun deaths in the i-frame—that it is a problem of "bad people" as opposed to bad policy. This, as well as the NRA's repeated insistence that the problem of violence can be traced to issues of mental health (while not actually applying its influence on policy toward increased spending on mental health), represents an attempt to put the responsibility for the problem of gun violence squarely on the individual.

Nonetheless, might some i-frame interventions make inroads into the problem of gun violence? This has been an area where behavioral scientists have been relatively quiet. A network of researchers centered at the University of Chicago Crime Lab has helped conduct randomized controlled trials of various intervention programs for young men in underserved communities with high crime rates, part of a program known as Becoming a Man (BAM). One influential paper, led by economist Sara Heller, drew particular attention to the possibility that helping individuals in tough neighborhoods respond to conflicts thoughtfully and proportionately, rather than reacting rapidly and intuitively, might help reduce gun crime.[52] The authors note that one of the programs being evaluated included exercises such as asking one person to get a ball from another (where the aim is to learn cooperative rather than confrontational styles of interaction). While the initial results of this intervention were promising (and highly touted), recent follow-up research seems to show that, when the BAM program was scaled up, its efficacy waned. The authors note that it had little to no impact on the number of arrests (and, in particular, arrests for violent crimes).[53]

It remains possible that similar interventions in troubled communities might be valuable and cost-effective (despite their relatively high cost) given the huge economic, social, and human impacts of violent crime. But their impacts will surely be limited, and it is important that excessive optimism about such approaches does not reduce the focus on addressing the fundamental cause of super-high rates of violence in the US—the widespread availability of firearms. Without dramatic reform of gun laws, the prospect of addressing gun violence in the US will remain remote.

———

Across the world, car accidents kill more than 1.3 million people each year and injure millions more. Increasingly, the victims are pedestrians and cyclists, especially in the United States. From 2010 to 2021, while traffic fatalities increased in the US by an already alarming 25 percent, the rate of pedestrian deaths increased even more—nearly doubling in the same period—from 4,302 to 7,624 deaths per year. This appears to be chiefly an American problem and a recent one; in a wide range of other countries, automobile-related deaths declined over the same period. Back in the 1990s, the US and France had similar per capita fatality rates, but today Americans are three times as likely to die in a traffic accident.[54]

In his insightful book *A Brief History of Motion*, journalist Tom Standage addresses the question of how and why such a monumental level of destruction is met with such complacency. Adaptation provides one obvious explanation; we don't react to the carnage until it affects us or people we care about, because we have gotten so used to it. Standage identifies another mechanism: that the automobile industry consistently attributes accidents to individual folly rather than to the nature of cars themselves. Standage notes that in the early days of motoring there *was* a public outcry about pedestrian deaths: "Cars become demonized as child-killing death machines in the early 1920s," which began to hurt sales. "At that point the industry is absolutely terrified and realizes it has to do something about safety. Or at least appear to do something about safety if it's going to go on selling more of its product."

What does the car industry do? You guessed it—blame the victims for getting themselves killed or maimed. According to Standage, the car industry "comes up with this very interesting strategy. It essentially says what we need to do is double down on education. And the problem here is uneducated pedestrians. It's not the drivers. It's not the cars. It's not the road design. In particular what they do is they weaponized in America one particular word, which is the word 'jaywalker.'"[55]

Pedestrian deaths, like all the other problems we have examined, vary across places and times in a way that gives clues about both causes and potential remedies. Consider, for example, the striking contrast between the increase in pedestrian deaths since 2009 in the US and the continuing fall in such deaths in the UK (see

Pedestrian fatalities per 100,000 people, 1979–2022

—— US —— UK

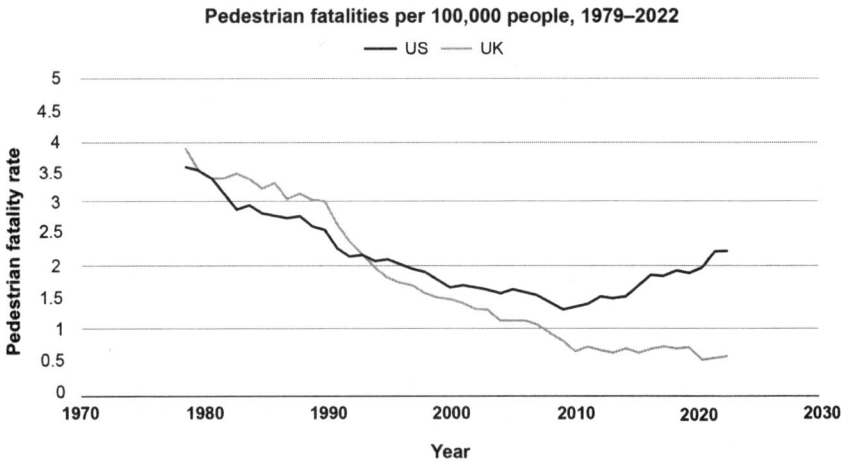

Figure 6.2. As safety regulations and enforcement have diverged between the US and the UK, so have, predictably enough, levels of pedestrian fatalities. While rates were roughly equal as recently as the early 1990s, the death rate in the US in 2020 was four times higher than in the UK. (US figures from Insurance Institute for Highway Safety, "Pedestrians: Fatality Statistics," 2024, www.iihs.org/topics/fatality-statistics/detail /pedestrians; UK figures from the Department for Transport, *Reported Road Casualties Great Britain: Pedestrian Factsheet 2021*.)

Figure 6.2). This seems unlikely to be the product of changes over time in pedestrian irresponsibility in the two countries. In fact, it appears to result, at least in part, from increase in vehicle sizes in the US, in contrast to the UK and Europe. Since 1980, according to the US Environmental Protection Agency's *Automotive Trends Report*, the average weight of a personal vehicle in the US increased by one thousand pounds, a more than 30 percent increase, and the length and width have increased commensurately.

One might expect that the auto industry would be relentlessly focused on increasing safety, if only to reduce the potential for public opposition to cars. But nothing could be further from the truth. The industry, in fact, has a history of fighting new safety measures tooth and nail. In the early part of the twentieth century, automakers resisted seat belts, padded dashboards, and collapsible steering columns.[56] In the 1970s and '80s, the industry continued to oppose mandatory seat belt laws and resisted rules to require the use of airbags. Most recently the US motor industry has fought against proposed regulations requiring automatic emergency braking and speed limiters. The industry has also not been above "dirty tricks": When campaigner Ralph Nader exposed safety problems at General Motors in his 1965 book *Unsafe at Any Speed*, the company's response was to hire private investigators to try to uncover information that might discredit him.[57]

The American Automobile Association, which was founded in 1902 to advocate for drivers' interests, has mainly (at least until recently) sided with the car companies against safety measures such as airbags. The UK Automobile Association has, likewise, frequently opposed the imposition, and tightening, of speed limits even in the face of rising public concern about road fatalities.[58] More recently, an auto industry trade body, the European Automobile Manufacturers' Association (ACEA), lobbied to weaken new EU legislation that would have imposed powerful (s-frame) regulations on speed limiters, requiring new car models to automatically detect, and respect, local speed limits. ACEA advocated instead for technology that simply would inform drivers if they violated local speed limits (a classic i-frame intervention)—which it argued would be equally effective in reducing speeding and fatalities. This claim is challenged by analyses of the UK's independent Transport Research Laboratory, which estimates that EU-wide adoption of the speed-limiting technology would save roughly thirteen hundred lives annually across Europe.[59]

Improving traffic safety has been a key goal of different nudge interventions, and in fact was one of the applications discussed in Thaler and Sunstein's original *Nudge* book. One such initiative is discussed in a white paper published by Behavia, a nudge unit centered in Berlin and Riyadh, that presents three illustrative options as possible solutions to encourage drivers to slow down: (1) a "shock nudge" consisting of graphic billboards next to highways, (2) an "optical nudge" in which horizontal lines that get progressively narrower are painted on highways to "amplify the feeling of speeding," and finally, (3) a "noise nudge" consisting of raised strips coated on asphalt to increase noise in cars.[60] The white paper proposes that all three interventions *could* be tested against a control group with no intervention, then, somewhat bizarrely, presents hypothetical data (with no explanation of where it came from or how it was collected) showing that the shock nudge would reduce average speed by 5 percent, the optical nudge by 8 percent, and the noise nudge by 6 percent. Extrapolating these figures to predicted accidents and fatalities (which fall by 13 percent, 24 percent, and 20 percent, respectively), and taking account of the costs of each nudge ("EUR 43,000 for each shock nudge, EUR 120,000 for each optical nudge and EUR 125,000 for each noise nudge"), the paper concludes that the shock nudge is the most cost-effective, saving eighty lives per million euros spent—a somewhat arbitrary number given it is only based on illustrative data.

Automobile-related safety is, though, a good domain for illustrating the potential for s-frame perspectives and solutions. Consider Sweden's long-term strategy for road safety, "Vision Zero," described as "an ethical stance stating that it is not acceptable for human mistakes to have fatal consequences. [Vision Zero] can be viewed as a paradigm shift, where the ultimate responsibility for road safety is shifted from the individual road-user to those who design the transport system. . . . It is human to make a mistake, but mistakes should not cost a person's life or health. Instead, [the aim is to design] the transport system so that accidents will not lead to serious consequences."[61]

Vision Zero was put into practice by the Swedish parliament in 1997. Practically, the plan has involved steps such as equipping roads with central barriers to prevent head-on accidents, giving police the ability to monitor with cameras the speed of cars, replacing four-way intersections with roundabouts, and enacting safety regulations for cars. The policy has been a success. When Vision Zero began to be implemented in Sweden, the number of fatalities caused by road accidents was seven per one hundred thousand inhabitants, which was a low figure by international standards. Since then, however, the number of traffic fatalities in Sweden has been more than halved at the same time that the volume of traffic has increased dramatically.

Another obvious solution is to actually enforce speed limits. George recently spent five weeks in New Zealand and discovered how effective such a policy can be. Not only are speed limits strictly enforced, but the automobile he rented displayed the prevailing speed limit prominently on the dashboard. Remarkably—for an American used to elastic speed limits and sparse enforcement—he rarely saw other cars exceeding the speed limit, even by a few kilometers per hour.

Technology is an obvious part of the solution to improving safety. We noted earlier that the European motor industry lobbied intensively against proposals to require vehicles to include technology that would directly enforce local speed limits (e.g., by cutting out the accelerator, the obvious s-frame solution). Still, from July 2024, all new cars sold in the EU are required to have mandatory speed limiters of some kind (typically by providing warning signals to the driver), and new vehicles must have automated lane-keeping and autonomous emergency braking.[62] These and similar developments are vigorously opposed by large sections of the motor vehicle industry (as well as by the governments of some nations in the EU).[63] But clearly the solution to road safety has to come through better systems (whether from better laws, road designs, or technology) rather than by vainly hoping for "more responsible people" at the wheel or on the sidewalk.

———

The common thread running through this chapter, and the first part of the book, should by now be clear. Many of our persistent social problems arise not from the failings of human nature (although people do have manifest limitations), nor primarily from public policies implemented with poor "ergonomics," leaving people struggling with badly designed forms, overcomplex procedures, or confused communications. To be sure, getting the implementational details right is an area where behavioral insights can help—but it is rarely the root of the problem. The real reason that many such problems don't get fixed is that there are powerful, typically corporate, interests that benefit from them *not* getting fixed. These powerful interests concentrate their own efforts on the s-frame, making sure that the "rules of the game" work in their favor. But at the same time, those same interests are keen to promote the idea that the social problems that they're enabling are issues of individual responsibility and should be addressed by i-frame interventions, supposedly to help individuals manage their responsibilities more effectively.

In Part Two, we trace the ideological roots of the i-frame perspective. And we show how the new field of behavioral economics, which should have been a natural enemy of the antiregulation approach, was co-opted into supporting it. Then we will begin to sketch out how behavioral science can help solve social and environmental problems by targeting the s-frame.

Part Two

HOW WE GOT INTO THIS MESS (AND HOW TO GET OUT)

Chapter 7

THE BIG MYTH

The only sure bulwark of continuing liberty is a government strong enough to protect the interests of the people, and a people strong enough and well enough informed to maintain its sovereign control over the government.

—Franklin D. Roosevelt, "fireside chat," April 1938

Government is not the solution to our problem; government is the problem.

—Ronald Reagan, first inaugural address, January 1981

George teaches a course on public policy each year at Carnegie Mellon, covering many of the topics in the first half of this book. As the semester goes by, students begin to notice a striking pattern—indeed, it is hard *not* to notice: Most of the problems discussed in class either originated or became much worse right around the year 1980. Why 1980? What went so badly wrong?

The answer, we believe, is deeply connected to the i-frame/s-frame distinction that is the central theme of Part One. A big part of what went wrong was that a powerful story about how society works—or should work—took hold in many parts of the world. International institutions such as the International Monetary Fund and World Trade Organization promoted a vision of an open and radically deregulated market economy both for the former Soviet Union and across the developing world. In this vision, rules and regulations were largely an impediment to social and economic progress and needed be cleared away so that individual people and businesses could flourish. As Joseph Stiglitz, a Nobel Prize–winning economist who was chief economist and senior vice president of the World Bank from 1997 to 2000, has influentially argued, the process of deregulation and privatization has had at best mixed and at worst disastrous impacts on the countries affected, ranging from greater economic instability and financial crises to increased corruption, asset-stripping, the creation of monopolies and oligarchies, and higher levels of inequality.[1] He notes, though, that the process of rapid and thoroughgoing liberalization has been highly profitable for the Western countries imposing this agenda. So, for example, the deregulation of public services and the elimination of tariffs, currency controls, and other barriers to trade opened up opportunities for Western firms— from consultancies, accountants, and banks to retailers and manufacturers looking for new markets and cheap labor.

Western countries advocating openness and deregulation for others don't always quite believe their own rhetoric, of course. Indeed, many have maintained strict restrictions on their own markets, especially in agriculture, where they deem this to be expedient. More generally, the powerful Western nations that largely control the international trade rules have, predictably, rigged the international rules governing trade and access to capital in their favor. This is, as usual, just what would be predicted from political economy 101: The rich and powerful will work to shape the rules to further entrench their wealth and power. We should not expect the rules of trade, as elsewhere, to be fair. Hence, a top priority for helping to create a fairer world requires, as usual, shifting to fairer rules.

Predictably, the rich and powerful tell a very different story; they argue that the "liberalization" they impose on others will actually be helpful rather than destructive. Rather than changing the rules (in their favor), the story is that they are merely sweeping away rules and creating a world in which merit prevails and people and firms can take responsibility for themselves. The question of *which* rules we live by (and whom they favor) is replaced with the question of *whether we really need rules at all.* And the suggested answer is, of course, that we do not—or at least that we should manage with as few rules as possible. In this presumed utopia of free enterprise, free speech, free trade, unlimited political donations, and freedom to concentrate media ownership, control of information, and technology, each person has the responsibility to look out for their own interests, unmolested by bothersome rules and regulations.

We call this story the "i-frame narrative." As in any good story, the i-frame narrative has heroes and villains. The heroes are self-reliant, innovative, and ingenious *individuals* (both actual people and those "honorary" individuals, corporations).[2] The primary villains are the advocates and implementers of taxation, legislation, regulation, and systemic changes of all kinds: *governments.* According to the i-frame narrative, social, economic, and environmental problems will evaporate once the government steps aside and individuals are empowered to stand up, take responsibility, and generally look out for themselves. Once freed from the shackles of regulation and government meddling, these heroic individuals (including, especially, entrepreneurs and CEOs) can create something close to utopia.

Inspired by the rise of this i-frame narrative (and, yes, note the irony here) came vast and systemic s-frame change in tandem on both sides of the Atlantic—a radical reshaping of the rules of society that systematically favored powerful businesses as well as the wealthy, who owned an increasing fraction of those businesses. These radical s-frame changes were supposedly—according to the i-frame narrative—just returning us to the "natural" state of society, which is as close as possible to a world with no rules at all. Once the thicket of rules and regulations had been cleared out of the way—the red tape cut and the "nanny state" sent packing—individual enterprise and innovation would take off.

Let's look at what happened in the US. The transition around 1980 did away with the so-called New Deal consensus that had reigned for the past half century: progressive taxation, high levels of unionization, highly regulated labor and financial sectors, and relatively high levels of welfare spending. Roosevelt's vision of a strong government protecting, and being guided by, its citizens was essentially an s-frame vision: The government sets up the "rules of the game" to benefit its citizens, and the role of citizens is to "maintain [their] sovereign control over the government" (to quote Roosevelt's words from the head of this chapter)—essentially to make sure that the rules aren't distorted to favor the few rather than the many. Of course, the reality was imperfect, and will always be imperfect. Governments will overreach, overspend, and generally promote the expansion of government for its own sake; and there will always be the danger that government officials and politicians will be subject to the influence and money of powerful business interests. But the New Deal consensus was that the answer was not *less* government, but *better* government.

Ronald Reagan and his supporters had other ideas.[3] Once the fortieth president took office in January 1981, he attacked unions and slashed taxes on corporations and the rich (cutting the top marginal income tax rate from 70 percent when he took office to 28 percent when he left). When these tax cuts predictably led to huge budget deficits, Reagan responded by increasing taxes—not income taxes, but excise taxes and payroll taxes that fell disproportionately on the poor, because rates did not depend on income.[4]

Reagan also enacted policies that cut millions of recipients from welfare (Aid to Families with Dependent Children), Food Stamps, and school lunch programs.[5] He gutted business regulations and antitrust enforcement and appointed Supreme Court justices who locked into place decades of consequential pro-business rulings. The core antigovernment tenet of the Reagan revolution became so entrenched that Bill Clinton, a Democrat elected in 1992, was able to win reelection in 1996 by enacting policies that pushed Reagan's agenda forward—further deregulating the financial sector, championing the North American Free Trade Agreement (NAFTA), and putting an "end [to] welfare as we know it." While he put a more positive spin on Reagan's view that government was "the problem," Clinton nonetheless declared proudly in his first State of the Union address that "the era of big government is over."[6]

There is, inevitably, more to the story. While we believe the transition from an s-frame to an i-frame political narrative is particularly central to explaining the radical upheavals around 1980, such historical inflection points have many elements and many intertwined causes. For example, it has been argued that the transition away from the New Deal consensus was speeded by, among other things, the fallout from the oil crisis of the 1970s; a reaction against government and union overreach; and the rise of, and focus on, civil rights, feminism, and hostility to the Vietnam War, leading to a perceived deprioritization of the economic interests of white working-class voters and laying the foundations for "culture wars" politics.[7] Likewise, the revolution that Ronald Reagan instigated didn't spring up abruptly; for example, Jimmy Carter, who was denied a second term by Reagan's ascension, deregulated airlines, trucking, rail, and long-distance phone services during his single term of office.[8] Still, Reagan accelerated the shift toward a more individualistic conception of society, policy, and politics.

The same pattern was occurring in the UK. During her tenure as prime minster from 1979 to 1992, Margaret Thatcher oversaw similar antiunion, antiregulation, and antigovernment measures—against a backdrop of economic and social malaise similar to that in the US. Some reforms were, admittedly, successful and almost certainly broadly beneficial; for instance, the radical deregulation of the City of London in 1983 known as the "Big Bang" led to the rapid rise of London's status as a global financial center. But the privatization of large sectors of the economy had mixed results—sometimes yielding dynamic and competitive markets (e.g., telecoms) while in other cases producing sclerotic natural monopolies (e.g., water). As in the US, later governments, whether Conservative or Labour, largely continued in the same direction: less government, less regulation, more emphasis on individual responsibility and enterprise.

The Reagan–Thatcher revolution has a mixed and disputed legacy. There were undoubtedly some bad regulations and ineffective government programs that were rightly challenged. But the social problems that we have been considering in this book, whether obesity, health care costs, inequality, or retirement, have hardly evaporated with the dismantling of regulation and the rollback of government. Indeed, quite the opposite: Many of these problems emerged around 1980, or became substantially worse. And the steady rise in people's expectations of living more prosperous lives than those of their parents—the sense that a rising tide would lift all boats—came to an abrupt halt (Figure 7.1).

What *has* improved since 1980 is the bottom line of many big businesses and the share of total wealth owned by the superrich. This is not an accident—it is the culmination of a multipronged effort by powerful commercial interests to embed the i-frame in the public mind. This campaign, we believe, is not merely being waged on an issue-by-issue basis. Rather, it is in the interest of those profiting from the current system to promote a vision of society that prioritizes individual self-reliance as the solution to

Average share of US 30-year-olds who earn more, after adjusting for inflation, than their parents did at age 30

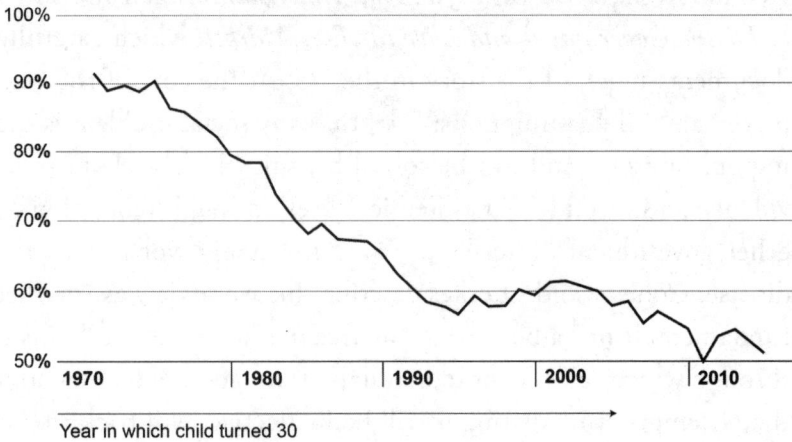

Figure 7.1. When the rising tide stopped rising. In the 1970s, the vast majority of people had higher real earnings than their parents; economic prosperity was benefiting almost everyone. But by the 2010s, such generalized upward progress across the generations had stopped entirely. Now for each person better off than their parents, another is worse off. (Figure redrawn from Jim Tankersley, "Barely Half of 30-Year-Olds Earn More Than Their Parents, Economists Find," *Wall Street Journal*, December 8, 2016. The original academic research paper is Raj Chetty et al., "The Fading American Dream: Trends in Absolute Income Mobility Since 1940," *Science* 356, 2017.)

any problem and rejects systemic solutions through government action or regulation.

————

Where does the antigovernment (and hence pro-individual-responsibility) narrative come from? Is it perhaps the inevitable outcome of a natural human impulse to live freely and take control of one's own destiny? Or perhaps it is the expression of a specific culture or historical tradition—the spirit of the Enlightenment, or the early settlers in the US, or even the Wild West? None of the above. The i-frame story about how society works did not emerge organically from the ground up but is a carefully nurtured narrative sponsored by powerful business interests. As we mentioned in the Introduction, our eyes were opened, in particular, by a recent and important book: Erik M. Conway and Naomi Oreskes's *The Big Myth: How American Business Taught Us to Loathe Government and Love the Free Market*, which carefully documents much of the story in the US. At the core of the "big myth" are twin assumptions: first, that any social problem is the responsibility of, and can be solved by, suitably self-reliant individuals; and second, that systemic "cures" through regulation or other government "interference" are inevitably worse than the disease. Conway and Oreskes describe this worldview as "market fundamentalism," a belief that the free market is the mechanism through which self-reliant individuals attain good outcomes, and that attempts at regulating it will be ineffective, will backfire, or have serious undesirable consequences.

Oreskes and Conway document how this antigovernment agenda was promoted in the US from the 1930s and 1940s, initially sponsored by the National Association of Manufacturers (NAM), which mounted sustained and well-funded campaigns, with billboards, pamphlets, and even radio shows—including a popular radio series called *The American Family Robinson*, created by Harry A. Bullis, a senior executive at General Mills (creators of the Wheaties and Cheerios breakfast cereals) and chair of NAM's Public Relations Committee. The show depicted the heroic efforts of individuals, and especially individual business leaders and their companies (their vigor and ingenuity arising, supposedly, from their i-frame spirit of self-reliance), fighting for the good of their communities against a relentless tide of obstructive, self-serving, and incompetent government initiatives (i.e., the crushing burdens imposed by the s-frame).

The central role of government in creating public goods—from infrastructure (railroads, canals, roads) and generating technological advances (from the machining revolution that led to the "American system of manufacturing" in the nineteenth century, to the creation of the computer and the internet in the twentieth)—was not, of course, part of the story. Indeed, as illustrated in the innovative and widely viewed NAM short movie *Your Town* (viewed by an estimated six million people in 1940), the entire prosperity, civic virtue, and spiritual well-being of a typical American town could be traced to the public-spirited and unaided efforts of its local businesspeople—embodied in the heroic individual entrepreneur. More broadly, according to this i-frame narrative, a successful community springs, in essence, from good, hardworking, self-driven individuals taking responsibility for their own lives and being subject to the minimum possible external constraints.

As documented by Oreskes and Conway, these popularization efforts included creating, for adult subscribers of *Reader's Digest*, a simplified version of Friedrich Hayek's "Road to Serfdom" attack on regulation and even a cartoon version for kids. A central member of NAM, the General Electric Corporation, had a TV show, *General Electric Theater*, which ran from 1953 to 1961 and was hosted by none other than Ronald Reagan, promoting stories about the importance of individual enterprise and the pernicious effects of government and unions.[9] Reagan's work for GE also included touring the company's plants to deliver inspirational speeches conveying the relentless narrative that good things come from individual self-reliance and hard work, unencumbered by interference (or assistance) from government or unions.

Reagan's work for GE turned out to be hugely consequential. Conway and Oreskes note that "GE transformed Reagan's political fortunes. . . . He emerged from his time there with powerful backers in corporate America who helped him launch his career in elected office."[10] As governor of California and then as president, Reagan became the reassuring and avuncular voice of an i-frame narrative that would change America, and the world.

Conway and Oreskes enumerate the diverse tactics employed in NAM's well-funded campaigns. These included supporting and popularizing the views of writers and thinkers who agreed on the idea that entirely unfettered individuals (including individual corporations) are the engines of prosperity and the basis for healthy and happy communities, and that even the hint of s-frame regulation is grit in those engines. These writers and thinkers included "Austrian school" economists Ludwig von Mises and Friedrich Hayek, as well as Chicago school economists Milton Friedman and George Stigler. Support was also extended to the polemical economics popularizer Leonard Read and the influential and controversial political novelist Ayn Rand. A particularly important figure was Harold Luhnow, who managed the William Volker Fund, a charitable foundation, during the period between 1947 and 1964. According to one enthusiastic historian of the process, Luhnow, as director of the fund, which previously had been used for more conventional philanthropic causes,

> paid Mises' salary at New York University; he paid FA Hayek's salary at the University of Chicago; he funded lectures that Milton and Rose Friedman turned into *Capitalism and Freedom* [a bestseller proposing the primacy of individual action and the ineffectiveness and undesirability of regulation]; and he approved the grant that enabled Murray Rothbard to write *Man, Economy and State* [a key libertarian text]. Inspired by Hayek, Antony Fisher provided the seed money for the Institute of Economic Affairs in London and then helped to establish free market institutes around the globe.[11]

To get a sense of the Chicago version of the i-frame narrative, here is Milton Friedman, writing in 1955: "I shall assume a society that takes freedom of the individual, or more realistically the family, as its ultimate objective, and seeks to further this objective by relying primarily on voluntary exchange among individuals for the organization of economic activity. In such a free private enterprise exchange economy, government's primary role is to preserve the rules of the game by enforcing contracts, preventing coercion, and keeping markets free."[12]

In his bestseller *Free to Choose*, Friedman criticized government as curtailing freedom and producing inefficiency; blamed the Great

Depression on government; advocated against public aid to the poor, public housing, Medicaid, Medicare, and Social Security; advocated for privatization of education; and proposed to abolish the Food and Drug Administration, the Consumer Product Safety Commission, Amtrak, and the Environmental Protection Agency.

To bolster the claim that individuals could be, and should be, "left alone" to pursue their self-interest, a mainstay of the Chicago school of economics was the idea that individuals are rational and self-interested. Combined with Adam Smith's notion of the "invisible hand"—that self-interested individuals interacting with one another to pursue their own goals would inadvertently promote the public good—the assumption of rational self-interest was taken to suggest that individuals would be best off if left to their own devices.

Such a perspective presents a highly simplified picture. For example, it ignores the crucial problem of *externalities*, which have loomed large throughout this book: i.e., cases in which Person A's free actions may damage Person B. Thus, A's free decision to drive a heavy (and polluting) car or truck may substantially endanger B's safety in a variety of ways (a serious problem in the US, whether B is a pedestrian, cyclist, or small-car driver).[13] And A's free actions can also damage the social or ecological environment on which we all depend—for example, by causing health-damaging smog, generating greenhouse gases, and so on.[14]

The simplified Chicago school picture also brushes aside problems of "asymmetrical information"—that markets may fail when sellers know more than buyers. In markets for, say, pensions or health care, the asymmetries will be hugely consequential: As we stressed in Part One, people can't possibly have the knowledge to make the right choices, and hence will all too often be lured into options that are most profitable to the seller. The Chicago school ignores, too, the very starting point of behavioral economics: People don't have the time or calculating expertise to assess the full consequences of their actions—and are forced to use crude, and fallible, mental shortcuts (or heuristics) to make decisions (thus compounding the problem of asymmetry of information). This makes regular citizens ripe for exploitation by other, better-funded interests, including corporations.

Perhaps even more important, what this picture of free exchange between individuals leaves out is that people interact with each other within a legal system that circumscribes what interactions can occur and what rules apply (from safety and environmental standards to constraints on false advertising, rights to return if dissatisfied, systems for approving medicines, airline safety protocols, rights of legal recourse, and so on). Modern capitalism works smoothly and effectively only when it is governed by an incredibly complex system of laws, regulations, and standards, and when there are governments and legal systems that enforce them. Without proper regulation, the system rapidly collapses into distrust and dispute. If even the basic rules of society begin to fray, life can rapidly degenerate into a brutish war of all against all.

Ignoring such complications, the Chicago school launched arguments about why free enterprise, unencumbered by government, was the best of all possible arrangements, and also provided a range of reasons why regulations of different types would fail. The prominent economist Albert Hirschman referred to these as *"perversity* arguments."[15] A perversity argument will be familiar to anyone who has taken introductory economics: If you control rents, there will be a deficiency of housing supply, which will ultimately *raise* rents. If you impose a minimum wage, employers will stop hiring precisely those whom the minimum wage is intended to help. If you provide people with unemployment insurance, or provide financial assistance to people with low incomes, they will work less. If you insure people against hazards, they won't bother to protect themselves from those hazards.

One of the most notorious arguments along these lines, by Chicago economist Sam Peltzman, aimed to show that automobile safety measures such as seat belt mandates did not decrease automobile fatalities, because they led drivers to make riskier driving decisions.[16] Peltzman's original analysis turned out to be flawed, and later, more careful analyses have found that, as any sensible person would guess, seat belts do reduce road deaths, substantially.[17]

More generally, as we saw in Chapter 6, safer vehicles and changes in road design have actually led to spectacular reductions in road deaths across many countries in the world, despite huge increases in passenger miles. But the supposed "Peltzman effect" is a perversity argument that is too surprising (and rhetorically persuasive) to be abandoned; it is one of many "zombie ideas" that, while long dead in academic circles, still stalks the land of political discussion and is used to defend the i-frame ideology.[18]

An even more far-reaching perversity argument was the "regulatory capture" theory advanced by another Chicago economist, George Stigler. The curious rhetorical strategy underlying Stigler's viewpoint is striking: While (correctly, we believe) viewing big business with a jaundiced eye, Stigler ends up promoting the very antiregulatory agenda that big business favors. Stigler drew on Mancur Olson's *The Logic of Collective Action*, familiar from our discussion in Part One, to argue that economic regulations rarely operate in the public interest but instead are typically shaped by industries and professions themselves to advance their own interests.[19] Olson had argued that concentrated, homogeneous, well-organized groups of firms (or in some cases wealthy individuals) tend to dominate political processes at the expense of larger groups of uncoordinated individuals. Stigler used Olson's analysis to justify the assumption that any regulations will tend to advance the interests of business.

We don't need to look very far to find evidence supportive of such a perspective. To take a particular high-profile example, the devastating global financial and economic crisis of 2008 came after decades of relentless lobbying from the finance industry that allowed firms to take wild risks (and reap wild profits). Once the bubble burst, moreover, those same firms that had previously argued that the government should butt out of financial markets now lobbied for bailouts, leaving taxpayers and ordinary investors to foot the bill. Once the dust had settled, lobbying to loosen regulatory oversight and restrictions on the financial services industry resumed as intensely as ever. Indeed, key elements of the 2010 Dodd-Frank Act, introduced to reduce systematic risk in the US financial sector, had already been rolled back a mere eight years later, potentially with destabilizing results.[20]

It might seem obvious that the answer to regulation that has been subverted by corporate interests is to aggressively root out the mechanisms by which corporate interests unduly influence the policymaking process. But Stigler employs a masterful rhetorical trick. Olson rightly warns that business interests can co-opt regulation (and we've seen that they often do). Stigler and his followers go even further and argue that pretty much *all* regulation serves business and not the public interest. Given that regulations will always be "captured," the Stigler perversity argument concludes, the best regulation is as little regulation as possible. Whether intended by Stigler or not, this conclusion is great news for big business because it dismisses as futile the task of buttressing democracy against the power of corporate interests, and leaves the levers of power in their hands.

The "big myth" that all good comes from individuals and businesses, and that government is the root of all (or at least most) social evil, has become so strongly embedded in media and political discourse that it has far outlasted the Reagan–Thatcher era. As we've seen in Part One, the political agenda has increasingly focused on handing individual and social problems over to the individual: seeing public health problems as requiring individual restraint (e.g., the obesity crisis, addiction to prescription drugs, tobacco, gambling, and more); shifting the problem of financial security in old age to individuals through individualized "defined benefits" private pension schemes; and (in the US especially) privatizing health care. As Conway and Oreskes note, "The myth spread, influencing American presidents from Jimmy Carter and

Ronald Reagan to Bill Clinton and Barack Obama and, most recently, Donald Trump."[21]

How did the collapse of confidence in "big government," and the embracing of the free-market ethos, contribute to the emergence of the problems discussed in Part One of the book? Some of the problems emerged as a result of a failure to intervene as problems got worse. For example, the government stood by as private industry dismantled the pension system that had prevailed for over half a century, and the population was hoodwinked by the health insurance industry to fear the "socialized medicine" that has achieved so much better results at much lower costs in virtually all other economically advanced nations. The slashing of the highest marginal tax rates, as well as effective undermining of unions, likewise contributed to a drastic worsening of inequality, with fallout, as we discussed in Chapter 5, for virtually all the other problems we review.

But the movements spearheaded by Reagan and Thatcher did more than weaken government—they established a culture that idolized self-interest, as embodied in the infamous statement that "greed is good" by the fictional Gordon Gekko in the 1987 film *Wall Street*.[22] John F. Kennedy's famous statement in his 1960 inaugural address, "Ask not what your country can do for you— ask what you can do for your country," would sound downright quaint just a few decades later.

So, yes, something big happened around 1980, as George's students noticed as the semester progressed, though the pattern could only be seen long after it began to unfold. This was the turning point when the i-frame narrative started to dominate political discourse, spreading its influence across the political spectrum. S-frame interventions were increasingly painted as old-fashioned, coercive, stultifying, and inevitably ineffective. But throwing responsibility back to the individual did not have the promised benefits. Instead of fixing problems, abandoning a systemic approach only made those problems much worse.

Chapter 8

SLEEPWALKING INTO
THE ENEMY'S RANKS

Although the world seems to be becoming increasingly polar-
ized, we continue to believe that libertarian paternalism can be
a promising foundation for bipartisanship and for simple problem
solving. Better governance often requires less in the way of government coercion and more in the way of freedom to choose.

To borrow a phrase from the late Milton Friedman, libertarian
paternalists urge that people should be "free to choose."

—Richard H. Thaler and Cass R. Sunstein,
Nudge: The Final Edition

By a curious coincidence, just as Reagan's and Thatcher's political revolutions focused attention on the "i-frame"—promoting
deregulation and trickle-down economics while demonizing the
role of government—the field of economics was beginning a revolution of its own. In 1979 (when Thatcher took office in the UK)
and 1980 (the year Reagan was elected president), two foundational papers were published that kick-started a new field called
behavioral economics.[1] On the face of it, the emerging discipline
seemed directly opposed to the antigovernment, antiregulation

perspective of the influential Chicago school. The theories of the right-leaning Chicago school economists were built on the foundational idea that economic "agents" (as people are commonly referred to in this rarefied world) rationally pursue their own self-interest. The Chicago school argued that, if these rational agents were unencumbered by government regulation—were "free to choose"—they would make rational decisions that would benefit themselves and, by the logic of Adam Smith's "invisible hand," society. By pushing back on this narrative, the early founders of behavioral economics, including George, saw themselves as embarking on a distinctly left-of-center agenda directly opposed to that of the Chicago school.

Paradoxically or not, Chicago was also where many of the early proponents of behavioral economics coalesced. George's first job was at the University of Chicago business school; Cass Sunstein spent a decade at its law school; and Richard Thaler, who arrived at Chicago's business school shortly after George left, is still a professor there as this book goes to press.

One of George's fondest memories from his time in Chicago was attending the imposingly named "Rationality Seminar," held Tuesday nights in an always-packed seminar room in one of the university's neo-Gothic buildings. Critics of strong assumptions about the extent of human rationality in economics, like George and Thaler, were invited to make their case, and Chicago school luminaries like Gary Becker, George Stigler (the proponent of regulatory capture we met in the last chapter), and Sherwin Rosen, as well as legal academics Richard Posner and Frank Easterbrook, defended the faith. The debate was invariably lively, and—characteristic of Chicago—surprisingly unpredictable.[2] Though the two groups had fundamentally different views on the key topic of rationality, both the stalwarts and their young critics saw the emerging field of behavioral economics as a threat to the Chicago school; the rationality seminar was a chance for the old guard to bolster their defenses against these new upstarts.[3]

With this historical background, one might expect that as behavioral economists became more involved in thinking about the implications of their new perspective for public policy, there would be a pushback against the antigovernment, deregulation agenda of the Chicago school and its allies. Surely, behavioral economists—who study the limitations of human rationality—should be especially well attuned to the importance of creating stronger, systemic regulations to compensate for the shortcomings they had exposed in human judgment and decision-making. Behavioral economics could have been—and, we argue, still can and should be—used to promote *more* and, crucially, *smarter* regulation, not less. But something very different happened. Ultimately, and perversely, in our view, behavioral economics ended up playing a role that bolstered the Chicago stance on regulation and the role of government.

How did this happen? That strange story begins around the year 2000, when two groups of behavioral economists (with a law professor on each team) proposed a new approach to public policy. One team was made up of economist Richard Thaler and law professor Cass Sunstein. The other included George, fellow behavioral economists Matthew Rabin, Colin Camerer, and Ted O'Donoghue, and the legal scholar Sam Issacharoff. The approaches advocated by the two groups were largely equivalent, which is not surprising, since the central idea was proposed by the economist Matthew Rabin at a weekly seminar at the Center for Advanced Study in the Behavioral Sciences, where George, Richard, Matthew, and Colin were in residence for the academic year 1997–1998.[4]

The new approach recognized that people's individual-level imperfections could be used to justify paternalistic policies in which the government in some cases restricted citizens' freedom of choice for their own good. We don't allow children to eat whatever they want, one of the papers noted; once one recognized that adults, like children, cannot be relied on to always do what is in their self-interest, wouldn't similar logic dictate that adults' options should be justifiably limited? But the concern of both teams was that such "hard" paternalistic measures, however well-intentioned, would provoke ire among conservatives. The solution was a form of "light" paternalism that, they hoped, would have appeal across the political spectrum. The titles of each of the two teams' papers, both published in 2003, clearly convey their central goal of appealing specifically to conservatives. Thaler and Sunstein titled their paper "Libertarian Paternalism," or in another version, "Libertarian Paternalism Is Not an Oxymoron," though their program was later branded with the much catchier term "nudge." George and his coauthors titled their paper "Asymmetric Paternalism: *Regulation for Conservatives*" (emphasis added).[5]

The key idea developed in these papers was that people who might naturally behave in self-destructive (or, given the existence of externalities, in other-destructive) ways could be steered in beneficial directions using the tools of behavioral economics, such as defaults and framing effects, without actually limiting their freedom of choice.[6] As George's team put it, such an approach made it possible "to have one's cake and eat it too" by creating what they called "asymmetrically paternalistic" regulations. The asymmetry came from how these regulations affected different types of people. Those inclined to make the "wrong" choice—such as failing to save for retirement or choosing an unhealthy diet—stood to benefit greatly from these nudges. Those already inclined to make the "right" choice, in contrast, would be hardly affected. And, importantly, whether they wanted to do what was best for themselves or not, everyone was left entirely "free to choose."

George's team argued that most earlier (s-frame-style) regulations broke down into two broad categories. The first category involved redistribution, most directly where tax revenue is taken from the rich and given to the poor in the form of welfare benefits. In this case, one group is helped at the expense of another. The second category involved "restricting behavior in a way that imposes harm on an individual basis but yields net societal benefits."[7] An example of this would be taxing citizens to fund public goods like roads, parks, or the judicial system. While a person may *individually* be better off if somehow exempted from the tax, everyone (that person included) still benefits from having a safe road to drive on, parks to walk in, and the maintenance of law and order. The paper then proposed that a "third form" of regulation is possible: "paternalistic regulations that are designed to help on an individual basis." Both papers argued that this form of regulation could in fact be implemented without limiting people's freedom of choice.

This third form of regulation was popularized in Thaler and Sunstein's bestseller *Nudge*, published five years after the original papers: "A nudge, as we will use the term, is any aspect of the choice architecture that alters people's behavior in a predictable way without forbidding any options or significantly changing their economic incentives. To count as a mere nudge, the intervention must be easy and cheap to avoid."[8]

In *Nudge*, the debt to the Chicago school perspective is even more explicit than it was in the academic papers that spawned the original idea. Indeed, as shown in the opening quotations for this chapter, Sunstein and Thaler make several admiring references to Milton Friedman's *Free to Choose*. The reader will recall from the last chapter that Friedman advocated eliminating virtually every government program protecting individuals.

Libertarian/asymmetric paternalism caught on beyond its proponents' wildest dreams. *Nudge* became required reading for politicians and policymakers around the globe. "Behavioral Insights Teams" or "nudge units" sprang up in Britain under conservative Prime Minister David Cameron and, later, in President Obama's White House. Soon, academic and professional conferences brought together researchers, bureaucrats, and policy wonks (including the two of us) who hoped to find individual-level solutions to social problems.[9]

What we, along with most of our colleagues who jumped onto the nudge bandwagon, did not take into account was that this approach to public policy, while designed to help people, also implicitly blamed them for problems they neither caused nor had any real power to fix.

Other social scientists, especially sociologists, had already identified this pattern and anointed it with the clever label of *responsibilization*: making individuals feel personally responsible for issues or problems that have systemic causes.[10] Responsibilization can show up in policies, political and commercial campaigns, and any discourse that emphasizes the responsibility of individuals, typically as consumers, for problems such as climate change, income inequality, exploitation of child labor, or the environmental damage caused by pesticides. Responsibilization aims to deflect attention away from larger systemic factors that might better be addressed via government policy.

On the basis of personal observation and documents at World Economic Forums in Davos from 2004 to 2012, the consumer sociologists Markus Giesler and Ela Veresiu identified a range of domains in which responsibilization is being advocated by the economic elite, often top corporate executives.[11] The strategy of responsibilization is to encourage individuals—when, say, shopping for food—to take account not only of price and quality but also of the impact of their purchases on ecological sustainability, biodiversity, energy conservation, worker safety, living wages, and, most important (in this example), the preservation of small farms and a rural way of life.[12]

While it is admirable that many consumers take such issues into account, it is wildly optimistic to believe that there is much scope for addressing these deep underlying problems purely via changes in individualistic food choices. Individual actions do matter for all these problems, but mainly via the actions individuals take as voters and in pressing for governments to change the rules by which businesses operate. Voters are likely to vote for changing the rules if they feel outrage about the ways those rules are currently working and they feel compelled to demand change. The trick of responsibilization is to help people view the rules as a mere neutral backdrop and to focus on the choices they and their fellow citizens make. If responsibilization works, any outrage should be directed at oneself and one's fellow consumers for persistently making "unethical" choices. According to the responsibilization viewpoint, for example, the problems caused by the food industry do not arise because loose regulation allows a plethora of environmentally and socially damaging practices. The problem instead stems from consumers not being careful enough to buy the very most "ethical" foods.

The strategy of responsibilization goes far beyond agribusiness. It is a completely general tactic for those who wish to deflect any regulation that might disturb the status quo. Recall that oil companies say they want us to consider going on a low-carbon diet, keep track of our carbon footprint, and generally "own the problem" of climate change. Recall, too, Exxon's CEO Darren Woods squarely blaming the consumer in Chapter 1. The oil industry would like us to believe that climate change is the product of our individual (and, they imply, selfish) choices.

Similarly, employers exhort individuals to build and manage their own personal investment portfolios, and express concern that so many of them seem strangely unable to do so, while offloading the burden of saving for retirement and of managing their savings to those individuals. The private US health care system, too, throws the challenge of managing vast medical and financial uncertainties over to each individual—"your health is your problem!" is the message (while reminding Americans to be thankful that they aren't stuck in one of those highly popular and effective collective health schemes that the rest of the rich world has for some reason adopted). It's the same story for inequality, of course: Anyone at the "sharp end" of rising inequality needs simply to buckle down, get an education, put in the hours, and reap the rewards.

The behavioral revolution in public policy played into this narrative, with the presumption that people are, and should be, responsible for the problems they face, and that the solution is to nudge them to make better, more responsible, decisions. But this leaves the rules of the game, where the real problems lie, intact, and propagates the illusion that with the right i-frame adjustments, radical s-frame policy changes will scarcely be necessary.

———

It is hard now to recapture the sense of possibility that was in the air as the new behavioral approach to solving society's, and the world's, problems began to gain ground. In 2010, the new UK prime minister, David Cameron, inspired by reading *Nudge*, gave the go-ahead for the creation of a Behavioural Insights Team within the government's Cabinet Office, led by the policy strategist and former Cambridge psychologist David Halpern, and staffed with a small but exceptionally talented group of civil servants. As we mentioned earlier in this book, Nick and George first met as members of the BIT advisory board in those early, heady days. Similar developments occurred in the US only a few years later, under the auspices of the Obama administration. One of the authors of *Nudge*, Cass Sunstein, took a leading government role in the Obama administration as head of the White House Office of Information and Regulatory Affairs in 2009, and was commonly referred to as the "regulatory tsar."[13] (Quite appropriately, Sunstein's work in this role extended far beyond nudges and mostly concerned conventional regulations.) Six years later, the cognitive scientist Maya Shankar founded a cross-governmental Social and Behavioral Sciences Team.[14] In parallel with these developments in the US, teams applying behavioral insights started popping up in local and national governments from Germany to Australia, from Singapore to Peru.[15]

Suddenly, it seemed, the empirical study of human nature, as it really is, had found a way into the policymaking process. Given that almost all policy aims, in one way or another, to shape human behavior, this shouldn't have been such a novel development. But, in practice, politicians and many of their advisers typically trust their "common sense" about how people will think and behave rather than looking for academic insights. And treasury officials and government economists often assume that they already possess a perfectly adequate account of human nature, as embodied in the perfectly rational utility-maximizing agents described by neoclassical economics. But now people inside governments started to feel that there might be something to be gained by talking to scientists who actually studied human nature and especially the quirks and foibles of human decision-making. Time for cognitive psychologists (like Nick) and behavioral economists (like George) to step into the spotlight.

This was very cheering for us personally, because (possibly due to the influence of *Nudge* and the bestselling *Thinking, Fast and Slow* by Nobel Prize–winning psychologist Daniel Kahneman) the spotlight was very much on the narrow realm of behavioral quirks and biases studied in the psychology of decision-making and behavioral economics rather than the full gamut of the social and behavioral sciences (encompassing everything from neuroscience to sociology to communication studies). For us, this initial emphasis on our own academic "patch" could at times be a little discomfiting, as colleagues from neighboring fields (say, from health, environmental, educational, or clinical psychology, mainstream economics, the law, political science, and more) could feel rather sidelined by "upstarts" such as ourselves with our narrow focus on individual behavioral quirks. Indeed, Nick can remember many slightly tense meetings on policy questions where some academics from other disciplines pushed back against the idea that targeting individual behavior could lead to radical social change. Nick suspected that these "s-framers" (as he would now see them) were rather stuck in the old-fashioned world of laws, regulations, subsidies, and taxes and hadn't yet grasped how much could be done by the exciting "modern" strategy of targeting the individual.

Contributing to our sense of excitement was the belief that nudges promised direct, speedy, uncontroversial, and low-cost solutions to difficult policy challenges. In the wake of the 2007–2008 financial crisis, the prospect of impactful change at low cost was particularly appealing to all kinds of stakeholders. Somewhat to our astonishment, we found politicians suddenly willing to listen to academics researching human bias and mental frailty, and to invite us onto committees and advisory boards.

At a personal level, we still feel a tinge of nostalgia for the days when it seemed that a behavioral revolution in public policy was imminent—in which cognitive psychologists and behavioral economists would rush to help people lead better lives, without getting stuck in political deadlock. Yet revolutions so often disappoint, and sadly this was no exception.

———

The first major problem we had with the "nudge" approach to public policy was pretty basic. Though applying our best efforts to devising and testing nudges, we noticed to our dismay that many behavioral i-frame interventions just didn't work—or when they did work, they didn't work very well. The reader will have observed this pattern throughout the book, but we've lived it.

George's major efforts were in the domain of health. Teaming with brilliant colleagues at the University of Pennsylvania such as Kevin Volpp and David Asch, he tested innovative incentive schemes to get people to lose weight. These individual-focused schemes did, in fact, succeed in getting them to do so; but in most studies, when the incentives ceased, participants not only didn't continue to lose weight, but actually gained back most or all of the weight they had lost. Other studies tested schemes to encourage people to take their medicine as prescribed. These schemes were also initially remarkably successful, but less so when rolled out to larger populations.

With his talented colleague Julie Downs and various graduate students, George also tested how displaying nutrition information or presenting food in different ways could get consumers to change their food choices. Examples included giving people traffic signals (green, yellow, or red) for the total calories in a meal they ordered online, informing them about how long they would have to work out on a treadmill to burn off the calories in a sugary drink, and having them order their meals ahead of time (when they weren't already hungry).[16] While some of these studies accomplished their narrow goal, and most got published in top journals and helped the graduate students get jobs, George started to get the uneasy feeling that they were unlikely to move the needle on any of the problems they targeted, and worse, that the whole approach was flawed and was providing Band-Aids for problems that could really only be addressed with surgery. He first articulated his growing misgivings in a 2010 *New York Times* opinion piece coauthored with his longtime collaborator and friend Peter Ubel. The editors titled the piece "Economists Behaving Badly."[17]

Nick was experiencing similar doubts even as he was trying to give practical policy advice. For six years, Nick was a member of the UK's Climate Change Committee, the small, dedicated, and impressive team that oversees and evaluates the UK's progress (or, quite often, lack of progress) toward meeting its legally binding goal of achieving net zero greenhouse gas emissions by 2050. Nick had hoped, as the representative of behavioral science, that he might be able to throw in i-frame insights about how to encourage individuals to reduce their carbon footprints—to reduce meat consumption, switch to electric vehicles, cut back on flying, and more. But he soon found that all the real action was at the s-frame: decarbonizing power generation, building a fully integrated electric vehicle infrastructure, kick-starting the take-up of heat pumps with appropriate subsidies, and so on. Yes, understanding human nature still mattered—but as an enabler for building support, and effectively implementing, system-level measures.

The two of us came to recognize that nudging—by defaulting people into green-energy tariffs, giving them smaller plates at the cafeteria, helping them spot disinformation, or any of the other myriad interventions that we and our colleagues devised and tested—had only marginal impacts (where they had any impact at all). With the benefit of hindsight, this should not have surprised us: When people are playing multiple games of 3D chess, often against corporations with way more time and resources than they have, they are going to lose, however much well-intentioned nudging and helpful advice they receive.

Ironically, businesses have proved far more adept at exploiting individual weaknesses, as well as the power of behavioral methods, for their own purposes than have governments in promoting the public good. Who has not struggled to make sense of the abstruse language of privacy disclosures, struggled to disenroll from subscriptions that automatically renew, or resisted the many temptations carefully designed and positioned to lure us at times when we are most vulnerable?

As ever, the "game" is rigged. The powerful business interests and wealthy individuals who benefit are perfectly aware of this, but they don't want us to be aware of it. The i-frame narrative has provided them with a useful "cover," telling us to focus on the individual and to distrust the potential of rules and regulations (and the governments that enforce them). Behavioral economists and psychologists (including ourselves) are natural and potentially forceful advocates for reform of s-frame policies. Yet we have instead inadvertently contributed to the creation of an individualist perspective on social problems.

How can we do better? In the next chapter, we ask how the study of human nature could encourage—rather than distract us from making—the deep systemic reforms required to address our social and environmental challenges. We'll see that the answer is not primarily about inventing new, innovative, policies: For most of the problems we have discussed, there are examples of successful policies implemented in other countries that could provide almost off-the-shelf solutions. Social and environmental problems exist not because we can't figure out how to solve them, but because powerful interests benefit from the status quo. So the key question is how to build support for, and to frame, those policies in ways that can attract the coalition of support required to drive change.

Chapter 9

THE WAY FORWARD

If we could turn back time and rethink the role that behavioral economics and behavioral science more generally should play in public policy, what would we do differently? Our agenda in this chapter is to at least begin to answer this question. Although we have so far deliberately steered clear of offering specific policy prescriptions, we propose, in broad strokes, a new vision for how behavioral science could help drive social change. We divide this vision into four broad categories: (1) circumventing rather than fixing human limitations; (2) protecting people from exploitation; (3) educating people *about policy*; and (4) using behavioral insights to guide the design and implementation of policies to maximize both their acceptance and effectiveness (sometimes called "behavioral mechanism design").[1] Each of these four elements calls on a mix of insights and research methods that is different from what the nudge agenda has drawn upon until now.

———

Instead of trying to nudge people toward making better decisions about complex issues, why not just save them from having to decide in the first place? Perhaps the most significant aspect of human psychology with implications for public policy—one that might seem obvious were it not assumed away by the Chicago school of economics—is the observation that the human mind is limited. We have limited attention spans, calculating ability, and memory, and our capacity for deliberative decision-making is often impinged upon by our emotions, our concerns about the opinions of other people, and a host of other factors. Many of the decisions that ordinary citizens are asked to make are ridiculously burdensome and require time, knowledge, and expertise that none of us have.

Consider financial provision for retirement. As discussed in Chapter 3, there are many bad features of current retirement savings plans (assuming you work for an employer who offers a plan at all), including the failure of many employers to offer substantial match rates; the ease with which people can withdraw their funds (leading to the problem of "leakage"); and the inequality-amplifying tax deductions on retirement savings (with almost all benefits accruing to high-income individuals yet having, according to the limited research that has investigated the issue, almost no impact on actual saving).[2] Perhaps the most important implication of limited rationality is, however, that it makes no sense to require individuals to decide how to invest their retirement nest egg: It is patently unrealistic to think that individuals, as they are (or as they could be following any conceivable financial literacy training), would be in a position to sensibly make these investment decisions. Although the psychologist Daniel Kahneman eventually became a big supporter of nudges, in a commentary with Terry Odean and Brad Barber he made exactly this argument:

> We are not optimistic that privatization will provide for adequate retirement incomes. Research indicates that decision biases, a lack of understanding of financial markets and too much personal discretion are likely to turn average workers into bad managers of their retirement accounts—to an extent that should not be ignored in discussions of privatization policy. . . . When people are psychologically disposed to make poor trading decisions, and insufficiently educated to do otherwise,

[controlling their own retirement planning] is as much an opportunity to do harm as to do good.[3]

In the US, workers are often not just given the option, but are *required* to make their own decisions about how to invest their nest egg. Research has documented the hazards of this approach. A study by Henrik Cronqvist and Richard Thaler showed the wealth-destroying decisions that large numbers of Swedish workers made when required to invest—fortunately only a fraction of—their own retirement funds.[4]

The same insight applies to myriad other decisions, such as the lunacy of requiring people to shop for insurance plans on an open market. Recall the lesson of the study we described in Chapter 4, in which George and colleagues found that the majority of the forty-eight health insurance plans offered by a Fortune 25 company (mistakenly following the guidance of a consultant) made no sense for anyone, regardless of their health needs and expenditures. As one would expect, most employees, including a disproportionate number of lower-income employees, chose the wrong plan for themselves. Indeed, the paper showed that *almost every employee would have benefited from being placed in the same insurance plan*— i.e., from having been given no choice of plans at all.[5]

When George's own son needed to buy insurance on the Obamacare exchange, George offered to help, confident that he could provide useful guidance, given the diverse research he has done on health insurance. Reality quickly intruded: Perusing the available options, George couldn't make sense of how they differed, exactly what each covered, or, ultimately, which plan his son should choose. If, as we discussed in Chapter 4, consumers don't understand the most basic elements of medical insurance, how can they possibly choose a plan to fit their requirements? And if consumers don't have a clue when choosing among plans, what is the chance that their decisions will drive insurance companies to provide better, lower-cost options? The low quality and high cost of medical insurance strongly suggests that choosing among incomprehensible health insurance plans is not a decision that individuals should be required to make.[6]

Limited rationality is only one of several reasons to eliminate many of the diverse choices people are currently required to make. A second is that people have only a limited amount of time and attention. Spending these precious resources on decisions such as investing one's nest egg or choosing among complex health insurance plans inevitably means having less bandwidth for other worthy endeavors, including work, leisure activities, childcare, and so on. Economists know very well that "time is money"—but those responsible for public policy seem to forget this when proposing policies that require people to grapple with problems of inordinate complexity.

Minimizing worry and regret is a third reason for limiting the decisions individuals face. When people are asked to make a complicated and consequential decision, they naturally worry whether they made the right choice. Then, when they discover they made a mistake—when their retirement funds portfolio tanks in a market downturn, or when it turns out that the small print in the health insurance policy they subscribed to denies coverage for exactly the procedure they urgently need—they may experience bitter remorse, blaming themselves and not the system that failed them.

Fourth and finally, reducing the complexity of the decisions people face is important for those decisions that are inherently distasteful to make. Illustrating the point again with health insurance: If you are going to be healthy in the upcoming year, a high-deductible insurance plan is likely to be most cost-efficient, but if you are not so fortunate, a low-deductible policy is likely to be more advantageous. For the large numbers of individuals who can't predict their health in the upcoming year (and health is somewhat uncertain for us all), this means that choosing a medical insurance plan is, in effect, a bet on one's own health—scarcely a bet that most people want to make.

Worse, to the extent that people *can* predict their own health, their decisions can undermine the very purpose of health insurance, which is to spread the burden of poor health by pooling together those fortunate enough to be—and remain—healthy with those who are less fortunate. Ironically, interventions designed to nudge people to make better choices for themselves can end up harming disadvantaged, less healthy, consumers. When healthy individuals opt for cheaper plans, the cost of more comprehensive plans typically rises, making them even less accessible to those who need them most.[7]

When different people have different preferences—e.g., for food, music, houses, cars—it makes great sense to give them choices. But people are often given decisions not because they have special information—e.g., about their own preferences—that experts don't have access to, but because experts don't agree among themselves. This is, once more, well illustrated by health care. Take, for example, amniocentesis, a procedure that involves removing amniotic fluid with a needle to test fetuses for genetic abnormalities. Whether and when to get amniocentesis *is* a decision that it probably makes sense to give to expectant parents, because there are meaningful differences between parents when it comes to their aversion to miscarriages (a possible consequence of the test) and their feelings about terminating a pregnancy or about bearing and raising a child with disabilities (a possible consequence of *not getting* the test). In contrast, it makes no sense to ask cancer patients to decide between chemotherapy and radiation just because battling medical specialists—oncologists who administer chemotherapy and radiologists who administer radiation—can't reach agreement about which is better for a patient. The general rule is: Where the experts can't agree, we need a process to require that they do agree (or some process—like an independent panel—that adjudicates between them). Yet the spirit of responsibilization puts the burden of decision on the hapless patient.

Technology offers another set of opportunities to introduce s-frame policies that can circumvent the frailties of human thinking and behavior. Obvious examples include devices on cars to prevent them from being operated by someone who is inebriated—eclipsing the more individualistic and less effective approach of deterring drunk driving via after-the-fact punishment—and software that would prevent cars from being driven over the legal speed limit (as discussed in Chapter 6). In the domain of gun violence, fingerprint-based locks on guns would surely dramatically reduce unauthorized use, leading to fewer accidental shootings by youths as well as fewer school shootings. In the United States, mandating fingerprint locks might well be more acceptable to Second Amendment defenders than outright bans.

———

Beyond critiquing the use of i-frame practices to solve public policy problems, we have argued that industry often uses i-frame interventions far more effectively than governments, exploiting elements of human psychology for commercial ends.[8] For example, George and his colleagues proposed and tested the idea of "enhanced active choice." Instead of defaulting individuals into a company's preferred option, enhanced active choice requires that they make a choice, but purposefully describes the superior option in positive, and the inferior option in negative, terms. Though he doubts they got the idea from his research, whenever George books airline tickets, he can't help noticing that the sales pitch for notoriously bad-deal travel insurance includes exactly such a pitch (as well as other strategies adopted from behavioral economics, such as social norms—e.g., informing the traveler of how many other customers purchased the insurance in the last week).[9]

We have already noted, too, that processed foods are engineered to be maximally tempting to consumers (and to suppress cues of satiation), and that slot machines (and other gambling products and services) are deliberately designed to keep gamblers gambling, capitalizing on, for example, human vulnerability to intermittent reinforcement and the tendency to chase losses. Arguably, large sections of entire industries—from alcoholic drinks, cigarettes, and gambling to payday lending—are at least partially dependent on "hooking" consumers on products that offer little, and sometimes negative, value. The circle is, of course, wider still. "Clickbait," "fake news," and the propagation of extreme opinions by social media algorithms all use insights from the behavioral sciences to keep our collective eyeballs on our screens; for example, day-trading platforms encourage unsophisticated investors to "burn" their money by over-trading specific stocks rather than holding diversified index funds.

———

The nudge agenda involves tackling problems by "fixing" individual limitations, or by exploiting people's decision biases for their own benefit. While this is *not* our focus in this book, we do believe that these limitations and decision biases are relevant and important for a different reason: They make people vulnerable to exploitation. This is an issue of great practical importance. Indeed, a good chunk of the work of many "nudge units" is actually focused on identifying and recommending ways to combat such exploitation (rather than proposing positive nudges). The status quo bias, for example, is regularly used by diverse subscription services to extend subscriptions that people don't want or use. As we were close to finalizing this book, an October 2024 Federal Trade Commission "Click-to-Cancel" rule was put in place which mandates that companies make canceling subscriptions as straightforward as signing up for them. In its press release announcing the rule, the FTC noted that it had received more than sixteen thousand complaints from March 2023, when it proposed the rule, to when it actually implemented it only eight months later.[10]

Likewise, crafty health insurance companies exploit the status quo bias by introducing cheap, high-value insurance plans in one year, then jacking up prices in the following years, relying on consumers who have gone through the ordeal of picking an insurance plan to leave well alone.[11] And credit card companies exploit present bias by offering "teaser" rates, while financial firms offer investment funds with no charges or commissions for buying and selling shares (factors that are highly salient to amateur investors), but that have high annual fees (which are much less salient).[12]

In theory, nudges could be devised that would at least attempt to reduce the impact of every one of these psychology-exploiting tactics. However, given limitations on individuals' time and attention, these defensive efforts would probably not offer much protection. As illustrated by FTC rules that make it simpler to unsubscribe, the policies that will be most effective in mitigating these threats are those that eliminate "bad nudges" rather than those seeking to fortify individuals against them.

As discussed throughout the book, we are skeptical of the benefits of educating people in specific domains to help them make impossibly complex choices—whether it's bringing them up to the level of "financial literacy" required to make sensible decisions about how to invest their nest egg, or raising their "health-insurance literacy" to the point where they can make reasonable choices among incomprehensible health insurance policies. Recall Lauren Willis's paper critiquing financial literacy education, which we discussed in Chapter 3, in which she argues that "the pursuit of financial literacy poses costs that almost certainly swamp any benefits" and "should be replaced by a search for policies more conducive to good consumer financial outcomes."

In contrast with our skepticism toward literacy training as a substitute for addressing problems best solved with s-frame reform, we see no substitute for providing people with the information and understanding they need to throw their weight as citizens, and in democracies as voters, behind beneficial s-frame reforms, and, of course, against destructive ones. A major reason that we so often end up with terrible public policies is that most people have no understanding of the details, or even the broad strokes, of the public policies that play such a key role in their lives.

Consider taxes and their consequences for income inequality in the United States. Perhaps the simplest distinction in the US tax system is the difference between a tax deduction and a tax credit. Curious whether students understood these concepts, George asked his class of forty-seven advanced undergraduates and master's students in public policy if they knew the difference: A single student raised his hand. So, for the benefit of the other forty-six, George explained this arcane but crucial difference. A tax *deduction* reduces an individual's taxable income by the amount of the deduction, so the actual benefit depends on the individual's tax bracket. A $10,000 tax deduction for a higher earner in a 30 percent tax bracket will reduce their taxes by $3,000, but the same deduction would only be worth $1,000 to a low earner in a 10 percent tax bracket. A tax *credit*, on the other hand, simply reduces every individual's tax by a specific amount (receiving a $2,000 tax credit cuts everyone's tax bill by the same amount—i.e., $2,000). The distinction between a tax deduction and a tax credit is critical for inequality, because a tax deduction will generally be far more valuable to a high earner, who, given progressive taxes (i.e., marginal tax rates that increase with income), faces a higher marginal tax rate. The fact that the tax breaks on 401(k) contributions take the form of a deduction at the time of contribution is hugely advantageous to high-income individuals.[13] This is true not only because they face higher marginal tax rates, but because they generally save more, and 401(k) plans also shield individuals from paying taxes on capital appreciation of assets (at least until they retire and spend the money, at which point they are likely to be in a lower marginal income-tax bracket). One much-discussed policy option would be to eliminate these tax breaks and shift the additional tax revenue ($380 billion annually, in 2022) to shoring up

Social Security (which disproportionately benefits lower-income Americans).[14] But because very few Americans understand how tax deductions work—and that almost all of the existing tax breaks go to the wealthy—there seems to be little public pressure to shift away from the status quo.

Continuing on the theme of taxation, two of the most egregious loopholes that undermine the potential inequity-reducing impact of taxes are the "stepped-up basis" of asset valuations and the tax treatment of so-called carried interest. The stepped-up loophole involves taxes paid upon death, but is different from inheritance tax. In the current US tax system, investors are taxed on capital gains, the increase in value of stocks, and other assets such as real estate, when they are sold. Capital gains are generally taxed at a lower rate—20 percent—than the top marginal tax rate on income, which is, as we write this book, 37 percent in the US. When a person dies and passes an asset on to an heir, however, the taxable value—"basis"— of the asset is "stepped up" to its current value.

This means that someone who, say, buys a stock for $10, then sells it for $30 right before they die will pay a tax of $4—the 20 percent tax rate times the $20 capital gain. If the same person passes the stock on to their child as part of an estate, however, the child can sell the stock immediately and pay zero in capital gains (or sell later, and pay only on gains above $30—the "stepped-up basis" of the stock). This loophole is hugely beneficial to the wealthy: 21 percent of the benefit goes to the top 1 percent of earners, and 55 percent goes to the top 10 percent. Eliminating it would generate an enormous amount of tax revenue—an estimated $20 billion per year.[15] And eliminating the stepped-up basis would also eliminate a source of economic inefficiency caused by people holding appreciated stocks until they die in order to avoid paying capital gains taxes on assets they would really prefer to sell.

The "carried interest" loophole refers to compensation earned by investment managers—e.g., hedge-fund billionaires. Such managers typically receive a management fee based on the total value of assets they manage, and a payment based on the profits generated by their trading activities. The former is taxed at the normal rate for income—i.e., 37 percent for most investment managers. But the latter is only taxed at the capital gains rate of 20 percent, and only after profits are realized—i.e., after the assets are sold. It has been estimated that eliminating this tax loophole, almost all of which accrues to the superwealthy, could generate more than $6 billion per year in additional taxes.[16]

Proposals to eliminate both of these tax breaks arise periodically in Congress but are routinely defeated, probably because, failing to understand them, low- and middle-income individuals don't pay attention to how their representatives vote. The affluent do, on the other hand, understand them perfectly (or, at least, their tax advisers do), and hence they lobby assiduously to prevent their elimination. For example, the Saving America's Family Enterprises (SAFE) organization, which claims to be "a nonprofit, nonpartisan educational organization" (but in fact represents the interests of the superwealthy), announced, in February 2023, "an initial six-figure paid media campaign" to oppose "proposals to tax unrealized capital gains."[17] Similarly, in the US and the UK, the private equity industry has long lobbied to preserve the carried interest loophole, although in both countries there are indications that the loophole may soon finally be closed.[18]

———

Attempts to apply the cognitive and behavioral sciences to the big policy questions that face the world have, to a large extent, been focusing on the wrong problem. We have implicitly assumed that a deeper understanding of human nature should be applied to helping policymakers inform, educate, and nudge people to do the "right thing." But tackling climate change, for instance, requires fundamental systemic changes across almost every aspect of the economy, not nudging individuals to behave in a more pro-social fashion. A deep understanding of human nature can and should be applied to the problem of getting the systemic changes right.

All policies have huge numbers of moving parts, small and large, and these need to be designed in a way that takes account of human nature and of political realities. A carbon tax, for example, can be implemented "upstream"—on fossil fuel companies, say—or downstream—on consumers. Which is easier to implement? And which will be more palatable to citizens? And, regardless of who is taxed, how should the vast revenues raised by such a measure be spent, both to maximize its environmental impact and to generate support for the policy among voters? Psychology and behavioral economics can help answer these questions.

Any carbon tax that raised the price of energy would inevitably hit lower-income individuals harder, since they spend a high proportion of their earnings on items such as gasoline, food, heating, and cooling. To avoid creating a fully justified popular uproar, those designing such a tax will need to figure out how to use the vast tax revenues that would be generated so as to mitigate the tax's inequality-exacerbating effects. Selling a carbon tax to the public will almost certainly involve not using the generated revenue to simply increase government revenues (and reduce the deficit), but rather spending it on something (e.g., enhancing Social Security) that people can get excited about. Selling a carbon tax to the public would (and, ideally, *will*) involve a combination of economics and psychology—since subjective perceptions matter as much as objective realities. Economists and psychologists have conducted extensive research on issues of fairness, which should inform the specifics of how such a tax should be implemented and its revenues spent.

More broadly, we need to use i-frame insights to make s-frame policies more effective and more popular. "Behavioral insights" have been at the heart of the i-frame interventions that define the nudge movement. But individual-level psychology is equally important in designing s-frame interventions that not only will be palatable to the public (the topic of the previous section) but will also accomplish their goals.

Recall the "crying Indian" ad with which the book opens. This campaign demonstrated the power of marketing—in that case, to generate strong negative emotions about pollution and give an attentional shove toward i-frame responsibilization. To counter the i-frame focus generated by corporate marketing, s-frame communications also need to be designed with the same level of skill as those deployed by private-sector actors.

Just as in the case of the corporate world's most beloved brands, good s-frame marketing would associate policies with desirable images, thoughts, feelings, attitudes, and experiences—beginning with a policy name that concretely communicates its benefits in ways that matter to its target audience.[19] (Think the "Combating Counterfeit Products Act," rather than the actual Canadian policy name "An Act to amend the Copyright Act and the Trade-marks Act and to make consequential amendments to other Acts.")[20] Such marketing would be supported by a coherent brand (policy) narrative—a story of the policy's purpose that prompts emotional engagement, activates a desire for change, and lends itself to positive word of mouth.[21] And, as in the case of the crying Indian, good marketing would align the policy with people's social and moral identities, raising the likelihood of loyalty over time.[22]

Consider a recent (as we write this) success story: the introduction of the "Trade Regulation Rule on Unfair or Deceptive Fees" by the Federal Trade Commission (FTC). To get the regulation approved, lawmakers' first smart marketing step was to rebrand the initiative in the public sphere as the much punchier "Junk Fees Rule."[23] By doing so, the policy's targets became immediately associated in consumers' minds with emotionally charged words such as "scam," "annoyance," "waste," and "garbage," communicating the unfairness of the status quo. The FTC, the Consumer Financial Protection Bureau (CFPB), and the Biden administration's subsequent media blitz also took a page from the corporate play-book, using approachable, authentic social media messaging to present the rule as a solution to a shared problem for all Americans, bridging identity and socioeconomic status. Further, the FTC made the rule's benefits directly relevant to individuals' lives, writing that it would "save Americans more than $11 billion over the next decade and over 53 million hours in time." The final rule, though narrower than originally envisioned, passed in December 2024 with unusual bipartisan support.[24] A worrying coda to this story is that there are currently active plans to undermine or defund both the FTC and the CFPB; hence consumer protection may be reduced significantly.[25]

One uncontroversial point is that, like i-frame policies, implementation of s-frame policies should be as ergonomic—or easy to use and understand—as possible. Many current s-frame policies fail badly in this regard. For example, tax credits or benefits (classic s-frame policies) often involve bureaucratic processes of baffling complexity and exclude a substantial proportion of the population that, at least in theory, they are intended to benefit;[26] and financial, medical, environmental, or nutritional information can often be uninterpretable to consumers and hence does not help inform their choices.[27]

In our view, one of the most valuable lessons from the existing focus on behavioral insights has been that the ergonomics of government policies, both in their design and implementation, are just as important as the ergonomics of the personal computer or the smartphone.[28] Indeed, successfully designing such policies around the consumer can frequently make the difference between success and failure. This is not to imply that policy design should be handed over to behavioral insights specialists, still less to those focusing purely on conventional behavioral economics. The process of policy design, like the design of any complex good or service, is likely to be best handled by a multidisciplinary team, including designers, user-experience specialists, ethnographers, anthropologists, and psychologists, all of whom can incorporate input from experts in behavioral insights.

Improving the quality of individual decision-making has, of course, been a primary focus of i-frame behavioral insights. But often the most powerful way to help people make better decisions is not merely to modify their "choice architecture" but to fundamentally change the rules of the game within which individuals operate. Thus, eliminating conflicts of interest between doctors and patients, or between financial advisers and their clients, is likely to be much more effective than requiring that conflicts be disclosed or educating consumers to detect them.[29] Similarly, when it comes to designing regulations for certain safety-critical industries (such as airlines or medicine), we should not see the challenge as helping individuals simultaneously balance competing priorities of safety and business, but rather as creating separate chains of command (e.g., for managers and safety specialists) and binding protocols that eliminate such conflicts in the first place.

Nonetheless, s- and i-frame approaches to changing individual behavior can potentially be complementary and mutually reinforcing. For example, as we noted in the Introduction, an i-frame measure, such as adding health warnings to cigarette packets, or engaging in antismoking public information campaigns, may serve to increase public support for s-frame measures such as banning cigarette advertising and banning smoking in public places.[30] But social, economic, and organizational change comes primarily not from helping individuals cope better with a broken system but from fixing the system in the first place.

———

Even the cleverest and most effective policy won't stand a chance if it doesn't gain the support of the public. And behavioral science can again play a key role when designing policies to be as politically attractive as possible. Take the carbon tax. Its very label sounds like a vote loser: Who ever heard of a popular tax? Clearly turning this around is going to be a huge challenge. But a number of well-established insights about human behavior can help.

Fairness is one key factor affecting both carbon taxes and almost every other area of public policy—and a topic that has been a major focus of research in behavioral economics, even if it has rarely been applied to public policy. Thus, to see the virtues of a carbon tax or regulations to reduce greenhouse gas emissions of all kinds, we first need to communicate the profound *unfairness* of the status quo, in which a relatively small number of companies profit from polluting the atmosphere with greenhouse gases that damage the climate for all of humanity. The "polluter pays" principle seems, to the two of us and probably to most people, to be the epitome of fairness—whoever benefits from an activity that hurts the rest of us should pay the price. And, under the current policy regime, polluters are typically not paying the price for the damage they do to the rest of us. Fixing this in a fair and transparent way is exactly what a carbon tax achieves: The more a company—or an individual—damages the climate, the more tax they pay.

The sense of fairness can be strengthened further, of course, by making a carbon tax revenue-neutral for the government, as implemented in Canada since 2019.[31] In such a system, businesses and individuals who pollute the least actually benefit through direct payments or rebates funded by the carbon tax. The polluters pay, and the rest of us get the benefits. And so the carbon tax becomes a "carbon transfer"—with more winners than losers.

The question of fairness arises when we consider our individual lifestyles, too. As an illustration, note that a carbon tax large enough to have an appreciable impact on the problem of climate change would likely put frequent flying—an activity that most Americans, and people in many countries throughout the world, view as virtually a right—beyond the budget of a large fraction of the population. Implemented badly, this consequence of a carbon tax could seem profoundly unfair: stopping regular families from visiting distant relatives while the jet set just keep on jet-setting.

But other implementations might work, and be perceived, very differently. One could imagine, for example, a policy in which each individual is given the same tradable flight quota authorizing the holder to fly a certain number of miles, so everyone can fly (a little) if they want or need to. While financial pressure may push some lower-income people to sell their flight quota—making the effects not all that different from a carbon tax that simply raises the cost of flying—people would probably feel a whole lot better about a quota system. In a system of tradable quotas, a person selling their quota gains an obvious benefit from doing so, choosing to swap the possibility of flying for, likely, much-needed, and much-appreciated, ready cash.[32]

Loss aversion—the tendency to experience losses more intensely than equivalent gains—contributes to the public's resistance not just to a carbon tax, but to a host of other proposals that could have big benefits.[33] After all, almost all shifts in policy entail both gains and losses. That means that the opposition from the people who stand to lose will be greater than the support from the people who stand to gain. And the same is true within a single individual, who might gain from a policy change in some ways but lose in other ways. If losses weigh more heavily than the equivalent gains, this will bias us to stick to the status quo, whatever it happens to be.

Loss aversion, though, is a double-edged sword when it comes to public policy. For example, banning the use of single-use plastic bags might be perceived as an excessive intrusion into individual rights, not to mention engendering rage in consumers who forget to bring their own bags and can't easily carry their shopping home. But a very elegant set of studies has shown that loss aversion can also be harnessed to make changes work better.[34] As discussed in Chapter 6, charging consumers a token amount for using single-use plastic bags is remarkably effective in reducing their use; although the cost is small, our aversion to even small losses makes us highly motivated to avoid the charge by bringing our own reusable bags when we go shopping.[35] Charging for a plastic bag might be resisted in the short run by people who are used to plastic bags being free. But the idea that it is appropriate to be charged for an object (in this case a plastic bag) is sufficiently ingrained that acceptance of such a tax can be rapid—and indeed small charges have led to very rapid reductions in disposable bag use in many countries, as we noted earlier.

Tangibility and *credit* are also psychological factors that could play a major role in motivating politicians to enact new policies. Everyone likes to get credit for positive outcomes and to minimize blame for negative outcomes. And this may be especially true for politicians, who know they will be held accountable by the voters for the perceived results of their policies. Naturally, then, policymakers will favor policies that produce not only positive outcomes, but positive outcomes that people notice, so they can receive credit for them. If credit were proportionate to the magnitude of positive outcomes achieved, even crudely, all would be fine, but this is far from the case. In fact, many of the most valuable policy interventions (e.g., childhood vaccination programs) produce outcomes that are virtually invisible—intangible—while policies that deliver some of the most tangible outcomes (e.g., neighborhood beautification initiatives) actually fail to deliver much real value.

Perhaps the most obvious cause of intangibility is the existence of random fluctuations in the severity of the underlying problem. Such randomness interferes with observers' ability to detect the "signal" of policy effects. Most of the problems that policymakers seek to solve, or desirable outcomes they seek to achieve, are the product of myriad factors. Because many of these factors are unobservable or even unidentified, they come across simply as "noise"—i.e., random variation. As such noise increases, there is a diminished likelihood that those experiencing the desirable outcomes will be able to detect the contribution of any policy on those outcomes. Climate change may provide the most dramatic illustration. It's already difficult even for climate scientists (let alone laypeople) to assess whether a particular heat wave, hurricane, or flood is the result of climate change. So it's very unlikely that people will be able to discern the benefit of even the most far-reaching policy (such as a worldwide carbon tax) over an extended interval. The lack of tangible benefits that they can point to is likely a factor contributing to many politicians' reluctance to enact policies, many of which would, in contrast to their intangible benefits, have very tangible immediate costs for constituents. A possible solution to this problem when it comes to climate change would be to focus on carbon emissions rather than on temperature. But even here, the right measures are crucial. The Scottish government got itself into political hot water with targets for *annual* carbon emissions reductions. But annual targets were misconceived (and later abandoned) because carbon emissions inevitably bounce around year to year because of random changes in the weather—cold winters, for instance, cause people to use more heating, which leads to higher emissions.[36]

There is an even more fundamental cause of intangibility in policy outcomes: People rarely if ever receive "counterfactual" information about how bad—how much worse—the situation would be had a policy not been implemented. Writing about this problem in the context of charitable giving, George and his coauthors note that "efforts at prevention suffer from a dual handicap: First, given that the problem has not yet emerged, there are no existing victims toward whom potential donors can feel sympathy, and second, it is difficult to provide details that increase the feeling of impact since the outcome is not remediation of a problem, but is the non-occurrence of a problem that otherwise would have materialized."[37]

Judgments of credit and blame are further complicated by the fact that many policies change the *probability* of negative events rather than the extremity of those events when they do occur. For example, repairing a bridge reduces the *probability* of its collapse, and implementing an antiterrorism policy reduces the *likelihood* of a terrorist attack. Policymakers are far more likely to get credit for a shiny new bus or bridge than for maintenance policies that reduce the likelihood that new buses or a new bridge will be needed. Here, publicly available monitoring of otherwise intangible factors is potentially of crucial importance: No politician wants to preside over a visible rise in some trusted measure of risk. Public monitoring can make invisible problems become tangible to voters, campaigners, and journalists.

Yet another potential problem is that decision-makers will tend to receive greater credit for policies that produce abrupt, rather than gradual, results. This is true both because abrupt changes are more tangible and because abrupt changes front-load benefits. Front-loaded benefits have immediate political payoffs, and politicians often have limited time horizons, in part owing to limited anticipated terms in office. In addition, the psychology of time discounting (people's tendency to care more about immediate than delayed benefits) further reduces the impetus for policies conferring benefits that unfold gradually over time. Over and above these well-studied elements, time delay can also reduce tangibility. When effect follows cause instantaneously, the causal connection is easy to identify. As time passes, however, or if benefits are distributed over time, the signal/noise problem just discussed becomes more severe.

All these policy-level effects also occur at the level of the individual. For example, people are probably discouraged from making advantageous lifestyle changes such as eating more healthily, stopping smoking, or increasing exercise because there is little tangible and immediate benefit; health benefits will accumulate almost imperceptibly over long periods of time. Here again, getting the monitoring right is crucial. For example, anyone trying to maintain an exercise regimen likely needs the motivation of noticing small daily or weekly improvements; similarly, for public policies, the possibility of an indiscernible impact on health in the far future won't be enough.[38]

———

When George gives public lectures, he always looks for, and usually finds, a friendly face—a member of the audience who seems onboard with what he is saying—conveying this, typically, with head nods and smiles. This individual is, more often than not, female (women just tend to be, let's face it, friendlier). When he presented his "boilerplate" i-frame/s-frame seminar to an audience at the University of Vienna in 2022, however, quite the opposite happened: The severe scowl and violent headshakes of a young middle-aged man in the audience were impossible to ignore. During the Q&A following the seminar, George's perceptions were validated by the audience member's question, which was really more of a statement (paraphrased here, from fallible memory): "You've succeeded in persuading me that all the research I've done for the past decade is worthless. I feel more depressed than I've ever been."

Less disturbingly, a common question we get from audience members who are currently doing i-frame research but are persuaded by our arguments is how could or should they reorient the focus of their research toward s-frame issues. Here, mainly for the benefit of fellow researchers (others may want to skip this section), we summarize some of the points we made in a paper we coauthored with Dan Connolly, a PhD student in George's department.[39]

Researchers have reasons for doing i-frame research, and one of the most important is that it is the type of research they are trained to do. Because i-frame interventions, such as sending text messages, are oriented toward individuals, they are generally easy to study using standard behavioral science methods—e.g., randomly assigning some individuals to get one kind of text message, others to get a different kind of text message (or no message at all), and monitoring if the two groups behave differently on some dimension one cares about (e.g., applying to college or showing up to a scheduled court appearance). S-frame public policies, in contrast, focus on societal rules and institutions, such as how medical care (and potentially health insurance) are organized, or whether and how fuel standards for vehicles are set.

Research focusing on the s-frame will typically address a set of questions entirely different from those in i-frame research. It will ask, for example, which types of policies are most effective—i.e., most beneficial across populations. Or, having identified a beneficial policy, what is the most effective way to frame it to the public to increase its likelihood of being supported and, ideally, implemented? S-frame-oriented research can and should also focus on issues of policy implementation. Note that this is subtly different from "choice architecture," a central aspect of nudges; instead of focusing on how to design the individual's environment so they make self-beneficial choices, s-frame research can and should focus on how to make policies that are beneficial to citizens.

Asking different questions will necessarily entail employing different research methods. Most, although not all, s-frame research questions will not be best addressed via randomized controlled trials (RCTs), but instead, often, by quasi-experimental and even qualitative observational approaches aimed not at the individual level but rather at variations and changes in policies across countries and over time.

Currently, there appears to be a virtual consensus among practitioners of behavioral public policy that RCTs are the best methodology for testing new policy interventions.[40] Indeed, when advocates of i-frame approaches have come to recognize the limited impact of the interventions they have historically supported, they sometimes seem to retreat from advocating specific interventions to the ostensibly more impregnable position that policies should be empirically tested with RCTs. We are, however, in agreement with a number of criticisms that have been leveled against RCTs and their enshrinement as the gold standard.[41] In a 2018 paper, for example, Angus Deaton and Nancy Cartwright note that most of the changes in economic policy that have led to substantial improvements in economic well-being have resulted from "large" shifts in policy, but that RCTs have been, and by necessity are only capable of, testing the impact of "small" innovations.[42] Green-energy nudges can be tested with an RCT; a carbon tax cannot. Interventions to help people make better health insurance choices can be randomized; single-payer insurance cannot. Modified trash bins (e.g., with "watching eyes") can be tested using RCTs; sweeping and complex regulations based on, for example, extended producer responsibility to reduce packaging cannot.

Even when it is conceivable that an s-frame policy could be tested with an RCT, practical considerations almost invariably prevent that from happening. As Richard Thaler notes (interestingly, in a critique he wrote of our i-frame/s-frame paper),

> the range of interventions studied by behavioral scientists is truncated by what I call permission bias: you can only test what you can get the approval to try. It is wrong to infer from this fact of life that behavioral scientists are using the wrong "frame." Rather, they face constraints! It also makes it problematic to judge the potential impact of possible behavioral policy interventions based on the set of randomized control experiments behavioral scientists have been allowed to run.

It is, indeed, a "fact of life" that conservatism on the part of policymakers, as well as cost considerations, will limit the types of policies that get tested to those that are cheap and easy to implement, such as changes in emails or mailings. And if testing with an RCT is a requirement for implementing a nudge, then "permission bias" will limit the range of nudges not only to those that can be tested cheaply and easily, but also, by extension, to the extremely limited subset that can be tested with an RCT. As Stanford sociologist Michelle Jackson writes, "It is hard to imagine how the welfare state reforms of the last century could have been introduced under current evidentiary standards for policy implementation: these reforms were simply too expansive in their scope, and there was certainly no body of experimental or quasi-experimental evidence to support an overhaul of multiple institutions."[43] The Harvard economist Dani Rodrik likewise notes that a wide range of policy reforms that led to dramatic improvements in quality of life—such as the introduction of a market economy in China, which lifted a large fraction of the world's population out of poverty—could not have occurred if they first had to be tested with RCTs prior to implementation.[44]

While running experiments, much like i-frame policies themselves, might seem uncontroversial, to the extent that experimentation is viewed as the gold standard there will be a tendency not only to devote resources toward RCTs that could go toward other methods, but also, perhaps even more seriously, to downplay the validity or relevance of results obtained using other methods. Enshrinement of the RCT will therefore inevitably direct attention away from the types of policy interventions for which RCT evidence cannot be obtained—which often means those that are substantive and far-reaching.

This is not to argue that RCTs should play no role in s-frame-oriented policy research. For example (as touched on above), in cases where strong policy solutions exist but are constrained by public support, experimentation on how to maximize public support by reframing or redesigning policy elements is likely to be highly productive and is probably most often best accomplished with RCTs. But RCTs are unlikely to be able to answer many other important policy questions, such as: Which of two potential policy solutions is likely to lead to the largest increase in welfare? Which factors best predict whether an economically efficient policy will be politically stable? Why are good policies adopted in some countries and not in others?

Addressing these and other s-frame questions will require embracing a far greater diversity of methods, including those that are already widespread in economics and sociology, but not offer the same degree of rigorous causal inference as RCTs, including quasi-experiments such as event studies, regression discontinuity, and synthetic control studies, as well as methods that used to have more of a home in the behavioral sciences, such as historical and comparative research. Perhaps the main difference between experiments and quasi-experiments is that the latter are often well suited to analyzing the impact of real-world problems and the policies designed to address them. For example, these methods have been used to analyze both the effects of air pollution and the effects of a cap-and-trade market designed to limit air pollution.[45]

The potential gains from historical approaches are also expanded by new machine-learning techniques for investigating the psychological and social constructs within significant historical periods through automated text analysis. These techniques have enabled researchers to use archival text to understand peer influence during the French Revolution, the concept of "rationality" during the Industrial Revolution and its aftermath, and the women-led development of abolitionist arguments in pre-emancipation America.[46] The analysis of bodies of text in marketing and political campaigns could similarly help policy researchers understand the development of successful policy initiatives like smoking bans and seat belt laws.

In addition to embracing a broader variety of existing methods in the behavioral sciences, we believe that researchers and policymakers should more explicitly embrace a "learning agenda" of policy development. The psychology of human learning and the parallel discipline of machine learning provide a powerful counterweight to the current emphasis on RCTs and other controlled experimentation, and provide the foundation for an observational approach that extends beyond a single historical or cross-national comparison. RCTs are designed to test which of two or three fully fledged variations is most successful (e.g., drug vs. placebo; tax letter X, Y, or Z)—a direct test that quasi-experimental, historical, and comparative methods can only approximate. But s-frame policy design, implementation, and communication require creating and continually adjusting complex and highly interdependent programs of actions and messages, continually buffeted by ever-changing social, economic, commercial, and political forces. RCTs allow us to play "Twenty Questions with Nature" (assuming that Nature is stable enough for us to learn and then apply the answers), which can sometimes usefully inform aspects of i-frame implementation. But s-frame interventions are complex, concerted, and interacting programs of action, operating in an unstable and reacting world, which cannot be navigated with a tree of binary or ternary choices.[47]

The broader insight to draw is that practical policymakers need not "turn off" their natural modes of intelligent engagement with the world because of a lack of evidence generated from RCTs. In the real world of business and government, policymakers continually draw on intuitions and insights from beyond the restrictions of knowledge gained from RCTs—they employ the full range of strategies that make human intelligence successful in dealing with an often overwhelmingly complex world. As Franklin D. Roosevelt famously said, "The country demands bold, persistent experimentation. It is common sense to take a method and try it: If it fails, admit it frankly and try another. But above all, try something."[48] Of course, intuition can mislead; critical analysis and carefully curated evidence are vital; and experimentation can play a critical role in teasing out causal mechanisms. But if researchers and policymakers adhere rigidly to the gold standard of RCTs, they will be forgoing almost all the techniques that make human intelligence successful.

Given this book's focus on systems, it would be a mistake simply to exhort individual researchers to pursue only the s-frame agenda. Shifting behavioral public policy research toward s-frame applications requires a change in systems—in research culture and norms—moving beyond tightly controlled laboratory experiments and in-field RCTs to the full range of strategies by which human intelligence grapples with a complex and uncertain world. Changing culture in this way will require several systemic changes:

- Broadening the methodological training of graduate students will require coursework that goes beyond experimental methods to include quasi-experimental, historical, and comparative methods.
- Journals should develop guidance for how to successfully publish s-frame research: standardized methods for comparing not just effect sizes but scope for total impact, a tolerance for trading off strict assumptions of causal identification for an accumulation of less-causal evidence, and special issues that focus strictly on s-frame research.
- Policymakers and professional organizations should support the s-frame agenda, financially and publicly, by integrating researchers into their operations and supporting administrative data access for s-frame research. While academic research constitutes only one corner of the marketplace for ideas, these reforms will help behavioral public policy researchers contend with the corporate interests that have successfully framed public policy debates in individualistic terms.
- Politicians, governments, and their agencies need to have powerful incentives to genuinely evaluate which s-frame policies work and which do not, despite the real possibility that many policies will be found to have failed.

Beyond these institutional changes, there needs to be a shift toward encouraging and rewarding the imagining of radical possible policies and futures.[49] The invention or modification of new rules and institutions is surely at least as important for the social sciences as the creation of conventional technology (from engineering, computer science, or pharmaceuticals) has been for the natural sciences. Indeed, campaigners for unionization, universal suffrage, civil rights, and radical political, health, and educational reforms have historically been able to imagine very different futures and help make them a reality. Yet conventional social science has, in past decades, remained largely silent as these reforms have unfolded. A focus on conceiving and evaluating radically different policy proposals will pull the field away from theoretically "cute" findings and the search for rigorously evidenced "tweaks." Instead, we believe that there should be an imperative to focus on understanding the systemic changes, and the processes by which those changes are framed and debated, that will be required to create a future that promotes, rather than undermines, the common good.

———

The battle against cigarette smoking in the United States (and similar successes across many other nations) illustrates our proposal. It is a story of mutually reinforcing public health advocacy, government regulation, and changing social norms. The story begins with the rise of cigarette popularity in the early twentieth century, boosted by mass production and aggressive marketing on the part of the cigarette industry, and further popularized during the two world wars when cigarettes became so ubiquitous that they were included in soldiers' rations. By midcentury, nearly half of US adults smoked. During this period, the health risks associated with smoking were not widely known or publicized. Despite some early warnings from health professionals, the tobacco industry thrived using marketing strategies that linked smoking with youth, health, and vitality. Cigarettes were advertised as aids for weight loss, relaxation, and even social success.

The first major challenge to the dominance of smoking came in the 1950s when scientific research began to establish a link between smoking and serious health issues, including lung cancer and heart disease. Indeed, the tobacco industry's own research had, as early as 1953, concluded that there was a causal link between smoking and cancer. Not surprisingly, however, cigarette companies suppressed the information and mounted a huge PR campaign involving celebrity endorsements along with pervasive advertising—to the tune of $250 *billion* from 1950 to 2005 (adjusted for inflation to 2022 dollars).

Perhaps most notorious (and publicized assiduously by the cigarette industry) were the views of the eminent statistician R. A. Fisher, who made fundamental contributions to statistical methods, the design of randomized controlled experiments, and mathematical genetics. Fisher famously (and despite a huge amount of strong evidence to the contrary that already existed at his time) challenged the view that smoking causes cancer, with the bizarre proposal that the undeniable correlation between the two was an example of reverse causality: People with cancer-induced pain (or an "itch") in their lungs turned to smoking to ease their discomfort.[50] In a 1957 lecture to the American Association for the Advancement of Science, Fisher characterized campaigns against smoking as "terrorist propaganda." Curiously, Fisher himself does not appear to have been "on the take" from the cigarette companies. Indeed, historians of science have conjectured that he was influenced by being a smoker himself, and perhaps also, according to one historian, motivated by an attempt to regain public attention in the waning years of his academic career.[51]

Fisher himself may not have been on the take, but thousands of other academics have, over the decades, proved more than happy to sell out. As Stanford historian of science Robert Proctor puts it, cigarette companies have "shoveled hundreds of millions of dollars to compliant scholars in exchange for cigarette-friendly research, cigarette-friendly testimony both in court or in regulatory hearings, and cigarette-friendly popular writings."[52]

One of the most notorious documents that surfaced during the lawsuits against the tobacco companies is the 1972 "Roper Proposal" written by Fred Panzer, then vice president of the Tobacco Institute (a trade group funded by major US cigarette manufacturers). Panzer outlined the three-pronged strategy that the cigarette companies had used to establish doubt about the link between smoking and cancer. In his words,

- creating doubt about the health charge without actually denying it;
- advocating the public's right to smoke, without actually urging them to take up the practice;
- encouraging objective scientific research as the only way to resolve the question of the health hazard.[53]

Panzer noted, however, that "on the public opinion front . . . our situation has deteriorated and will continue to worsen." To reverse this trend, Panzer wrote, the public must be made to "perceive, understand, and believe in evidence to sustain their opinions that smoking may not be the causal factor."[54] Panzer proposed two possible strategies. The first, which by now should be familiar to the readers of this book, was to blame not cigarettes or the industry that creates them for the increase in cancer deaths, but individual smokers—their genetics, "patterns of life," and "pressure under which they live"—for their increased propensity to contract cancer. The second strategy was to blame other factors, such as "air pollution, viruses, food additives, occupational hazards and stresses." Panzer then proposed what he called a "scenario for action" based on recruiting academics to conduct supportive research. The scenario involved six steps:

1. Select a panel of prestigious experts to consult on the design of a study and who would be willing to endorse the study publicly.
2. Conduct a pilot study.
3. Present the results to members of key groups, which Panzer lists: the Senate, the House, the Cabinet, the White House, state governors, medical schools, university presidents, and scientific bodies.

4. Conduct a full-scale survey.
5. Release the findings from the survey as a book.
6. Market and promote the book on TV and in radio talk shows, newspaper reviews, etc.

Turning the tide against the coordinated and well-funded efforts of the tobacco industry required considerable bravery, which was provided by US Surgeon General Dr. Luther Terry in a groundbreaking 1964 report that concluded that smoking was a major cause of lung cancer and other diseases. George was only nine at the time but still registered the momentousness of the occasion. The announcement was a watershed moment in public health—the first time the federal government publicly recognized the dangers of smoking. In the wake of the announcement, and in response to mounting evidence, public health campaigns began to emerge advocating for awareness about the risks of smoking. The tobacco industry pushed back energetically, including by funding a huge surge of research questioning the link between smoking and cancer. But within little more than a year after the surgeon general's report, the Federal Cigarette Labeling and Advertising Act required health warnings on cigarette packs and ads.[55] In 1971, cigarette advertising was banned from radio and television. And in 1984, the Comprehensive Smoking Education Act required even more explicit warning labels. Throughout this whole period, public perception of smoking shifted dramatically, and smoking rates began to drop.[56]

Grassroots advocacy also played a crucial role. Nonprofit organizations representing patient interests, such as the American Cancer Society, the American Lung Association, and the American Heart Association, campaigned tirelessly to educate the public about the dangers of smoking. They lobbied for stronger regulations and pushed for smoke-free environments. As a result, smoking bans in public places began to take hold, starting with airplanes and restaurants, and eventually expanding to workplaces and other indoor spaces.

The rise of secondhand smoke as a public health concern further fueled antismoking efforts. Research showing the harmful effects of passive smoking galvanized public support for smoke-free laws, which became increasingly common across states and cities.

The 1990s were marked by a series of legal battles that held the tobacco industry accountable for its role in promoting smoking while hiding its dangers. The 1998 Master Settlement Agreement (MSA) between the tobacco industry and forty-six states was a landmark victory. Under the MSA, the tobacco companies agreed to pay billions of dollars to cover health care costs related to smoking and to fund antismoking campaigns. The agreement also imposed restrictions on tobacco advertising, especially that targeting youth, and banned billboard advertisements and promotional giveaways. Higher taxes on cigarettes, combined with smoking bans and public education, made smoking less accessible and less appealing. Cigarette smoking rates in the US dropped dramatically, from a peak of 42 percent of Americans in 1964 to its current level of around 10 percent.

While illustrating a success story in changing policy in the face of concerted opposition by enormous concentrated economic interests, the case history of the battle against smoking also illustrates a number of other points relevant to our argument.

The first is a reminder of just how powerful and vicious industry can be to preserve its prerogatives. This does not imply that individual executives involved in the tobacco industry are unusually amoral (although some may very well be). To believe this would be to fall into the i-frame trap. Rather, the problem is much more fundamental: When pursuing the common good would damage the economic interests of an industry, that industry will fight against the common good with whatever tools it can muster. Few executives gain promotion by proposing and overseeing the rapid demise of their business. And the incentives for those executives to push against (and, often, far beyond) the confines of ethics, and indeed the law, will be substantial. The problem for campaigners isn't battling a few amoral businesspeople; it is reshaping a system in which the interests of the industry have become deeply entrenched. In the face of such ferocious opposition, positive, systemic change is likely to be hard-fought and hard-won. But change is possible.

Note, too, the story provides yet another example of one of the themes of this book: how industry will be anxious to advance a popular narrative that holds individuals responsible for the systemic problems it creates. Ominously, this story also illustrates how easily academics can be bought off and led to support such a narrative, no matter how baseless and damaging it is.

Another issue that the case of cigarettes helps to highlight is the sometimes porous border between the i-frame and the s-frame, a point we introduced in the Introduction of the book. Some of the policies that have helped to combat smoking—such as very high taxes on tobacco and bans on smoking in or even near public places—fall clearly under the umbrella of the s-frame. Others, such as bans on advertising and graphic warning labels, are mandated through s-frame regulations but target individual consumers. In these cases, instead of banning smoking altogether (changing the rules of the game), the aim is to educate and encourage people not to smoke (helping people play the game better). As we noted earlier, the i-frame/s-frame distinction is not absolute; it depends on which of the relevant social and economic games we are considering. But some measures, such as public health campaigns (and, indeed, disinformation campaigns sponsored by the industry) are pretty clearly i-frame: They aim to shape behavior by influencing individual hearts and minds.[57] The successful effort to regulate the tobacco industry nicely illustrates the point that i-frame and s-frame measures need not be in competition—they can be mutually reinforcing.

So i-frame measures that influence public attitudes to smoking will impact support for s-frame measures (tax increases, restrictions on smoking in public places, and so on); and s-frame measures that reduce smoking may, in turn, change public attitudes (e.g., by signaling that society disapproves of smoking).

Last, we should note that the battle against the cigarette industry, even in the US and similar nations, is by no means a "done deal." At the time of writing, smoking remains the largest cause of preventable deaths in the US, the UK, the EU, and many other rich nations. Moreover, the tobacco industry's power is still intact, and its sales are buoyant in many regions across the world. Twenty-three percent of the world's population were smokers in 2020, and smoking still causes one in seven deaths globally.[58] And even where the tide of smoking has been reversed, a new challenge has emerged in the form of electronic cigarettes, or vaping. Marketed as a safer alternative to smoking tobacco, vaping products have rapidly gained in popularity, especially among young people. While the cover story for the vaping industry has been to help smokers quit, companies like Juul have used sleek designs and fruity flavors to attract a new generation of users—echoing tactics used earlier by the tobacco industry to promote smoking. Clearly, the battle is ongoing, and there is more work to be done. The story is a reminder that public health battles—and, indeed, battles over public policy more generally—are rarely ever completely won but require sustained effort and adaptation to new challenges.

———

Behavioral science has tended to take the rules of the game as fixed, for good or ill, and the field has focused on the remedial task of trying to retrain the players, one at a time. Behavioral scientists have spent too long helping people make marginally better choices for the climate, their health, or their financial futures, while facing impossible odds. In this chapter, we've pointed to a different approach: We need an understanding of human nature to help the democratic process work better—to inform public and political debate to help us choose better rules, with better outcomes. Behavioral science is needed not only to help nudge the players, but to change the game. We take our perspective a step further in the next chapter, where we examine implications of the i-frame/s-frame distinction for politics.

Chapter 10

DEMOCRACY HACKED

It is hard to talk about any social or environmental problem without playing the blame game. For every dilemma and crisis that we've discussed in this book, one could easily create a villain. Climate change? Blame the oil companies. Gun violence? Decry the influence of the NRA. Income inequality? Rail against the 1 percent. Retirement crisis in the US? Point the finger at corporate America and the greed of the financial services industry. Spiraling health care costs? It's the insurance and drug companies' fault.

Certainly, there are bad corporate actors and wrongdoing by rich and powerful individuals. But to blame individual players in the game is to miss the source of the problem—that the social, economic, and political games we play all too often provide powerful incentives to damage the common good. If the concentrated interests that Mancur Olson highlighted can enact policies that benefit themselves at the cost of the population, this should tell us that there is something wrong with the functioning of the *political process* that allows them to do so. And if there is something wrong with the political process, it is unlikely to be entirely an accident. The concentrated interests that might benefit from being able to manipulate politics to their advantage will, of course, work hard to maintain and increase their power.

Democratic politics, however imperfect, is supposed to allow us—we the people, not we the rich and powerful—to govern. But it should come as no surprise that politics is being "hacked" by powerful interests to serve their ends rather than those of the population at large. And to the extent that the game of politics itself is hacked, then the social and economic games concerning climate change, health care, retirement savings, inequality, gun control, and so on, won't get fixed.

In this chapter, we turn the spotlight on the political process itself—on the ways in which powerful interests continually work to rig the political system in their favor, and on the types of *s-level* reforms to our political system that could ultimately result in overcoming the resistance by concentrated interests to long-overdue systemic change.

———

In the world of computer security, the most effective approach to fighting hackers is to think like a hacker. In fact, organizations often hire former hackers or even teams of hackers to continually attempt to break into their own systems and ferret out vulnerabilities. This process helps organizations design countermeasures, such as automatically generated strong passwords, two-factor authentication, automatic message encryption, spam filters, and more restrictive protocols for storing personal data.

Strategies for hacking political systems—like those for computer hacking—have undergone continual innovation. The long and rich history of political hacking includes flagrant vote-buying, interfering with elections, bribery, threats of violence, and corruption of endlessly varied kinds. While such strategies remain active in many notionally democratic states, the most egregious forms of corruption have largely been blocked in the US, the UK, and other mature democracies (although many continue in the shadows). But a wide range of *legal* hacking strategies remain, which can be grouped into four broad, overlapping categories.

First, *networks of influence.*

If you're a billionaire or corporate CEO, you probably have some powerful personal connections to exploit, but hiring a firm of lobbyists to work on your behalf is also likely to pay dividends. Consider the many government subsidies on, for example, oil drilling (Chapter 1) and corn and corn syrup (Chapter 2), or consider regulations such as the prohibition of plastic bag bans (Chapter 6), or preventing renegotiation of drug prices (Chapter 4), or the dismantling of financial regulation before, and indeed even after, the 2008 financial crash. The key to this hacking strategy is to ensure behind-the-scenes influence on the decisions that matter for you most, often through "networks of influence" among business leaders, lobbyists, and politicians. A particularly striking demonstration of this effect is the relentless rollback, at least until very recently, of so-called antitrust legislation in the US, such as that curtailing anti-competitive practices that benefit big business.[1] Careful academic analysis has found that such policies are driven not by intellectual argument, and certainly not by public demand, but most likely by the hidden influence of business interests on judicial decisions.[2] Unfortunately, despite the public's horror of high prices (which, of course, is the main consequence of monopolistic concentration of industry), for most of the American public antitrust legislation and its target—monopolistic industrial concentration—are abstractions of little apparent relevance to "real life."

Or, to focus on the interests of the superrich more directly, consider the low marginal tax rates for the very wealthy, and the innumerable tax breaks, offsets, and byzantine systems of offshore ownership that safeguard the assets of the very wealthy. These loopholes in the tax systems of the US, the UK, and other countries are hardly the products of a groundswell of public enthusiasm. They appear to be outcomes of highly successful—and profitable—behind-the-scenes lobbying efforts.[3]

Existing legal remedies to networks of influence tend to be weak, and the very interests that benefit from these networks have been successful in shifting the rules to remove the last remaining restraints. The most notorious recent development in the US is the 2010 *Citizens United* case, in which a 5–4 majority on the Supreme Court ruled that corporations and other outside groups can spend unlimited money on elections. Anthony Kennedy, who crafted the majority opinion, wrote that limiting "independent political spending" from corporations and other groups violates the First Amendment right to free speech.[4] Perhaps the most consequential developments, however, have been regulations that permit unlimited spending so long as it is not coordinated with a candidate's campaign—an almost meaningless restriction. The result has been a massive increase in political spending by wealthy donors, corporations, and special-interest groups, channeled through PACs and "super-PACs."[5] According to the Brennan Law Center, this empowering of the wealthiest donors has "helped reinforce the growing sense [quite accurate, in our view] that our democracy primarily serves the interests of the wealthy few, and that democratic participation for the vast majority of citizens is of relatively little value."[6] The change in political financing has, almost surely not coincidentally, accompanied the sharp turn in the rewriting of the rules in favor of corporate interests and the superrich that we described in Chapter 7. What is, or is not, on the political agenda can be heavily influenced by the superrich. Proposals that work against the interests of the rich and powerful can be—and often are—quietly squelched.

Many, if not most, countries other than the US have greater restrictions on lobbying and donations. So, if we want the kind of policies that address deep-rooted social problems, there is an obvious necessary first step: Take money out of politics as comprehensively as possible.[7] US politics, where the rules are especially lax and few, is both an outlier and a warning to other countries. Radical reform of campaign financing in the US, where the volumes of money are so vast and rising, seems especially urgent. But money is an ever-present danger for democracies across the world. Democracies, like computer systems, require constant vigilance.

Taking money out of politics is a necessary first step. But it is unlikely to be a full solution because, as anthropologists and social psychologists have long argued, human social life is not a matter merely of momentary transactions but also of ongoing relationships.[8] These relationships, which are cemented by innumerable implicit rules, norms, and expectations, have a powerful sway on their participants. The creation and maintenance of such relationships provides, therefore, a second powerful route through which external interests can directly influence the political process. There have been recent (as we write this) revelations that, during his three decades on the US Supreme Court, Clarence Thomas received gifts in the form of at least thirty-eight "destination" vacations on yachts, access to premium suites at sporting events, at least twenty-six private jet flights, and, from ultra-right-wing Texas real estate billionaire Harlan Crow, the purchase of Thomas's mother's house in Georgia. Many of these were not disclosed, as required by federal law. In a statement defending these gifts, Thomas wrote that the Crows "are among our dearest friends," and "As friends do, we have joined them on a number of family trips."[9]

Beyond political contributions, outright gifts, and personal relationships, there is the notorious "revolving door" in which individuals who staff government regulatory agencies leave to take lucrative positions in the industries they were responsible for regulating—in some cases making repeated back-and-forth switches. Such practices are widespread and only weakly regulated, at least in the US.[10] As touched on in Chapter 6, this revolving door seems to have played a central role in the opioid crisis in the US.

In many governments across the world there are, quite rightly, rules to combat the power of networks of influence crossing from the private to the public sector. But these rules are often weakest where they matter the most—at the very most senior levels of government and the judiciary.[11] The fundamental attribution error (our tendency to pin responsibility on individuals, not systems) is a useful ally for any hacker of democracy. Not only does it lead us to overestimate the importance of character in determining other people's behavior—and to commensurately underestimate the influence of relationships, favors, revolving doors, promotions, or campaign donations—it also helps those in positions of power to convince themselves that their own decisions are unbiased and unaffected by the incentives they face; participants in networks of influence can all too easily maintain a clear conscience.

For those interested in hacking democracy, it will be important to maintain these networks of influence, of course. Thus, we should expect any reform to meet with substantial opposition—including, of course, from those politicians, lawyers, and public servants who benefit from being part of these networks. The most senior figures, with the most powerful networks of influence, will be especially well-placed to block such oversight—and incentivized to do so. For prospective hackers of democracy, this is ideal—it means a few, well-placed meetings at the most senior levels will pay substantial dividends.

If we are serious about addressing the social and environmental problems that confront us, a first priority should be exposing and breaking up these networks of influence. All parties can deny that their judgment is corrupted by such networks (and some may believe this to be true), but what we know about human nature tells us the very opposite.

The second hacking strategy involves *the small print*.

In policy, as in life, our brains are not designed to notice things that *don't* happen. One of the techniques that hackers use to break through security barriers is to embed hidden code that slips past computer users unnoticed but can have a devastating impact. A parallel strategy exists for hackers of democracy. Governments and courts make a huge number of decisions, only a fraction of which are subject to legislative scrutiny or much (if any) public debate, in part because their often far-reaching consequences are not well understood, except by their crafters.

As an example of enormously consequential legislation that flies "below the radar," consider Section 230 of the "Communications Decency Act." According to the website of the Electronic Frontier Foundation (EFF, a left-leaning advocacy group that maintains its independence and claims it is not influenced by its donors, has been criticized with taking money from, and sometimes advocating for, large technology companies), this law "protects Americans' freedom of expression online by protecting the intermediaries we all rely on."[12] Although the EFF was not behind the insertion of Section 230, and actively opposed large parts of the Communications Decency Act, it has been a major supporter of Section 230 itself. The EFF website continues, "The law prevents most civil suits against users or services that are based on what others say." The description is accompanied by a graphic depicting a joyful person shouting into a megaphone held up by another joyful person. As depicted by the EFF, Section 230 sounds admirable. Who wants to be held responsible for lies that some reprehensible individual tells? But newspapers and book publishers have long been held to a much higher standard of liability for publishing lies and defaming others, and have done so while retaining their freedom of expression and, at least until recently, financial viability.

The EFF website states that "Congress passed this bipartisan legislation because it recognized that promoting more user speech online outweighed potential harms. When harmful speech takes place, it's the speaker that should be held responsible, not the service that hosts the speech." One can't help wondering whether Congress's determination that the benefits of internet freedom outweigh the costs of regulation may have had something to do with the multibillion-dollar corporations and their billionaire owners who would be protected from liability by this seemingly innocuous addendum to the Communications Decency Act. As with antitrust legislation, Section 230 of the Communications Decency

Act, and its far-reaching implications, are far too abstruse for most of us to pay attention to (or indeed be aware of). So the pressures exerted by the tech industry (with its deep pockets and lobbyists) will inevitably not be checked by any spontaneous outpouring of public concern.[13]

The third strategy: *controlling the agenda.*

Even though a CEO may wish that certain topics remain under the radar, some topics are unavoidably, or may suddenly become, matters of public debate. However much one's networks of influence can, for example, transform the tax system to give the lowest marginal tax rates to the superrich, tax levels are inevitably a matter of public concern. In such situations, a further hacking strategy comes into play. The key objective is to ensure that any policy threatening one's interests, however popular it might be with a well-informed and thoughtful public, remains completely off the political agenda. As already discussed, a good first move is through political campaign donations. If a party or politician benefits from your financial support, they are unlikely to propose policies that may damage your interests.

Another way to control the agenda is through the media. In the UK, there has long been a perception that no political party or policy is likely to succeed without the backing of the tabloid press, and especially its most influential titles, *The Sun* (part of the Murdoch family's Newscorp) and *The Daily Mail* (owned by the 4th Viscount Rothermere).[14] British Prime Minister Tony Blair's close and long-standing relationship with Rupert Murdoch, for example, was seen as crucial to his electoral success. Needless to say, almost any policy inimical to Murdoch (or to business leaders close to Murdoch) could scarcely be considered.[15] This Blair–Murdoch relationship seemed to be highly beneficial for both sides: Blair got *The Sun*'s backing in 1997, and the Blair government attacked backers of antitrust restrictions on the media industry, which Blair's Labour Party had previously supported and which were widely viewed as targeting Murdoch's businesses.[16] One well-known

British journalist, Anthony Hilton, has written that he once asked Rupert Murdoch why he was so opposed to the European Union. "That's easy," he replied. "When I go into Downing Street they do what I say; when I go to Brussels they take no notice"—a quote that Murdoch denies having made.[17]

The press, including Murdoch's *Sun*, strongly and consistently attacked the EU for decades, likely paving the way for a "Yes" vote in the Brexit referendum in 2016. Irrespective of the details, it seems clear that there is a serious potential problem for democracy: Rather than reflecting the deliberations of thoughtful and well-informed citizens, the democratic process can all too easily be "hacked" to reflect the interests of the rich and powerful.

In the US, too, the rolling back of antitrust legislation has led to the increasing concentration of news media ownership, including across platforms. Writing in 2024, journalist Phillip Longman traces two centuries of government regulation of the postal service, the telegraph, the press, and later TV to maintain diversity of expression against the dangers of monopoly power. He notes that "until about 40 years ago, both the courts and public opinion viewed the [First Amendment of the US Constitution], and the Constitution generally, as . . . requiring that government take positive steps to protect these freedoms [of speech and of the press] from interference by monopolists." But over the last forty years or so, media concentration has increased both via the growth of media empires such as Rupert Murdoch's (including Fox News, the *New York Post*, and *The Wall Street Journal* in the US, and many more news and media companies across the world) and through the growth of near-monopoly social media companies, especially Google and Meta (Facebook), which are frequently gatekeepers of access to conventional news content.[18]

The result is that a large majority of journalism is ultimately controlled by billionaires, and that s-frame changes that might harm those billionaires (or their networks of powerful allies) will scarcely be supported, if they are even mentioned at all.[19]

For example, given the vast flow of wealth in the US to the 0.1 percent, and the largely stagnant long-term real incomes for the working and middle classes, one might naturally imagine that large-scale redistribution of wealth might be the popular issue of the moment. Yet in mainstream political debate it is scarcely mentioned, and when it is, it is dismissed as wholly unrealistic. That is, of course, the way those billionaires want things. And, as we saw in Chapter 8, many have spent a great deal of money creating the political and journalistic climate in which the very thought of redistribution can be seen as antibusiness, antifreedom, and un-American.

Without radical decentralization of media ownership, including decreasing the power of a handful of big-tech companies—including Facebook, Google, and Twitter/X, which are taking over the role of the conventional media—reasoned democratic debate to address pressing social and environmental challenges will inevitably be hobbled.[20]

The fourth hacking strategy: *corrupting the debate.*

When debate of "threatening" policy options is unavoidable, and a member of the economic elite fears losing any debate decided by thoughtful, well-informed citizens, there's a fourth and final hacking strategy: to undermine the *very possibility* of thoughtful, well-informed debate. Businesses accomplish this by sponsoring "think tanks" and lobbying groups to promote their agenda; by hiring publicists to sell their message to a usually "business-friendly" and (as we've seen) often highly concentrated media; and by generating misinformation and disinformation, or propagating misinformation and disinformation generated by others. Similar motives might well underlie their sponsorship of academic research on related topics, hoping to indirectly skew the results while at the same time providing a useful veneer of respectability.

Earlier policy shifts with enormous implications for the functioning of democracy have made efforts to shape and disrupt public debate even easier. In 1987, for example, President Ronald Reagan's libertarian Federal Communications Commission chairman, Mark Fowler, repealed the "Fairness Doctrine," which had regulated news programs since 1949. Although Congress voted to reinstate the Fairness Doctrine, Reagan vetoed the bill with the rationale that "it shouldn't take the force of law to compel broadcasters to be fair."[21] As Longman writes, "Within a year, an obscure radio personality named Rush Limbaugh began broadcasting the unbalanced, hyper-partisan programming that launched nationally syndicated talk radio."[22] This was an important step toward the current, "post-truth" era, in which conspiracy theories are rampant and even basic historical and scientific facts are perceived by many as matters of opinion.[23]

A common strategy of propaganda and disinformation is to create new narratives, "alternative facts," and to instill distrust in (and damage) any institutions that might provide reliable anchors to reality (investigative journalism, news reporting, history, science, data of all kinds, the courts). The lesson for the prospective hacker: Democracy depends on people being able to *trust* each other and the institutions that serve them. If you can corrupt trust, you can get us (or substantial numbers of us at least) to believe just about anything (or, almost as good, believe in nothing). All you need is a big enough budget.

———

Throughout the book we have attempted to emphasize the bad-system over the bad-actor narrative, but sometimes it becomes difficult to suppress the perception that there really are evil actors out there. Asked whether his view of topics tends to change as he researches them, comedian John Oliver responded to *New York Times* reporter Lulu Garcia-Navarro: "But things are generally, with some of these systemic problems, worse than you thought when you start looking at them."[24] She then followed up by asking him whether this sometimes drives him to rage. His response:

Yeah, because things are so much worse than you thought they were, and you thought they were pretty bad. Then you have to work through that. Because nihilism is completely useless. The coward's way out. So you work through that. And I have found, generally, that the light at the end of the tunnel—albeit that light might be smaller than you would like it to be ideally—is that there are activists making small, incremental progress on the ground, and that progress is really, really important.

We certainly crossed our rage threshold when reading a *Guardian* piece documenting the steps that corporations have taken to muzzle exactly those activists who might otherwise have had a shot at instigating change. Under the headline "Revealed: How the Fossil Fuel Industry Helps Spread Anti-Protest Laws Across the U.S.," the article documents how fossil fuel lobbyists coordinated with lawmakers behind the scenes and across state lines to push and shape laws that crack down on peaceful protests against the actions of fossil fuel companies—laws that increased penalties for such protests and could lead to nonviolent environmental and climate activists being imprisoned up to ten years.[25] Clearly, the purpose of such legislation is to deter activists from protesting in the first place.

Almost exactly the same pattern has been playing out in the UK. Under former Prime Minister Rishi Sunak's Conservative administration from 2022 to 2024, draconian antiprotest laws were introduced, cracking down on anti-oil protests.[26] And the laws have been used in earnest: Several protesters from the campaign group Just Stop Oil received unprecedented multiyear prison sentences for stopping traffic flow on the M25 motorway around London in November 2022—sentences condemned by the United Nations High Commissioner for Human Rights Volker Türk as "deeply troubling."[27] The source of these laws turns out to be, at least in part, a right-wing think tank, Policy Exchange, which published a briefing paper in 2019 on the topic (titled "Extremism Rebellion"). Prime Minister Sunak later said that Policy Exchange's work "has helped us draft" the government's crackdown on protests.[28] Policy Exchange does not disclose its donors; but the media organization Open Democracy found a $30,000 donation from Exxon Mobil to the American arm of Policy Exchange in 2017.[29] One can only speculate how much other oil money may be backing a think tank providing such helpful input to government officials eager to close down protests threatening the fossil fuels industry.

Vested interests, it seems, are not only exploiting the political process to enact laws and regulations favorable to themselves, but are attempting to circumvent the political process itself to deter and incapacitate potential opponents who do manage to mobilize against them.

———

We've seen throughout this book that rigged rules, not flawed individuals, lie at the heart of many of society's most persistent problems. But if this is right, a natural question arises: Why aren't the rules reformed to work in the interests of the many, not the few, given that in a democracy the many have, by definition, the majority of the votes? The answer, as we've seen, is that the democratic process has been hacked by the powerful and wealthy. This corrupting influence of power and money on politics is an ever-present threat; democracies need continual and vigorous defense by campaigners, journalists, lawyers, and above all by citizens, if they are to survive as more than a hollow shell. This will mean taking money out of politics across the board; radical reforms of lobbying; coming down hard on mis- and disinformation both through algorithms and the law; greater plurality and transparency of political think tanks; arm's-length funding and independent oversight of any academic research potentially subject to conflicts of interests by commercial funders; and much more. As with computer security, restoring the integrity of the political process is a prerequisite for progress on just about anything else. Where the process for setting the rules has been hacked, the rules in any domain—climate policy, finance, health care, and so on—will all too often be good for the hackers and bad for the rest of us.

Chapter 11

GREEN EGGS AND HAM

In Dr. Seuss's classic children's story, the cheerfully persistent Sam-I-am repeatedly attempts to persuade a grumpy, unnamed narrator to try a strange dish: green eggs and ham.[1] Through rhythmic, repetitive text and playful illustrations, Sam-I-am's relentless enthusiasm and creative attempts to persuade the narrator to try the concoction lead to an unexpected and delightful conclusion: Taking a bite to mollify Sam-I-am, the curmudgeonly narrator finds to his surprise that "I do so like green eggs and ham!"

Written using only fifty words (based on a bet that Seuss made with his editor), the story illustrates an important truth about human nature: that people often resist things they would come to value, if only they gave them a chance.[2] The same is true, we'll see, not just for foods or new experiences, but also for the rules by which we live. Like green eggs and ham, policy changes are often met with resistance—even highly beneficial ones that people ultimately would (and, if implemented, do) come to support. To understand why, and how to overcome our excessive attachment to the familiar, we must understand the fundamental psychological mechanism of *adaptation*, the process by which we become less sensitive to a constant stimulus over time. Adaptation allows us to tune out nonessential stimuli, focus on changes in our environment that are often more important for survival, and respond to a much wider range of stimuli than we otherwise could. For example, photoreceptors in the eyes adapt to light levels, enabling vision across an astoundingly wide range of lighting conditions: When you enter a dark room, or suddenly walk into brilliant sunlight, at first you can't see anything, but your eyes quickly adapt. Olfactory receptors in the nose quickly adapt to persistent smells, which is why strong odors typically become less noticeable after prolonged exposure. In the same way, we can find ourselves "tuning out" noises that we initially find disturbing: Living by a busy road, railway, or under a flight path, we can soon find ourselves oblivious of a formerly intrusive noise, at least if it is sufficiently predictable and repetitive.

Adaptation also occurs for "hedonic" states, such as subjective feelings like happiness or sadness.[3] Whatever their material circumstances, level of health, etc., most people have a natural "happiness set-point" that they ultimately return to. More than forty years ago, a classic paper, "Lottery Winners and Accident Victims: Is Happiness Relative?," concluded that people who had won the lottery were, in fact, not happier—nor were accident victims (specifically, paraplegics) less happy—than a comparison group of people who had experienced neither outcome.[4] Although subsequent research has raised issues with, and improved on, the relatively crude research methods used in the original study (and has in some cases reached more nuanced conclusions), the core finding that humans are enormously adaptable even to truly momentous life-changing shocks has proved remarkably robust.

One of the quirks about adaptation is that people are very bad at predicting it—they tend to vastly underestimate their own powers of adjusting to good or bad news.[5] When it comes to positive changes, people don't appreciate how short-lived their elation will be: No matter how many times we experience the contrary, we seem to be hardwired to believe that the next promotion and/or pay raise will make us permanently happy and content, that our current feelings of passion toward another person will persist forever, or that a new car or house will permanently give us delight. When it comes to adverse changes, we radically underestimate our ability to adapt to negative circumstances—which often leads us to overreact to negative events such as getting "dumped" by a partner, convinced that we will never recover—and we believe that people who suffer from permanent disabilities must be far more miserable than they end up being, on average. As Adam Smith wrote in *The Theory of Moral Sentiments*, "The great source of both the misery and disorders of human life seems to arise from overrating the difference between one permanent situation and another."[6]

One important consequence of underpredicting how well we will adapt to change is that we often become excessively resistant to it. And, much like the fundamental attribution error, this psychological bias can be exploited by those resisting change: They will naturally frame any change that threatens their bottom line as one that will be intolerably—and permanently—disruptive.

———

Either because of our inability to predict adaptation or because of a hardwired preference for things to stay the way they are (what psychologists call the *status quo bias*), making sweeping change to the s-frame is hard.[7] Citizens come to view the status quo as a given, and understandably focus on improving their own situation while operating within the constraints of existing policy. A key step in addressing the distortion of the democratic process is recognizing that there is a problem at all; a second step is realizing just how far-reaching the problem is. Indeed, we would argue that it is *the* central problem that needs to be addressed to help unblock badly needed reforms essential to solving climate change, the obesity epidemic, the crisis of long-term saving, inequality, and so on. Fixing the rules of democracy is crucial to fixing just about anything else.

S-frame change is hard for another reason, too: People are afraid of, and often resist, change. This can lead policy experts and politicians to be so daunted by initial resistance that they rule out potentially beneficial changes as politically impossible, fearing that "people will never stand for it!" But once a policy has been put into place, things can change quite radically. Consider the smoking bans we discussed in Chapter 9. When first proposed, they faced vociferous objections. Detractors claimed they would limit personal freedom and hurt businesses like bars and restaurants. But in a remarkably short period of time people have come to prefer a smoke-free environment. Smoking bans are now popular even among smokers themselves.[8] And this public acceptance has in turn increased support for even more restrictive measures against smoking, including the UK's proposed "rolling" age ban (now in limbo after a change of government and furious behind-the-scenes tobacco industry lobbying), which would effectively outlaw the sale of cigarettes to anyone born after 2009.[9]

A similar pattern has occurred with onshore wind and solar energy. Opposition for aesthetic reasons—people not wanting solar panel arrays or wind turbines to mark the landscape—remains high in some places. For example, in the UK, fear of public outrage in rural areas has made it, until the 2024 change of government, almost impossible to get planning permission for onshore wind turbines—the UK's cheapest energy option—despite legally binding carbon reduction targets. Yet elsewhere we've seen people rapidly adapt to the installation of onshore wind turbines, even, in some cases, coming to find them visually attractive.[10] As with the arrival of the railroad in the nineteenth century, people dislike the change until it becomes part of the background of their lives.

Some of the most rigorous research addressing what could be called the "green eggs and ham" syndrome—opposition to policy change *until* it is enacted—focuses on congestion charges in densely populated urban areas. In a study of Stockholm's trial introduction of a congestion charge in 2006, residents completed surveys both before and after a congestion charge was implemented. Initially, there was strong public opposition to the policy, but public support increased dramatically once the policy was in place, which helped lead to its permanent implementation, after which support increased even more.[11] This pattern prevailed for a range of subgroups—for people who did not own a car, as well as for those who did, and for those who paid the charge seldom, sometimes, or often. A similar pattern occurred in London, Oslo, Singapore, Milan, and Rome; people tend to be negative toward the congestion charges at first, but, consistent with adaptation, opposition diminishes and support increases once people experience the benefits and get used to the changed circumstances.[12] In an especially rigorous laboratory demonstration of the phenomenon, environmental economist Nicholas Janusch and coauthors examined individuals' acceptance of a "congestion charge" before and after its implementation in a six-player, two-route congestion game—a radically simplified setup designed to capture the basic logic of congestion charging in an experimental context. Although the charge curbed congestion effectively, people often voted against it initially. But when the positive effects of the charge were experienced in playing the game, many embraced the very s-frame reform they had previously resisted.[13]

In so many cases, then, "objections" to a new policy are, to a large degree, objections to the fact that it is new, and they melt away once the changes are enacted.[14] Recent examples include making the use of seat belts compulsory, tighter drunk-driving rules, phasing out sales of gas-powered vehicles, and, in most countries where such rules have been implemented, decriminalizing homosexuality, legalizing gay marriage and abortion, abolishing the death penalty, and so on. In all these cases, the status quo bias was quickly overwhelmed by adaptation. As much as we may prefer what we are already used to, we are also remarkably adept at getting used to something new.

In its 2016 budget, the UK government introduced a tax on sugar in soft drinks. Two years later, the "soft drinks industry levy" came into effect: An eighteen-pence tax (about twenty-five cents US) was added to the price of each liter of soft drink containing more than fifty grams of sugar, and twenty-four pence (thirty-two cents US) to the price of each liter containing more than eighty grams.[15]

What happened? First, once the notice period for the tax was given, manufacturers scrambled to reformulate their drinks with less sugar, in order not to have to increase prices. Second, when the newly reformulated products were introduced, it turned out that consumers *didn't notice*—or, at least, they soon became entirely accustomed to, and equally happy with, the lower-sugar drinks. So this looks like a win-win for consumers, not a lose-lose: They enjoy their drinks as much as before, don't pay higher prices, and are healthier to boot.

Indeed, it turned out that after the sugar tax was implemented, soft drink consumption actually rose (good for business), while the total amount of sugar consumed through soft drinks fell substantially (good for consumers).[16]

From a policy point of view, this changes everything. From being arguably bad for consumers (because it pushes them away from their preferred, although unhealthy, sugary drinks), the policy now looks unequivocally good for consumers: improving their health with no noticeable loss in the pleasures of consumption. Knowing about human nature—and in particular knowing about the psychology of adaptation—changes the policy argument. What a libertarian may see as a welfare-destroying move suddenly looks rather benign. The libertarian is assuming that people's preferences are fixed, so that their current choices of unhealthy drinks must tell us that this is what they really want. And that seems to imply that any systemic intervention that pushes people away from their current preferred choices must cause them harm, at least by their own lights. But adaptation tells us that our preferences are not fixed at all; once we get used to something new (which we initially reject), we may find we like it just as much (or perhaps even more) than our original choice.

These same principles have applications to diverse aspects of public policy. Take a problem like hearing loss caused by excessive and avoidable exposure to noise. The perception of loudness is relative, but damage to our ears depends on absolute decibel levels. If we smartly regulated noise levels in concerts, clubs, and, perhaps most crucially, headphones, we could reduce hearing loss while causing little change to sensations of loudness.

A similar limit could be placed on the strength of recreational drugs like marijuana, which has been increasing over time. Given the nature of adaptation, users will inevitably get used to more powerful versions, meaning that any emotional or hedonic benefit will be lost over time, even as the risks of taking such potent drugs only increase. One advantage of legalizing and controlling certain drugs is that, as with sugar and salt, regulators could keep overall strength levels relatively low without severely diminishing the benefits to users.

Gambling is another area where adaptation-conscious policy might matter a great deal. A gambler can quickly become accustomed to the thrill of playing high-stakes slot machines, which offer much bigger payoffs but a greater risk of personal financial disaster. But as the extra thrill wears off (so that gamblers are getting little or no more excitement than when they were playing for "pennies"), the risk of financial disaster does not, and it can end up destroying the lives of many gamblers and their families. So legislating against high-stakes slot machines—and indeed high-stakes gambling of any kind—is likely to have only a modest negative impact on the enjoyment of gamblers but a substantial positive effect on their financial and mental well-being. Indeed, one could imagine a "duty of care" on gambling companies (as is becoming common in banking regulation in the UK, for instance) that would legally require that they do not allow people to endanger their financial well-being.[17] Needless to say, the gambling industry lobbies relentlessly against any such restrictions, precisely because they are very likely to work.

Finally, consider consumption and the environment. Environmental priorities—reducing greenhouse gas emissions, as well as protecting biodiversity, conserving soil, and keeping our air and water clean—seem to clash with the consumer demand for ever larger cars and houses, more extensive travel itineraries, and so on. Curtailing people's choices (for example, by regulating fuel efficiency, tightening standards of home insulation, or raising taxes on flying) might seem inevitably to be welfare-damaging—after all, people would be willing to spend a lot of money to obtain things that the restrictions might place beyond reach. But taking account of adaptation changes the picture completely.[18] Cars, for example, have been growing in size over the decades, both in Europe and even more so in the US.[19] But adaptation means that most of us haven't even noticed, let alone gained any discernible welfare benefit, from these larger vehicles, while the damage caused to the climate by ever-larger vehicles is all too real. So regulation to encourage smaller vehicles also starts to look like a win-win. Consumers pay less for smaller, and cheaper-to-run, vehicles without any discernible welfare loss; and there is less damage to the climate (and fewer pedestrian and bicycle fatalities).[20]

———

From the perspective of public policy, adaptation might seem to be unequivocally good news: Slowly tapering sugar and salt levels, for example, should be embraced by policymakers and the public. But the phenomenon of adaptation poses real dangers, especially when it comes to our ability to respond, as individuals and societies, to changes that are not merely incidental but insidious.

The problem is that adaptation makes us vulnerable to threats that build up slowly and imperceptibly. Such threats are rarely the immediate preoccupations of voters. Our emotional and motivational "alarm systems" are bypassed, in part because of the slow nature of the threat; and we continually adapt to the new normal, scarcely noticing as conditions continue to decline.[21] Environmental degradation provides a stark illustration. Forests are cleared, soils eroded, fish stocks are overexploited, air becomes increasingly polluted, the number of pollinators such as bees diminishes—but these processes often happen slowly, and almost imperceptibly. Once a critical point is reached, the impacts may sometimes be sudden and severe, but by this stage it is almost certainly too late for remedial action.

We see similar effects in public health. Resistance to antibiotics, the gradual buildup of human-caused toxic substances in the environment and food chain, and the shift of the food system toward ultraprocessed foods all occurred over many years, and these things may have long-lasting and, in some cases, devastating effects on current and future generations. But it is so much more difficult to marshal resources against a slowly building threat rather than, say, the immediate crisis of a global pandemic.

Inequality provides another striking example. In many developed nations, both income and wealth inequality have been gradually increasing over the past few decades (see Chapter 5). This has exacerbated many social problems and caused considerable social tension. But there has been surprisingly little public demand that it be reversed. Had such a massive transfer from the poor to the rich occurred at a single stroke, by contrast, one suspects it would have been viewed with outrage by the poor—and perhaps even by the rich. The problem of gradual change flying under our "cognitive radar" is particularly serious regarding existential threats, whether from climate change and collapses in biodiversity and soil fertility, or from the rise of artificial intelligence or the internal collapse of democratic societies into disorder.

There are, of course, many psychological reasons why large-scale existential problems evoke surprisingly little public concern, such as our individual sense of powerlessness and the fact that most of us are primarily absorbed in coping with our personal struggles in the immediate present rather than worrying about longer-term challenges for the world. Nonetheless, our ability to adapt to creeping catastrophe remains a major factor in why our response to problems often seems too little, too late.

———

Almost any proposal for s-frame change faces the implacable forces of the status quo. People won't like the new order; they'll never get used to it; they simply won't tolerate it. Best to leave things as they are. But, in truth, we've seen that people's beliefs, attitudes, preferences, and skills continually adjust to the society in which they live. Before the fact, it was all too easy to imagine that people would never accept smoking bans, seat belt legislation, plastic bag taxes, gay marriage, mask-wearing, and much more; going further back, it would have seemed doubtful that there would be general acceptance of widening the franchise, educating the poor, expanding civil rights, instituting strong health and safety measures, or even abolishing slavery—all of which were driven through against furious opposition. The challenges we face today are formidable, but they are no greater than many of those we have already overcome.

Conclusion

TAKING BACK CONTROL

We've argued in this book that many of our most pressing and persistent social and environmental problems remain unsolved not because we don't collectively know how to solve them, but because powerful interests benefit from their *not* being solved. Indeed, the powerful typically do everything they can to ensure that the rules of the game are rigged in their favor. The fossil fuel industry works hard to slow the shift to renewable energy; multinational food companies use their influence to expand their global markets for unhealthy ultraprocessed foods and to push back against legislative restrictions aimed at improving public health; the US health care sector lobbies relentlessly against reforming a failing, though very profitable (for them), model of medical care; the firearms industry pushes back against gun control; the packaging industry backs preemptive legislation to sabotage efforts to cut down on plastics; and so the list continues. The rich and powerful have had every incentive to consolidate and enhance their wealth and power, by skewing the tax system in their favor, deregulating financial services, allowing concentrated ownership and loose regulation of the traditional and digital media, and keeping money—and vast numbers of lobbyists—at the heart of politics.

We've seen that such rigging of the rules is typically disguised by two clever sleights of hand. The first is *responsibilization*—diverting public attention from the systemic issues responsible for a problem by pinning responsibility on individual choices and behavior. Worried about obesity? Go to the gym and monitor your calories. Worried about the retirement crisis? Become a prudent saver and canny investor. Worried about the climate crisis? Perhaps it's time to go on a low-carbon diet (to echo the campaign from oil giant BP). Of course, the appeal of responsibilization is a mirage. The climate crisis hasn't arisen because people have suddenly become especially greedy for carbon-intensive material goods; problems of obesity and retirement savings haven't arisen because people are suddenly so much more weak-willed than past generations. These problems arise from systemic factors, and need systematic solutions—but the beneficiaries of the status quo would rather we don't see the problems in such terms.

The second sleight of hand is to suggest that the most obvious and capable potential vectors of change—governments—are inherently corrupt, while in reality powerful special interests are attempting to corrupt them as much as possible. As we saw in Chapter 8, a well-funded libertarian ideology has been especially dominant in the US, the UK, and many other parts of the world since around 1980. According to this ideology, the answer to virtually every major social problem is not *better* government (and hence better systems) but *less* government. Since 1980, as we and many others have noted, the political and economic playing field has been increasingly tilted in favor of corporations and billionaires, with disastrous consequences.

As we saw in Chapter 9, many behavioral scientists, including the two of us, have been deceived by these sleights of hand. In line with the logic of responsibilization, we've implicitly assumed that we can address society's problems directly by changing individual behavior. And many of us have gone along with the idea that individual-level interventions (nudges, information, targeted education) can help people "play the game" more successfully to achieve better outcomes for themselves and society—no need for the heavy hand of government, with its traditional armory of taxes, subsidies, and regulation. Though these ideas may have been well-intentioned, they turned out to be very convenient for those trying to block reform. By spending all our effort fixing the individual, we distracted ourselves and others from a much more urgent mission: "unrigging" the rules by acting at the s-frame.

———

In confronting the ills of the world, our psychological bias to focus on the individual can take hold, and it is easy to find ourselves not just despairing of the world's problems, but despairing of human nature itself. And once we despair of human nature, we are not far from drifting into cynicism and apathy—we can conclude that humans are irremediably flawed, that society's problems are unsolvable, that there is no hope for us as a species, or even that the planet will be better off without us.[1] This is just what the purveyors of the responsibilization sleight of hand would like us to believe—that individual humans are (en masse) the root of society's problems, and that we have only ourselves to blame for our failings. Indeed, the entire purpose of responsibilization is to set off futile individual-level blame games in which people point fingers at each other (or humanity collectively) and leave the rules of the game unchanged. Cynicism, fatalism, and even despair can sometimes seem natural human reactions to our collective troubles. But once we refocus our attention on the s-frame, we will see that the situation is not as hopeless as it seems. Ordinary citizens, instead of futilely blaming ourselves and one another, can campaign, argue, and vote to change the rules.

The focus on the rules is crucial. A glance at history should remind us that the difference between well-functioning governments, societies, and organizations, and those that are awash with venality and corruption, lies at the level of the s-frame. The horrors of empire, slavery, totalitarianism, theocracies, or the near anarchy of failed or collapsing states, are illustrations of the dreadful outcomes that can result when the "rules of the game" go catastrophically out of control or break down entirely. The citizens of failing or thriving societies share a common human nature, but the rules of the social and economic games they are immersed in can differ tremendously.

In this book—and in the earlier academic articles that inspired it—we have tried to show how the rules of the game benefit a small group of powerful people and business interests. Some of our colleagues have interpreted our efforts as an exercise in "conspiratorial thinking"—claiming that we are blaming global problems on a cadre of evil, coordinated plotters for world domination or some similarly fanciful end.[2] This misses the point entirely: The problem isn't with individuals at all, but with the systems that govern economic, social, and political life. Conspiracy theories are stuck in the i-frame (it's the "bad people," whoever they are, who are supposedly the source of our woes). But the truth is more subtle. Where the rules of the game are broken, bad outcomes are pretty much guaranteed.

For political scientists, sociologists, legal scholars, or historians, this is all familiar ground, and many of even the most doctrinaire economists would agree. The conventional logic of political economy (including Mancur Olson's work that has underpinned so much of our analysis) is that powerful organizations and influential individuals will attempt to play the game, and where possible maintain or change the rules of the game, to further their own objectives. This is in fact one of the few propositions shared across the political spectrum, from Marxists to Chicago school economists. As the Scottish enlightenment philosopher David Hume wrote, when considering the design of a political system "every man must be supposed a knave."[3] And this is so not because humans are inherently knavish, but rather because badly designed games will allow knaves to thrive and take over, and will, indeed, turn even well-intentioned individuals into knaves. Systems that are corrupt, in which cheating goes unchecked and misconduct goes unsanctioned, can pull any of us into the vortex of knavish behavior. Almost everyone benefits from a political system that is accountable to the population at large, can't be captured by special interests, has proper checks and balances, and punishes knavish behavior without fear or favor. So we should set our sights—whether as citizens or as behavioral scientists—not on nudging the players, but on "unrigging" the rules of the game.

But if we are not being too cynical, perhaps the reverse is true? Perhaps the idea that we can collectively change the rules of the game is too ambitious—just "pie in the sky," as some other colleagues, including *Nudge* coauthor Richard Thaler, have suggested.[4] As Anand Giridharadas writes in *Winners Take All*, "Many millions of Americans, on the left and right, feel one thing in common: that the game is rigged against people like them. Perhaps this is why we hear constant condemnation of 'the system,' for it is the system that people expect to turn fortuitous developments into societal progress."[5] The objection is that fundamental change is just hopelessly unrealistic, particularly in times of political polarization. Isn't it better for people, as individuals, to focus on their own lives and what they can control? Isn't politics too broken to get fixed? Shouldn't each citizen just try to lead a prudent and ethical life, however much we may feel we are living in an unhinged world? Perhaps we behavioral scientists should be soldiering along with what we know how to do best—seeking to promote individual-level change, taking the system as given?

This is a seductive story, and it's just the story the powerful interests who are subverting politics for their own ends want us to tell ourselves, because disengaged citizens will be the least likely to protest or even notice the subversion of the democratic process.

But the truth is that systemic change *is* possible. The answer to broken politics is not despair but reform. The answer to rigged games controlled by special interests is to change the rules, step by step, to reflect the interests of the many, not the few. Any reforms will be vigorously opposed, of course, by those who benefit from the status quo. But a moment's reflection on the history of democratic policies should remind us that reform can and often does happen despite the fiercest opposition.

The birth, growth, and maintenance of democracy has been a story of continual, and often successful, struggles for power, with special interests fighting reform every inch of the way—from the rise of Parliament against the monarchy, the battle to widen the franchise, struggles for national independence, the abolition of slavery, through to the civil rights movement and beyond. The history of democratic politics across the world is, after all, one of continual and often convulsive struggle to wrest control of the political and legal processes from the few to the many. The results are usually partial and imperfect; consistent forward progress is by no means guaranteed. Yet democracies, for all their imperfections, have also been remarkably successful in delivering unprecedented levels of freedom, health care, education, and economic prosperity for their citizens. As Giridharadas writes,

> We must ask ourselves why we have so easily lost faith in the engines of progress that got us where we are today—in the democratic efforts to outlaw slavery, end child labor, limit the workday, keep drugs safe, protect collective bargaining, create public schools, battle the Great Depression, electrify rural America, weave a nation together by road, pursue a Great Society free of poverty, extend civil and political rights to women and African Americans and other minorities, and give our fellow citizens health, security, and dignity in old age.[6]

Democratic processes are the best mechanisms we have for allowing the concerns of the many to overwhelm the interests of the powerful few; we need to strengthen democracy rather than abandon it. But powerful special interests will always have an interest in hobbling or coopting the democratic process, often with considerable success. Building a coalition of support for change, in whatever political direction, is clearly the best way to overcome such special interests, as documented in David Cole's superb book *Engines of Liberty*—maintaining public pressure until change is driven through and cemented in place.[7] In the US, such popular coalitions have, on the progressive side, helped reshape civil rights and women's rights, led to the wide acceptance of gay marriage, raised environmental awareness, uncovered sexual abuses in the movie industry, and many more. On the conservative side, however, similar coalitions such as the Tea Party movement have pushed for a shrinking state; the large base of the National Rifle Association has shredded gun laws; and activist Christian groups have rolled back access to abortion (all moves, which, it should be apparent, we personally oppose).

We suspect there is considerable latent public enthusiasm for changes that would wrest control of the s-frame from powerful special interests. Indeed, perhaps ironically, many populist movements seem to call for systemic reform, claiming they want to "clean up" politics or "drain the swamp." Such enthusiasm partly drives the appeal of anti-elite "populism" in its many forms, evidenced in the Brexit referendum in the UK; the rise of populist leaders in Brazil, India, and Europe; and, as we write, a second term for Donald Trump as US president. Of course, in reality populist political platforms are often more corrupt and more easily controlled by powerful interests than the traditional political parties they replace. By whatever means, however—whether fueled by populist rhetoric or supported by logical argument—we need concrete action to weaken the hold of the rich and powerful whose interests so often diverge greatly from the common good. Changing the rules of the game is all the more important at a time of pressing social and environmental problems combined with the increasing fragility of democracy itself.

Writing this book has taken us in unexpected directions. We started out frustrated by the ineffectiveness of individual-focused behavioral interventions (including those that we ourselves were developing and testing) to make meaningful inroads into persistent social problems. But as we dug deeper into the question of why nudges often came up short, we began to see our work and that of many of our talented colleagues as unintentionally supporting the agenda of special interests, which try to distract the public debate by focusing on individuals rather than on rules and systems, where the real levers for change are found.

In the process of advancing these views, we discovered that, while our ideas are controversial, we are by no means alone. Partway through writing this book, we decided to crystallize and clarify our thinking by writing a journal article, "The i-Frame and the s-Frame: How Focusing on the Individual Has Led Public Policy Astray." These days, authors usually put their draft papers on online repositories while they go through the lengthy and often rather bruising process of peer review (where the journal asks our colleagues to evaluate our work, usually eliciting a mix of trenchant critiques and constructive suggestions). On March 11, 2022, we put our paper up on the Social Sciences Research Network repository, with every expectation that it would make few, if any, ripples in the behavioral public policy community. To our astonishment, though, we seemed to have struck a nerve. We learned from students and colleagues that our paper was picking up social media attention (social media Luddites ourselves, we had missed this entirely); an article on the paper—while it was still only an online draft—appeared in the *Financial Times*.[8] The paper has, as we write this, been downloaded 17,458 times, giving it a rank of 442 on SSRN. That might not sound all that great until you know that it is competing with 1,520,408 other papers, putting it in the top .03 percent of papers on SSRN.

This doesn't say much about the quality of our paper. As with pretty much everything else, the relation between "popularity" and quality is loose at best for academic papers. But it did tell us that we had indeed hit a nerve. We'd never had a reaction anything like this before, and probably never will again. Discussing it with our more enthusiastic colleagues, we found that our ideas were attractive not because of any staggering novelty, but rather because we had set out a viewpoint that had been bubbling up across the field for a while but had not before, as it were, been "spoken aloud." Perhaps not surprisingly, the reviews for our paper, solicited by the leading journal *Behavioral and Brain Sciences*, were mixed, ranging from the wildly enthusiastic to the vehemently critical. One bad review can often kill a paper's publication chances at a top journal. Happily for us, the journal took a chance and gave us the green light; and, as is usual with this journal, it then asked for commentaries from our academic colleagues from a wide range of disciplines (including, not surprisingly, Richard Thaler and Cass Sunstein, the authors of *Nudge*).

Exposure to our critics, and supporters, turned out to be extremely valuable in helping us to think through, and extend, our own arguments in this book. Perhaps the biggest surprise, however, was the incredibly positive reaction we got from so many people. We have been overwhelmed by the volume of positive emails we have received from colleagues saying they had long held just the reservations about the i-frame that we express in these pages. Academia is intended to be a forum for debate, and we hope this book will contribute to maintaining the vibrancy of the debate, by collectively considering, and where necessary changing, the rules of the game in a way that goes with the grain of human nature.

Like most people in our field, and perhaps like many readers of this book, we became entranced by the cognitive and behavioral sciences partly because we had the (admittedly nebulous) feeling that understanding human nature and human society should surely help change the world for the better. We've personally been on what, in retrospect, seems like a long detour, as we focused our sights on individual thoughts and choices, and took the rules of the game as fixed. The rules are, however, *not* fixed, but in continual flux and under perpetual strain—often by special interests with narrow agendas, rather than concern for the common good. We urgently need to fight back. We need to harness insights into human nature and society to help take back control of our democratic processes, clear away the influence of special interests in all their manifestations, and begin to rewrite the rules to help fix the urgent social and environmental problems we face.

ACKNOWLEDGMENTS

David Hagmann, Ralph Hertwig, Theresa Marteau, Katy Milkman, Joachim Vosgerau, and Donna Harsch read through the whole book and provided detailed comments and suggestions, which improved the book considerably. Critical friends and colleagues, who might disagree strongly with some of arguments, helped sharpen our thinking and strengthen our arguments. Both in written comments on the whole manuscript and in various in-person conversations, Max Bazerman helped us to identify weaknesses in our argument. Thanks, too, to Cait Lamberton for her valuable feedback and input, especially on Chapter 9. Katy Milkman provided a range of useful critiques in the course of two public debates (with George) over the paper that emerged as we wrote this book—the first of which she famously (at least in our small group of policy nerds) opened with the memorable statement "I despise this paper." David Laibson provided enormously helpful guidance (and corrected some of our misconceptions) on the topic of retirement. We also gained a wide range of insights from the thirty-four people who wrote commentaries on the original paper, many (although not perhaps a majority) critical. One of these, Cass Sunstein, whose commentary accused us of being conspiracy theorists, also wrote a more extended response, accusing us of being reactionaries. And this, while he and George were busy and happily writing papers together on other topics—a model, in our view, for constructive academic engagement. Christina Roberto and Troy Brennan provided invaluable feedback on Chapters 2 and 4, respectively. Warm thanks to Dan Connolly for his terrific input to the ideas in Chapter 9. Our thinking has been shaped by, and in reaction to, stimulating conversation with Todd Cherry, David Hagmann, Sam Issacharoff, Jules Lobel, Graham Loomes, Scott Morgenstern, Adam Oliver, Nachum Sicherman, Bob Sugden, Peter Ubel, Leaf Van Boven, and Kevin Volpp, among many others. Adam, and Craig Fox, have also helped establish the subfield of behavioral public policy, of which this book is an example.

We'd like to thank John Mahaney, our editor at PublicAffairs, both for backing this project from the outset and for his detailed suggestions on the manuscript, and T. J. Kelleher and his team, including Gillian Sutliff and Melissa Veronesi, for helping the book through the final stages. We'd also like to thank our wonderful agents, Catherine Clarke at Felicity Bryan Associates and George Lucas at InkWell Management. Thanks to Rebekah Yore for her excellent work on our figures, to Roger Labrie for his superb job line editing the manuscript, to Christina Sotirescu for her amazing work sorting out our footnotes, and to our excellent copyeditor, Glenn Novak. Thanks to David Hagmann, Sam Issacharoff, and Hildie Leyser for help with our title. And a special thank-you to Stephen Heyman, whose amazing literary skills did so much to knock this book into shape.

NOTES

Introduction: Change the Game, Not the Players

1. The behavioral sciences, of course, encompass a wide range of different perspectives. Behavioral decision research, which has provided the main underpinning of behavioral economics (and from which the latter gets its name), has focused on biases and errors of human decision-making—phenomena such as biases in judging the probabilities of events, overweighting immediate consequences of decisions, and overweighting (or in some cases ignoring) small probability outcomes. Other accounts of human judgment and decision-making have either not emphasized these issues of rationality or have assumed that, although people may make suboptimal individual choices, these reflect some kind of larger "ecological" rationality—e.g., Gerd Gigerenzer, Ralph Hertwig, Ulrich Hoffrage, and Peter Sedlmeier, "Cognitive Illusions Reconsidered," in *Handbook of Experimental Economics Results*, vol. 1 (Elsevier, 2008), 1018–1034.

2. Nor is the demarcation between i-frame and s-frame always clear-cut. For the consumer, for example, graphic health warnings on cigarette packages operate at the i-frame level, aiming to influence (but not constrain) individual choices. But for the tobacco industry, these labels represent s-frame change, being required by law.

3. Providing people with better information to make more-informed choices is the essence of an approach to public policy dubbed "boosting" by Ralph Hertwig, its central proponent: see Ralph Hertwig, "When to Consider Boosting: Some Rules for Policy-Makers," *Behavioural Public Policy* 1, no. 2 (2017): 143–161. For early discussions of the variety of behaviorally inspired policy interventions see, e.g., Adam Oliver, ed., *Behavioural Public Policy* (Cambridge University Press, 2013); Eldar Shafir, *The Behavioral Foundations of Public Policy* (Princeton University Press, 2012); George Loewenstein and Nick Chater, "Putting Nudges in Perspective," *Behavioral Public Policy* 1, no. 1 (2017): 26–53.

4. Jennifer Plebani Lussier, Sarah H. Heil, Joan A. Mongeon, Gary J. Badger, and Stephen T. Higgins, "A Meta-Analysis of Voucher-Based Reinforcement Therapy for Substance Use Disorders," *Addiction* 101, no. 2 (2006): 192–203.

5. George Loewenstein, Cass R. Sunstein, and Russell Golman, "Disclosure: Psychology Changes Everything," *Annual Review of Economics* 6, no. 1 (2014): 391–419.

6. Jessica Wisdom, Julie S. Downs, and George Loewenstein, "Promoting Healthy Choices: Information Versus Convenience," *American Economic Journal: Applied Economics* 2, no. 2 (2010): 164–178.

7. Charles J. Courtemanche, David E. Frisvold, David Jimenez-Gomez, Mariétou H. Ouayogodé, and Michael K. Price, "Chain Restaurant Calorie Posting Laws, Obesity, and Consumer Welfare," *Journal of the European Economic Association* (2025); see also Cass R. Sunstein, "Ruining Popcorn? The Welfare Effects of Information," *Journal of Risk and Uncertainty* 58 (2019): 121–142.

8. Richard H. Thaler and Cass R. Sunstein, "Libertarian Paternalism," *American Economic Review* 93, no. 2 (2003): 175–179; also Cass R. Sunstein and Richard H. Thaler, "Libertarian Paternalism Is Not an Oxymoron," *University of Chicago Law Review* 70, no. 4 (2003): 1159–1202; Colin Camerer, Samuel Issacharoff, George Loewenstein, Ted O'Donoghue, and Matthew Rabin, "Regulation for Conservatives: Behavioral Economics and the Case for 'Asymmetric Paternalism,'" *University of Pennsylvania Law Review* 151, no. 3 (2003): 1211–1254.

9. In this spirit, nudge has been labeled "the small BIG": Steve J. Martin, Noah Goldstein, and Robert Cialdini, *The Small Big: Small Changes That Spark Big Influence* (Hachette UK, 2014).

10. Barack Obama, "Executive Order—Using Behavioral Science Insights to Better Serve the American People," White House, September 15, 2015, https:// obamawhitehouse.archives.gov/the-press-office/2015/09/15/executive-order-using -behavioral-science-insights-better-serve-american.

11. "How Does 'Nudging' Work as an Intervention Technique?," World Economic Forum, October 15, 2021, www.weforum.org/agenda/2021/10/what-is-nudging-and -how-has-it-changed-over-time/.

12. Gerd Gigerenzer, "On the Supposed Evidence for Libertarian Paternalism," *Review of Philosophy and Psychology* 6 (2015): 361–383; Vincent Berthet and Benjamin Ouvrard, "Nudge: Towards a Consensus View?," *Psychology and Cognitive Science* 5 (2019): 1–5.

13. Cass R. Sunstein, "The Rhetoric of Reaction Redux," *Behavioural Public Policy* 7, no. 3 (2023): 828–829.

14. Justin Bank, "Palin vs. Obama: Death Panels," Factcheck.org, August 14, 2009, www.factcheck.org/2009/08/palin-vs-obama-death-panels/.

15. As Troyen Brennan, the longtime chief medical officer of CVS and decidedly not a socialist, writes, "The opponents of health care reform that would improve access through a government-controlled system often refer to the reformers' goal as 'socialized medicine.' The term is pejorative and was first used by the American Medical Association to attack health care reforms backed by the Truman administration more than 70 years ago." Troyen A. Brennan, *The Transformation of American Health Insurance: On the Path to Medicare for All* (Johns Hopkins University Press, 2024), ix.

16. Fossil fuel companies have been spectacularly successful in influencing governments around the world. A recent International Monetary Fund study finds that the fossil fuel industry benefits from hundreds of billions of dollars of direct subsidies annually, while at the same time creating damage to the climate estimated by the IMF to total an extraordinary $5.9 trillion per annum. "Fossil Fuel Subsidies," International Monetary Fund, accessed December 3, 2024, www.imf.org/en/Topics /climate-change/energy-subsidies.

17. Mancur Olson Jr., *The Logic of Collective Action: Public Goods and the Theory of Groups* (Harvard University Press, 1971). The implications of Olson's viewpoint, and indeed the perspective of our book, was prefigured by Adam Smith in 1776: "The proposal of any new law or regulation of commerce which comes from this order [of employers] ought always to be listened to with great precaution, and ought never to be adopted till after having been long and carefully examined, not only with the most scrupulous, but with the most suspicious attention. It comes from an order of men whose interest is never exactly the same with that of the public, who have generally an interest to deceive and even to oppress the public, and who accordingly have, upon many occasions, both deceived and oppressed it." Adam Smith, *The Wealth of Nations*, ed. Edwin Cannan (New York: Bantam Classics, 2003/1776), Book I, chap. 11, 339.

18. Daron Acemoglu and James A. Robinson, *Why Nations Fail: The Origins of Power, Prosperity, and Poverty* (reprint ed., Crown Currency, 2013); Simon Johnson and Daron Acemoglu, *Power and Progress: Our Thousand-Year Struggle over Technology and Prosperity* (Hachette UK, 2023).

19. Max Roser and Hannah Ritchie, "Share of Adults Defined as Obese," Our World in Data, accessed November 2, 2024, https://ourworldindata.org/grapher /share-of-adults-defined-as-obese?tab=table.

20. The solutions that emerge to solve these problems are often complex, involving turn-taking or quotas to limit individual use of the common resource; agreed systems for monitoring, punishment, and dispute resolution; mechanisms for ensuring that subgroups (or intruders) cannot subvert the system; and so on, as documented in a variety of detailed case studies by the Nobel Prize–winning work of political scientist and economist Elinor Ostrom and colleagues. These solutions often arise bottom-up within communities depending on the farmland, forestry, or fisheries, without imposition of central government control—and, indeed, the creation and maintenance of these systems are essential to the economic survival of the communities concerned.

21. Eric J. Johnson and Daniel Goldstein, "Do Defaults Save Lives?," *Science* 302, no. 5649 (2003): 1338–1339.

22. Alberto Molina-Pérez, David Rodríguez-Arias, and Janet Delgado, "Differential Impact of Opt-In, Opt-Out Policies on Deceased Organ Donation Rates: A Mixed Conceptual and Empirical Study," *British Medical Journal Open* 12, no. 9 (2022): e057107.

23. Another much discussed, and seemingly successful, nudge aimed to reduce the high rates of nonenrollment in the US's Earned Income Tax Credit (EITC). In "Psychological Frictions and the Incomplete Take-Up of Social Benefits: Evidence from an IRS Field Experiment," *American Economic Review* 105, no. 11 (2015): 3489–3529. Saurabh Bhargava and Dayanand Manoli reported a randomized controlled trial in which different individuals who were eligible to collect the EITC, but had failed to do so, were randomly assigned to receive different reminder mailings. The authors found that the nudge of merely receiving the reminder mailing, only months after receipt of an initial letter, led 22 percent of those who had previously failed to do so to take up the benefit. Moreover, comparing different letter formats they tested, the authors concluded that the most effective interventions they tested, if applied to the 35 percent of eligible nonclaimants, "could reduce incomplete take-up from 10 percent to 7 percent, among tax filers, and from 25 percent to 22 percent, overall," which "would result

in an estimated increase in annual disbursements of $503 million." Again, however, subsequent work has undermined these optimistic claims. In an especially comprehensive follow-up study also addressing EITC take-up, Elizabeth Linos and colleagues reported six large-scale field experiments that carefully varied the communications that households received, by content, design, "messenger" (e.g., government or an NGO), and mode (letter, text message). Dispiritingly, they concluded that there was "no evidence that [these messages] affected households' likelihood of filing a tax return or claiming the credit"; see Elizabeth Linos, Allen Prohofsky, Aparna Ramesh, Jesse Rothstein, and Matthew Unrath, "Can Nudges Increase Take-Up of the EITC? Evidence from Multiple Field Experiments," *American Economic Journal: Economic Policy* 14, no. 4 (2022): 432–452.

24. "Organ Donation: Lessons from the Spanish Model," *Lancet* 404, no. 10459 (2024): 1171; Michael Hobbes and Peter Shamshiri, hosts, *If Books Could Kill*, "'Nudge' Part 1: A Simple Solution for Littering, Organ Donations and Climate Change," May 4, 2023, 1:10:51, www.buzzsprout.com/2040953/episodes/12780949-nudge-part-1 -a-simple-solution-for-littering-organ-donations-and-climate-change.

25. Stefano DellaVigna and Elizabeth Linos, "RCTs to Scale: Comprehensive Evidence from Two Nudge Units," *Econometrica* 90, no. 1 (2022): 81–116.

26. Shlomo Benartzi, John Beshears, Katherine L. Milkman, et al., "Should Governments Invest More in Nudging?," *Psychological Science* 28, no. 8 (2017): 1041–1055.

27. Dennis Hummel and Alexander Maedche, "How Effective Is Nudging? A Quantitative Review on the Effect Sizes and Limits of Empirical Nudging Studies," *Journal of Behavioral and Experimental Economics* 80 (2019): 47–58.

28. The problem of publication bias is greatly exacerbated when large numbers of studies are conducted with small samples and hence suffer from so-called low statistical power. In a nutshell, the problem with small studies is that only big effects are detectable, and only the detected effects get published, so the average effect size of published studies is inflated, often greatly. To illustrate the problem, imagine that a researcher runs a small study with only fifty participants, half randomly assigned to receive a nudge and half assigned to a no-nudge control condition. Given the small number of participants, the study is only "powered" to detect an effect size of 10 percent or larger. Now imagine that one hundred of such studies are conducted, that five of them produce effect sizes of 10 percent or larger, and that these five studies are submitted for publication and duly published. This is an outcome that should be expected *even if there is no actual effect to be detected*. The average published effect size, then, will be larger than 10 percent (since only studies showing a 10 percent effect size or larger will be published). For a similar effect in daily life, think about how when scanning the night sky over a city, the "average" visible star is relatively bright (only the brightest stars are visible through the smog and light pollution); in the middle of the desert, the "average" star seems far fainter, because countless dim stars are visible.

29. Jesse Singal, "Daniel Kahneman's Gripe with Behavioral Economics," *Daily Beast*, April 26, 2013, www.thedailybeast.com/articles/2013/04/26/daniel-kahneman -s-gripe-with-behavioral-economics.html.

30. See Avishalom Tor and Jonathan Klick, "When Should Governments Invest More in Nudging? Revisiting Benartzi et al. (2017)," *Review of Law & Economics* 18,

no. 3 (2022): 347–376. Some nudges can also have unintended consequences that may offset their benefits: Linda Thunström, Ben Gilbert, and Chian Jones Ritten, "Nudges That Hurt Those Already Hurting—Distributional and Unintended Effects of Salience Nudges," *Journal of Economic Behavior & Organization* 153 (2018): 267–282; and Linda Thunström, "Welfare Effects of Nudges: The Emotional Tax of Calorie Menu Labeling," *Judgment and Decision Making* 14, no. 1 (2019): 11–25.

31. This is possibly due to sheer organizational inertia, which can be very difficult to overcome from within: see Stefano DellaVigna, Woojin Kim, and Elizabeth Linos, "Bottlenecks for Evidence Adoption," *Journal of Political Economy* 132, no. 8 (2024): 2748–2789.

32. Michael Hobbes and Peter Shamshiri, hosts, *If Books Could Kill*, "'Nudge' Part 2: Mr. Nudge Goes to Washington," May 19, 2023, 1:01:04, www.buzzsprout.com /2040953/episodes/12877671-nudge-part-2-mr-nudge-goes-to-washington.

33. Financial scams are a particularly shocking example. Insecure systems in the financial services sector have created a vast "industry" of fraud; yet victims often feel, and are encouraged to feel, individually culpable for falling for extremely sophisticated scams even where "red flags" have been missed by the banks (see, e.g., Tara Siegel Bernard, "Swindled Savings: How One Man Lost $740,000 to Scammers Targeting His Retirement Savings," *New York Times*, July 29, 2024, www.nytimes.com/2024/07/29 /business/retirement-savings-scams.html). Regulation in the UK, at least, is gradually shifting responsibility to the banks (e.g., "Banks Must Reimburse Bank Transfer Fraud Victims in New Refund Rules," ITVX, October 7, 2024, www.itv.com/news/2024-10 -07/banks-must-reimburse-bank-transfer-fraud-victims-in-new-refund-rules). Customer security is now becoming a higher priority for the financial services industry.

Chapter 1: The Corporate Boot That Made the Carbon Footprint

1. Michael E. Mann, *The New Climate War: The Fight to Take Back Our Planet* (PublicAffairs, 2021).

2. William Safire, "On Language: Footprint," *New York Times Magazine*, February 17, 2008, www.nytimes.com/2008/02/17/magazine/17wwln-safire-t.html.

3. Gregory Solman, "BP: Coloring Public Opinion?," *Adweek*, January 14, 2008, www.adweek.com/brand-marketing/bp-coloring-public-opinion-91662/.

4. The US Environmental Protection Agency has developed a carbon calculator, and major newspapers have guides for helping people take individual action (e.g., "How Can I Reduce My Carbon Footprint?," *New York Times*, November 28, 2015, www.nytimes.com/interactive/projects/cp/climate/2015-paris-climate-talks /how-can-we-slow-climate-change). BP's wider campaign won a Golden Effie in 2007, a major advertising industry award (http://current.effie.org/downloads/org_downloads /2007_Awards_Journal.pdf).

5. P. Wesley Schultz, Jessica M. Nolan, Robert B. Cialdini, Noah J. Goldstein, and Vladas Griskevicius, "The Constructive, Destructive, and Reconstructive Power of Social Norms," *Psychological Science* 18, no. 5 (2007): 429–434.

6. David Cameron, "The Next Age of Government," TED Talk, London, UK, February 2010, www.ted.com/talks/david_cameron_the_next_age_of_government.

7. George Lakoff, *The ALL NEW Don't Think of an Elephant!: Know Your Values and Frame the Debate* (Chelsea Green, 2014).

8. Joshua Schwartzstein and Adi Sunderam, "Using Models to Persuade," *American Economic Review* 111, no. 1 (2021): 276–323.

9. Pierre Bajgrowicz and Olivier Scaillet, "Technical Trading Revisited: False Discoveries, Persistence Tests, and Transaction Costs," *Journal of Financial Economics* 106, no. 3 (2012): 473–491; Nancy Pennington and Reid Hastie, "Explaining the Evidence: Tests of the Story Model for Juror Decision Making," *Journal of Personality and Social Psychology* 62, no. 2 (1992): 189–206.

10. Jane Thier, "Exxon Mobil CEO on the 'Dirty Secret' of Net Zero: 'People Who Are Generating the Emissions Need to Be Aware . . . and Pay the Price,'" *Fortune*, February 27, 2024, https://fortune.com/2024/02/27/exxon-ceo-darren-woods-interview-pay-the-price-for-net-zero/.

11. For examples of discussion of what needs to be done see, e.g., Peter Cramton, David J. C. MacKay, Axel Ockenfels, and Steven Stoft, *Global Carbon Pricing: The Path to Climate Cooperation* (MIT Press, 2017), http://library.oapen.org/handle/20.500.12657/26042; Jochen Markard, "The Next Phase of the Energy Transition and Its Implications for Research and Policy," *Nature Energy* 3, no. 8 (2018): 628–633; *Keeping 1.5°C Alive: Actions for the 2020s* (Energy Transition Commission, 2021), www.energy-transitions.org/publications/keeping-1-5-alive/; David Klenert, Linus Mattauch, Emmanuel Combet, et al., "Making Carbon Pricing Work for Citizens," *Nature Climate Change* 8, no. 8 (2018): 669–677; Thomas Hale, Thom Wetzer, Selam Kidane Abebe, et al., "Regulating Net Zero: From Groundswell to Ground Rules," *Nature Climate Change* 14, no. 4 (2024): 306–308.

12. Geoffrey Supran and Naomi Oreskes, "Rhetoric and Frame Analysis of ExxonMobil's Climate Change Communications," *One Earth* 4, no. 5 (2021): 696–719. The quotations from advertorials in the rest of this paragraph are taken from this paper.

13. Imogen Learmonth, "How the 'Carbon Footprint' Originated as a PR Campaign for Big Oil," *Thred*, September 23, 2020, https://thred.com/change/how-the-carbon-footprint-originated-as-a-pr-campaign-for-big-oil/.

14. BP's approach has been widely adopted by the media. For example, *The New York Times* has published dozens of articles focusing on the role of individual behavior in combating climate change, via individual decisions we make about what we eat, how and where we travel, and how we heat and light our houses. Environmentalists have developed sophisticated analyses of how individuals can change their behavior to reduce their carbon footprints: e.g., Chris Goodall, *How to Live a Low-Carbon Life: The Individual's Guide to Stopping Climate Change* (Earthscan, 2007).

15. Chris Goodall, "How to Reduce Your Carbon Footprint," *Guardian*, January 19, 2017, www.theguardian.com/environment/2017/jan/19/how-to-reduce-carbon-footprint. Goodall, a very thoughtful and well-informed analyst of the carbon transition, does also note the importance of political pressure; see also Debra Kamin, "What You Can Do at Home to Help Stem Climate Change," *New York Times*, July 26, 2023, www.nytimes.com/2023/07/26/realestate/homeowne-climate-change-tips.html.

16. For example, Nick Chater, "Nudging to Net Zero?," in *Delivering Net Zero*, ed. Ryan Shorthouse and Patrick Hall (Bright Blue, 2020), 188–192, http://brightblue.org.uk/wp-content/uploads/2020/05/Final-Delivering-net-zero.pdf. See also Hunt Allcott and Todd Rogers, "The Short-Run and Long-Run Effects of Behavioral Interventions:

Experimental Evidence from Energy Conservation," *American Economic Review* 104, no. 10 (2014): 3003–3037.

17. Ulf Liebe, Jennifer Gewinner, and Andreas Diekmann, "Large and Persistent Effects of Green Energy Defaults in the Household and Business Sectors," *Nature Human Behaviour* 5, no. 5 (2021): 576–585.

18. Cass R. Sunstein, "Green Defaults Can Combat Climate Change," *Nature Human Behaviour* 5, no. 5 (2021): 548.

19. Such a policy could not be applied universally, because there would not be sufficient green energy to "go round." Admittedly, if rolled out almost universally, the policy might generate a sufficient "premium" for green energy to increase long-term investment. But that very premium would cause more users to switch away from the green tariff, as well as generating a likely media and political backlash. Moreover, the cost of such investment would fall on consumers unequally, allowing free-riders to opt out of investing in the public good of green energy, which is likely to be politically divisive.

20. Anne Marike Lokhorst, Carol Werner, Henk Staats, Eric van Dijk, and Jeff L. Gale, "Commitment and Behavior Change: A Meta-Analysis and Critical Review of Commitment-Making Strategies in Environmental Research," *Environment and Behavior* 45, no. 1 (2013): 3–34; Wokje Abrahamse, Linda Steg, Charles Vlek, and Talib Rothengatter, "A Review of Intervention Studies Aimed at Household Energy Conservation," *Journal of Environmental Psychology* 25, no. 3 (2005): 273–291; Giacomo Marangoni and Massimo Tavoni, "Real-Time Feedback on Electricity Consumption: Evidence from a Field Experiment in Italy," *Energy Efficiency* 14, no. 1 (2021): 13.

21. Claudia F. Nisa, Jocelyn J. Bélanger, Birga M. Schumpe, and Daiane G. Faller, "Meta-Analysis of Randomised Controlled Trials Testing Behavioural Interventions to Promote Household Action on Climate Change," *Nature Communications* 10, no. 1 (2019): 4545. These conclusions, if anything, presumably *overstate* the likely potential of nudges. The authors report that the effects were even more disappointing when the sample was restricted to studies that were not vulnerable to self-selection bias—i.e., in which participants actively "opt in" to the study. Moreover, when studies that were vulnerable to "small-sample bias" were eliminated (resulting from the fact that small studies, by chance, are more likely to produce erroneous results), the effects of the nudges were not discernible.

22. David Hagmann, Emily H. Ho, and George Loewenstein, "Nudging Out Support for a Carbon Tax," *Nature Climate Change* 9, no. 6 (2019): 484–489.

23. Seth H. Werfel, "Household Behaviour Crowds Out Support for Climate Change Policy When Sufficient Progress Is Perceived," *Nature Climate Change* 7, no. 7 (2017): 512–515.

24. Tariq Fancy, "The Secret Diary of a 'Sustainable Investor'—Part 1," *Medium*, August 20, 2021, https://medium.com/@sosofancy/the-secret-diary-of-a-sustainable -investor-part-1-70b6987fa139.

25. Interestingly, even a trenchant critic of Fancy's position largely agrees with his analysis of the current state-of-play in ESG (taking this to be widely agreed in the ESG community) but is more optimistic about the future of ESG. Robert G. Eccles, "A Critique of Tariq Fancy's Critique of ESG Investing: An Interview with Clara Miller," *Forbes*, last updated April 21, 2022, www.forbes.com/sites/bobeccles/2021/10/01/a-critique -of-tariq-fancys-critique-of-esg-investing-an-interview-with-clara-miller/.

26. Tariq Fancy, "The Secret Diary of a 'Sustainable Investor'—Part 4 (Epilogue)," *Medium*, June 20, 2022, https://medium.com/@sosofancy/the-secret-diary-of-a-sustainable-investor-part-4-epilogue-f18304fd9db7.

27. This view is encapsulated in the title of his op-ed in Canada's *Globe and Mail*: Tariq Fancy, "BlackRock Hired Me to Make Sustainable Investing Mainstream. Now I Realize It's a Deadly Distraction from the Climate-Change Threat," *Globe and Mail*, last updated March 30, 2021, www.theglobeandmail.com/business/commentary/article-sustainable-investing-is-a-deadly-distraction-from-actually-averting/.

28. Tariq Fancy, "The Secret Diary of a 'Sustainable Investor'—Part 3," *Medium*, August 20, 2021, https://medium.com/@sosofancy/the-secret-diary-of-a-sustainable-investor-part-3-3c238cb0dcbf.

29. Brent S. Steel, "Thinking Globally and Acting Locally? Environmental Attitudes, Behaviour and Activism," *Journal of Environmental Management* 47, no. 1 (1996): 27–36. See also Peter Andre, Teodora Boneva, Felix Chopra, and Armin Falk, "Globally Representative Evidence on the Actual and Perceived Support for Climate Action," *Nature Climate Change* 14, no. 3 (2024): 253–259.

30. Classic psychological theories in which people (at least in part) infer their preferences and values from their actions include attribution theory, cognitive dissonance theory, and self-perception theory. See, respectively, Harold H. Kelley, "Attribution Theory in Social Psychology," in *Nebraska Symposium on Motivation* 15, ed. David Levine (University of Nebraska Press, 1967); Leon Festinger, *A Theory of Cognitive Dissonance* (Stanford University Press, 1957); and Daryl J. Bem, "Self-Perception: An Alternative Interpretation of Cognitive Dissonance Phenomena," *Psychological Review* 74, no. 3 (1967): 183–200. The literature of relevant experiments is vast; recent examples include demonstrations of "choice blindness," in Petter Johansson, Lars Hall, Sverker Sikström, and Andreas Olsson, "Failure to Detect Mismatches Between Intention and Outcome in a Simple Decision Task," *Science* 310, no. 5745 (2005): 116–119.

31. Moreover, we note that crowd-out is only a small and inessential part of our overall argument. The central elements of our argument are (1) that nudges and other i-frame interventions are too weak to address major public policy issues; (2) that s-frame reform is sorely needed, and there is often a policy consensus regarding the types of reforms that will work; and (3) that corporations and other vested interests have tended to publicly promote i-frame approaches while simultaneously lobbying against these s-frame reforms and, indeed, working to reshape s-frame policies to further benefit themselves.

32. Michael E. Mann, *The New Climate War: The Fight to Take Back Our Planet* (PublicAffairs, 2021), 82.

33. Oliver A. Williams, "118 Private Jets Take Leaders to COP26 Climate Summit Burning Over 1,000 Tons of CO^2," *Forbes*, last updated April 21, 2022, www.forbes.com/sites/oliverwilliams1/2021/11/05/118-private-jets-take-leaders-to-cop26-climate-summit-burning-over-1000-tons-of-co2/.

34. Shahzeen Z. Attari, David H. Krantz, and Elke U. Weber, "Statements About Climate Researchers' Carbon Footprints Affect Their Credibility and the Impact of Their Advice," *Climatic Change* 138 (2016): 325–338.

35. Amy Westervelt, "Big Oil Is Trying to Make Climate Change Your Problem to Solve," *Rolling Stone*, May 14, 2021, www.rollingstone.com/politics/politics-news/climate-change-exxonmobil-harvard-study-1169682/.

36. Aylin Woodward, "As Denying Climate Change Becomes Impossible, Fossil-Fuel Interests Pivot to 'Carbon Shaming,'" *Business Insider*, August 28, 2021, www.business insider.com/fossil-fuel-interests-target-climate-advocates-personally-2021-8.

37. Marc Kaufmann, Peter Andre, and Botond Kőszegi, "Understanding Markets with Socially Responsible Consumers," *Quarterly Journal of Economics* 139, no. 3 (2024): 1989–2035.

38. If they don't, the dampening problem arises more directly. If green-oriented Country A reduces fossil fuel use, the oil price falls; but then unscrupulous Country B, which has no such concerns, has an incentive to use more fossil fuels, as they are now cheaper; and, there is a net transfer of wealth from Country A to Country B.

39. Scaling up this general style of argument dramatically (beyond the level of the individual, for a moment), note that if most nations succeed in completely decarbonizing, this will significantly reduce the price of the remaining coal, gas, and oil—and thus encourage those nations that are willing to burn carbon to burn more of it, slowing the progress of decarbonization at a global level. Enforceable international agreements, probably with financial compensation for nations with cheaply extractable fossil fuel reserves, are almost certainly required to counter this type of problem. For wider discussion of the need for regulation to overcome "carbon lock-in" see Karen C. Seto, Steven J. Davis, Ronald B. Mitchell, Eleanor C. Stokes, Gregory Unruh, and Diana Ürge-Vorsatz, "Carbon Lock-In: Types, Causes, and Policy Implications," *Annual Review of Environment and Resources* 41, no. 1 (2016): 425–452.

40. Insulation is particularly cost-effective, though largely abandoned in the UK for opaque political reasons. Simon Evans, "Analysis: Cutting the 'Green Crap' Has Added £22bn to U.K. Energy Bills Since 2015," *Carbon Brief*, June 18, 2024, www.carbon brief.org/analysis-cutting-the-green-crap-has-added-22bn-to-uk-energy-bills-since -2015/.

41. Andrew Van Dam, "The Real Reason Trucks Have Taken Over U.S. Roadways," *Washington Post*, April 7, 2023, www.washingtonpost.com/business/2023/04/07 /trucks-outnumber-cars/.

42. Josh Gabbatiss, "'Drill, Baby, Drill': The Surprising History of Donald Trump's Fossil Fuel Slogan," *Carbon Brief*, March 18, 2024, www.carbonbrief.org /drill-baby-drill-the-surprising-history-of-donald-trumps-fossil-fuel-slogan/.

43. For a variety of recent perspectives varying in optimism see, e.g., David Wallace-Wells, *The Uninhabitable Earth: Life After Warming* (Tim Duggan Books, 2019); Mark Lynas, *Our Final Warning: Six Degrees of Climate Emergency* (Fourth Estate, 2020); Hannah Ritchie, *Not the End of the World: How We Can Be the First Generation to Build a Sustainable Planet* (Little, Brown Spark, 2024).

Chapter 2: Obesity: Blaming the Victim

1. Ali Rafei, Michael R. Elliott, Rebecca E. Jones, Fernando Riosmena, Solveig A. Cunningham, and Neil K. Mehta, "Obesity Incidence in US Children and Young Adults: A Pooled Analysis," *American Journal of Preventive Medicine* 63, no. 1 (2022): 51–59; Gianna Melillo, "Childhood Obesity Is Surging: What to Know About Rising Rates and Efforts to Curb Them," *Hill*, February 24, 2023, https:// thehill.com/changing-america/well-being/prevention-cures/3871475-childhood -obesity-is-surging-what-to-know-about-rising-rates-and-efforts-to-curb-them/.

2. Miao Liu and Ye Sun, "Understanding Blame in the Context of Childhood Obesity," *Health Communication* 39, no. 9 (2024): 1684–1704.

3. Rebecca M. Puhl and Chelsea A. Heuer, "The Stigma of Obesity: A Review and Update," *Obesity* 17, no. 5 (2009): 941; Rebecca A. Krukowski, Delia Smith West, Amanda Philyaw Perez, Zoran Bursac, Martha M. Phillips, and James M. Raczynski, "Overweight Children, Weight-Based Teasing and Academic Performance," *International Journal of Pediatric Obesity* 4, no. 4 (2009): 274–280; Sean M. Phelan, Diana J. Burgess, Mark W. Yeazel, Wendy L. Hellerstedt, Joan M. Griffin, and Michelle van Ryn, "Impact of Weight Bias and Stigma on Quality of Care and Outcomes for Patients with Obesity," *Obesity Reviews* 16, no. 4 (2015): 319–326.

4. Janet Polivy and C. Peter Herman have done seminal research on what they call the "false hope syndrome" among dieters, as well as on the mental health benefits (and lack of impact on weight) of an "undiet," in which people are encouraged to not diet: Janet Polivy and C. Peter Herman, "The Effects of Resolving to Diet on Restrained and Unrestrained Eaters: The 'False Hope Syndrome,'" *International Journal of Eating Disorders* 26, no. 4 (1999): 434–447; Janet Polivy and C. Peter Herman, "Undieting: A Program to Help People Stop Dieting," *International Journal of Eating Disorders* 11, no. 3 (1992): 261–268.

5. A. Janet Tomiyama, Deborah Carr, Ellen M. Granberg, et al., "How and Why Weight Stigma Drives the Obesity 'Epidemic' and Harms Health," *BMC Medicine* 16 (2018): 1–6; Rebecca Puhl and Young Suh, "Health Consequences of Weight Stigma: Implications for Obesity Prevention and Treatment," *Current Obesity Reports* 4 (2015): 182–190.

6. "Obesity Rates by Country 2024," World Population Review, accessed November 2, 2024, https://worldpopulationreview.com/country-rankings/obesity-rates -by-country.

7. *WHO European Regional Obesity Report 2022* (Copenhagen, World Health Organization Regional Office for Europe, 2022), www.who.int/europe/publications/i /item/9789289057738. In this chapter we set aside the wider and very serious problems associated with eating disorders such as anorexia nervosa and bulimia nervosa. It seems likely that these, too, are rising in response to some of the same factors underlying increases in obesity, although available data are patchy. More generally, the relationship between eating disorders and obesity is complex and not well understood: Eric Stice, Rebecca P. Cameron, Joel D. Killen, Chris Hayward, and C. Barr Taylor, "Naturalistic Weight-Reduction Efforts Prospectively Predict Growth in Relative Weight and Onset of Obesity Among Female Adolescents," *Journal of Consulting and Clinical Psychology* 67, no. 6 (1999): 967–974; Joel D. Killen, C. Barr Taylor, Chris Hayward, et al., "Weight Concerns Influence the Development of Eating Disorders: A 4-Year Prospective Study," *Journal of Consulting and Clinical Psychology* 64, no. 5 (1996): 936–940; Lori M. Irving and Dianne Neumark-Sztainer, "Integrating the Prevention of Eating Disorders and Obesity: Feasible or Futile?," *Preventive Medicine* 34, no. 3 (2002): 299–309.

8. Eating disorder rates in Japan are high and appear to be increasing: Yoshikatsu Nakai, Kazuko Nin, and Neha J. Goel, "The Changing Profile of Eating Disorders and Related Sociocultural Factors in Japan Between 1700 and 2020: A Systematic Scoping Review," *International Journal of Eating Disorders* 54, no. 1 (2021): 40–53.

9. Tara Templin, Tiago Cravo Oliveira Hashiguchi, Blake Thomson, Joseph Dieleman, and Eran Bendavid, "The Overweight and Obesity Transition from the Wealthy to the Poor in Low- and Middle-Income Countries: A Survey of Household Data from 103 Countries," *PLOS Medicine* 16, no. 11 (2019): e1002968. Even in the US the picture is somewhat more complicated, and differs by demographic group. For women, obesity is most prevalent in the lower two-thirds of the income distribution; for men it is most prevalent in the middle third and less prevalent in both the lowest and highest groups: Cynthia L. Ogden, Tala H. Fakhouri, Margaret D. Carroll, et al., "Prevalence of Obesity Among Adults, by Household Income and Education—United States, 2011–2014," *Morbidity and Mortality Weekly Report* 66, no. 50 (2017): 1369–1373, www.cdc.gov/mmwr/volumes/66/wr/mm6650a1.htm.

10. George W. Bush, "President Bush Highlights Health and Fitness Initiative," White House, July 18, 2003, https://georgewbush-whitehouse.archives.gov/news/releases/2003/07/20030718-6.html.

11. Ashlesha Datar and Nancy Nicosia, "Assessing Social Contagion in Body Mass Index, Overweight, and Obesity Using a Natural Experiment," *Journal of the American Medical Association: Pediatrics* 172, no. 3 (2018): 239–246; Ashlesha Datar, Nancy Nicosia, Amy Mahler, Maria J. Prados, and Madhumita Ghosh-Dastidar, "Association of Place with Adolescent Obesity," *Journal of the American Medical Association: Pediatrics* 177, no. 8 (2023): 847–855.

12. Alison M. Buttenheim, Anne R. Pebley, Katie Hsih, Chang Y. Chung, and Noreen Goldman, "The Shape of Things to Come? Obesity Prevalence Among Foreign-Born vs. US-Born Mexican Youth in California," *Social Science and Medicine* 78 (2013): 1–8; Nicholas A. Christakis and James H. Fowler, "The Spread of Obesity in a Large Social Network over 32 Years," *New England Journal of Medicine* 357, no. 4 (2007): 370–379.

13. David M. Cutler, Edward L. Glaeser, and Jesse M. Shapiro, "Why Have Americans Become More Obese?," *Journal of Economic Perspectives* 17, no. 3 (2003): 93–118.

14. Eric A. Finkelstein, Christopher J. Ruhm, and Katherine M. Kosa, "Economic Causes and Consequences of Obesity," *Annual Review of Public Health* 26, no. 1 (2005): 239–257.

15. Marion Nestle persuasively attributes the increase in obesity since 1980 in part to a decrease in the price of sodas and processed foods and an increase in the price of fresh produce. She argues further that this discrepancy in trends is partly attributable to federal agricultural policies and subsidies favoring crops used in processed foods, such as corn and soybeans, rather than fruits and vegetables. Marion Nestle, *Food Politics: How the Food Industry Influences Nutrition and Health* (University of California Press, 2013).

16. Filippa Juul, Niyati Parekh, Euridice Martinez-Steele, Carlos Augusto Monteiro, and Virginia W. Chang, "Ultra-Processed Food Consumption Among US Adults from 2001 to 2018," *American Journal of Clinical Nutrition* 115, no. 1 (2022): 211–221.

17. Grant Ennis, *Dark PR: How Corporate Disinformation Undermines Our Health and the Environment* (Daraja, 2023).

18. Boyd A. Swinburn, Vivica I. Kraak, Steven Allender, et al., "The Global Syndemic of Obesity, Undernutrition, and Climate Change: The *Lancet* Commission Report," *Lancet* 393, no. 10173 (2019): 791–846.

19. Ennis, *Dark PR*, 11.

20. Mike Russo, *Apples to Twinkies: Comparing Federal Subsidies of Fresh Produce and Junk Food* (MassPIRG Education Fund, 2011), https://publicinterestnetwork.org/wp-content/uploads/2012/01/MASSPIRG-Apples-to-Twinkies.pdf.

21. Russo, *Apples to Twinkies*, 8.

22. Christina Sewell, "Removing the Meat Subsidy," *Journal of International Affairs* 73, no. 1 (2019): 307–318.

23. Michael Moss, "The Extraordinary Science of Addictive Junk Food," *New York Times Magazine*, February 20, 2013, www.nytimes.com/2013/02/24/magazine/the-extraordinary-science-of-addictive-junk-food.html; Michael Moss, *Hooked: Food, Free Will, and How the Food Giants Exploit Our Addictions* (Random House, 2021).

24. Marion Nestle and Michael F. Jacobson, "Halting the Obesity Epidemic: A Public Health Policy Approach," *Public Health Reports* 115, no. 1 (2000): 12.

25. Azeen Ghorayshi, "Too Big to Chug: How Our Sodas Got So Huge," *Mother Jones*, June 25, 2012, www.motherjones.com/media/2012/06/supersize-biggest-sodas-mcdonalds-big-gulp-chart/.

26. Lisa R. Young and Marion Nestle, "The Contribution of Expanding Portion Sizes to the US Obesity Epidemic," *American Journal of Public Health* 92, no. 2 (2002): 246–249.

27. Home delivery and "drive-thru" are, according to the consumer research firm NPD, the fastest-growing dining options in the US: "Carry-Out Restaurant Orders Declining as Delivery and Drive-Thru Boom," *Convenience Store News*, May 2, 2022, https://csnews.com/carry-out-restaurant-orders-declining-delivery-drive-thru-boom.

28. Robert Rosenheck, "Fast Food Consumption and Increased Caloric Intake: A Systematic Review of a Trajectory Towards Weight Gain and Obesity Risk," *Obesity Reviews* 9, no. 6 (2008): 535–547; Janet Currie, Stefano DellaVigna, Enrico Moretti, and Vikram Pathania, "The Effect of Fast Food Restaurants on Obesity and Weight Gain," *American Economic Journal: Economic Policy* 2, no. 3 (2010): 32–63; Mika Matsuzaki, Brisa N. Sánchez, Maria Elena Acosta, Jillian Botkin, and Emma V. Sanchez-Vaznaugh, "Food Environment Near Schools and Body Weight: A Systematic Review of Associations by Race/Ethnicity, Gender, Grade, and Socio-Economic Factors," *Obesity Reviews* 21, no. 4 (2020): e12997; Julianne Williams, Peter Scarborough, Anne Matthews, et al., "A Systematic Review of the Influence of the Retail Food Environment Around Schools on Obesity-Related Outcomes," *Obesity Reviews* 15, no. 5 (2014): 359–374.

29. Anahad O'Connor, "Coke and Pepsi Give Millions to Public Health, Then Lobby Against It," *New York Times*, October 10, 2016, www.nytimes.com/2016/10/10/well/eat/coke-and-pepsi-give-millions-to-public-health-then-lobby-against-it.html.

30. William Neuman, "Save the Children Breaks with Soda Tax Effort," *New York Times*, December 14, 2010, www.nytimes.com/2010/12/15/business/15soda.html?searchResultPosition=2.

31. Jason Kessler, "Groups: NYC Soda Ban Unfair to Small, Minority-Owned Businesses," CNN, January 25, 2013, https://edition.cnn.com/2013/01/23/health/new-york-large-drinks/index.html?utm.

32. Marianne Bertrand, Matilde Bombardini, Raymond Fisman, Brad Hackinen, and Francesco Trebbi, "Hall of Mirrors: Corporate Philanthropy and Strategic Advocacy," *Quarterly Journal of Economics* 136, no. 4 (2021): 2675. It could be that a firm merely happens to donate to nonprofits that are, in any case, poised to argue in their favor. Indeed, the untraceability of direct links between lobbying dollars and nonprofit support is one of its attractions to industry.

33. Chase Purdy, "Coca-Cola and Pepsi Have a Strategy to Beat Soda Taxes: Confuse as Many Voters as Possible," *Quartz*, last updated July 20, 2022, https://qz.com/1451209/coca-cola-and-pepsi-have-a-tricky-strategy-to-beat-soda-taxes.

34. Julia Belluz, "Coca-Cola and Pepsi's Deceptive Tactic to Stop Soda Taxes Worked in Washington State," *Vox*, last updated November 7, 2018, www.vox.com/policy-and-politics/2018/11/7/18069890/washington-initiative-1634-results-soda-grocery-tax.

35. Daniel G. Aaron and Michael B. Siegel, "Sponsorship of National Health Organizations by Two Major Soda Companies," *American Journal of Preventive Medicine* 52, no. 1 (2017): 20–30.

36. These figures and those from the preceding paragraph are excerpted from O'Connor, "Coke and Pepsi Give Millions to Public Health."

37. Anahad O'Connor, "Coca-Cola Funds Scientists Who Shift Blame for Obesity Away from Bad Diets," *New York Times*, August 9, 2015, https://archive.nytimes.com/well.blogs.nytimes.com/2015/08/09/coca-cola-funds-scientists-who-shift-blame-for-obesity-away-from-bad-diets/.

38. "How Coca-Cola Disguised Its Influence on Science About Sugar and Health," Union of Concerned Scientists, October 11, 2017, www.ucsusa.org/resources/how-coca-cola-disguised-its-influence-science-about-sugar-and-health.

39. O'Connor, "Coca-Cola Funds Scientists."

40. Pedro Serodio, Gary Ruskin, Martin McKee, and David Stuckler, "Evaluating Coca-Cola's Attempts to Influence Public Health 'In Their Own Words': Analysis of Coca-Cola Emails with Public Health Academics Leading the Global Energy Balance Network," *Public Health Nutrition* 23, no. 14 (2020): 2647–2653, https://doi.org/10.1017/S1368980020002098.

41. Sarah Steele, Gary Ruskin, and David Stuckler, "Pushing Partnerships: Corporate Influence on Research and Policy via the International Life Sciences Institute," *Public Health Nutrition* 23, no. 11 (2020): 2032–2040.

42. Susan Greenhalgh, "Making China Safe for Coke: How Coca-Cola Shaped Obesity Science and Policy in China," *British Medical Journal* 364 (2019): k5050.

43. Aviva Shen, "How Big Food Corporations Watered Down Michelle Obama's 'Let's Move' Campaign," *ThinkProgress*, February 28, 2013, https://archive.thinkprogress.org/how-big-food-corporations-watered-down-michelle-obamas-let-s-move-campaign-85d09b60607b/.

44. Bee Wilson, "How Ultra-Processed Food Took Over Your Shopping Basket," *Guardian*, February 12, 2020, www.theguardian.com/food/2020/feb/13/how-ultra-processed-food-took-over-your-shopping-basket-brazil-carlos-monteiro.

45. Mélissa Mialon, Paulo Sêrodio, and Fernanda Baeza Scagliusi, "Criticism of the NOVA Classification: Who Are the Protagonists?," *World Nutrition* 9, no. 3 (2018): 176–240.

46. Kelly D. Brownell and Katherine Battle Horgen, *Food Fight: The Inside Story of the Food Industry, America's Obesity Crisis, and What We Can Do About It* (McGraw Hill, 2004).

47. "About Us," Center for Consumer Freedom, 2024, https://consumerfreedom.com/about/.

48. Though not generally signing on to the industry-promoted specific idea that the primary problem is lack of exercise and not diet.

49. Julie S. Downs and George Loewenstein, "Behavioral Economics and Obesity," in *The Oxford Handbook of the Social Science of Obesity*, ed. John Cawley (Oxford University Press, 2011); Kevin G. Volpp, Leslie K. John, Andrea B. Troxel, Laurie Norton, Jennifer Fassbender, and George Loewenstein, "Financial Incentive–Based Approaches for Weight Loss: A Randomized Trial," *Journal of the American Medical Association* 300, no. 22 (2008): 2631–2637; J. Jane S. Jue, Matthew J. Press, Daniel McDonald, et al., "The Impact of Price Discounts and Calorie Messaging on Beverage Consumption: A Multi-Site Field Study," *Preventive Medicine* 55, no. 6 (2012): 629–633; Gary Charness and Uri Gneezy, "Incentives to Exercise," *Econometrica* 77, no. 3 (2009): 909–931.

50. Eric M. VanEpps, Julie S. Downs, and George Loewenstein, "Advance Ordering for Healthier Eating? Field Experiments on the Relationship Between the Meal Order–Consumption Time Delay and Meal Content," *Journal of Marketing Research* 53, no. 3 (2016): 369–380.

51. Leslie K. John, George Loewenstein, and Kevin G. Volpp, "Empirical Observations on Longer-Term Use of Incentives for Weight Loss," *Preventive Medicine* 55 (2012): S68–S74.

52. Rachel A. Crockett, Sarah E. King, Theresa M. Marteau, et al., "Nutritional Labelling for Healthier Food or Non-Alcoholic Drink Purchasing and Consumption," *Cochrane Database of Systematic Reviews* no. 2 (2018).

53. Charness and Gneezy, "Incentives to Exercise"; Heather Royer, Mark Stehr, and Justin Sydnor, "Incentives, Commitments, and Habit Formation in Exercise: Evidence from a Field Experiment with Workers at a Fortune-500 Company," *American Economic Journal: Applied Economics* 7, no. 3 (2015): 51–84; Dan Acland and Matthew R. Levy, "Naiveté, Projection Bias, and Habit Formation in Gym Attendance," *Management Science* 61, no. 1 (2015): 146–160.

54. Anneliese Arno and Steve Thomas, "The Efficacy of Nudge Theory Strategies in Influencing Adult Dietary Behaviour: A Systematic Review and Meta-Analysis," *BMC Public Health* 16 (2016): 1–11.

55. Kelly D. Brownell and Kenneth E. Warner, "The Perils of Ignoring History: Big Tobacco Played Dirty and Millions Died. How Similar Is Big Food?," *Milbank Quarterly* 87, no. 1 (2009): 259–294.

56. "U.S. House Bans Quick-Serve Lawsuits," *QSR Magazine*, March 11, 2004, www.qsrmagazine.com/news/us-house-bans-quick-serve-lawsuits/.

57. "US House Bans Fast-Food Lawsuits," *China Daily* website, March 11, 2004, www.chinadaily.com.cn/english/doc/2004-03/11/content_313793.htm.

58. "Agribusiness Lobbying," *OpenSecrets*, accessed November 2, 2024, www.opensecrets.org/industries/lobbying?ind=A.

59. Andrew Jacobs and Matt Richtel, "How Big Business Got Brazil Hooked on Junk Food," *New York Times*, September 16, 2017, www.nytimes.com/interactive/2017/09/16/health/brazil-obesity-nestle.html.

60. Michaela Silvia Gmeiner and Petra Warschburger, "Intrapersonal Predictors of Weight Bias Internalization Among Elementary School Children: A Prospective Analysis," *BMC Pediatrics* 20 (2020): 1–9; Stephen J. Pont, Rebecca Puhl, Stephen R. Cook, and Wendelin Slusser, "Stigma Experienced by Children and Adolescents with Obesity," *Pediatrics* 140, no. 6 (2017): e20173034; Puhl and Suh, "Health Consequences."

61. Marie Galmiche, Pierre Déchelotte, Grégory Lambert, and Marie Pierre Tavolacci, "Prevalence of Eating Disorders over the 2000–2018 Period: A Systematic Literature Review," *American Journal of Clinical Nutrition* 109, no. 5 (2019): 1402–1413. Indeed, during the COVID pandemic, when obesity rates significantly increased, levels of eating disorders appear to have jumped as well. Outpatient visits for eating disorders, as well as phone calls inquiring about eating disorder treatment, approximately doubled from their levels prior to the pandemic in medical establishments contacted by reporters investigating the problem. See Tristan Barsky, "The Rise of Eating Disorder Behaviors During the COVID-19 Pandemic," *Student Well-Being* (blog), February 14, 2022, https://wellbeing.jhu.edu/blog/2022/02/14/the-rise-of-eating -disorder-behaviors-during-the-covid-19-pandemic/. An analysis of electronic medical records data from about eighty US hospitals found a sudden and dramatic increase in admissions for eating disorders among female adolescents starting immediately after the onset of the pandemic. See Dave Little, Adrianna Teriakidis, Eric Lindgren, Steven Allen, Eric Barkley, and Lily Rubin-Miller, "Increase in Adolescent Hospitalizations Related to Eating Disorders," Epic Research, April 29, 2021, www.epicresearch.org /articles/increase-in-adolescent-hospitalizations-related-to-eating-disorders.

62. In her *New York Times* article reviewing the Royal Society meeting on the causes of obesity, Julia Belluz writes, "Instead of viewing obesity as a societal challenge, the individual choice bias dominates. . . . People are simply told to eat more vegetables and exercise—the equivalent of tackling global warming by asking the public only to fly less or recycle. Diet gurus and companies mint billions off food and exercise fads that will ultimately fail." Julia Belluz, "Scientists Don't Agree on What Causes Obesity, but They Know What Doesn't," *New York Times*, November 21, 2022, www.nytimes .com/2022/11/21/opinion/obesity-cause.html.

63. Alyssa J. Moran and Christina A. Roberto, "A 'Food Is Medicine' Approach to Disease Prevention: Limitations and Alternatives," *Journal of the American Medical Association* 330, no. 23 (2023): 2243–2244.

64. Moran and Roberto, "A 'Food Is Medicine' Approach," 2244.

65. We draw here on an impassioned article by senior medical professionals (including a former US surgeon general): Bill Frist, Jerome M. Adams, and Jerold Mande, "Commissioner Califf Needs to Put the F Back in FDA," *STAT*, March 14, 2022, www.statnews.com/2022/03/14/commissioner-califf-needs-to-put-the-f-back-in-fda/.

66. "Prepared Remarks: Chairman Sanders Leads HELP Committee Hearing on Diabetes Epidemic and Obesity Epidemic in America," U.S. Senate Committee on Health, Education, Labor and Pensions, December 14, 2023, www.help.senate .gov/chair/newsroom/press/prepared-remarks-chairman-sanders-leads-help -committee-hearing-on-diabetes-epidemic-and-obesity-epidemic-in-america.

67. "Final Determination Regarding Partially Hydrogenated Oils," Food and Drug Administration, last updated October 1, 2024, www.fda.gov/food

/food-additives-petitions/final-determination-regarding-partially-hydrogenated-oils
-removing-trans-fat.

68. "Artificial Trans Fats Banned in U.S.," Harvard T. H. Chan School of
Public Health, June 19, 2018, www.hsph.harvard.edu/news/hsph-in-the-news
/us-bans-artificial-trans-fats/; "FDA Completes Final Administrative Actions on Partially Hydrogenated Oils in Foods," US Food and Drug Administration, December 13, 2023, www.fda.gov/food/hfp-constituent-updates/fda-completes-final
-administrative-actions-partially-hydrogenated-oils-foods.

69. E.g., Mayo Clinic Staff, "Trans Fat Is Double Trouble for Heart Health,"
Mayo Clinic, accessed November 14, 2024, www.mayoclinic.org/diseases-conditions
/high-blood-cholesterol/in-depth/trans-fat/art-20046114.

70. Eric J. Brandt, Rebecca Myerson, Marcelo Coca Perraillon, and Tamar S. Polon-
sky, "Hospital Admissions for Myocardial Infarction and Stroke Before and After the
Trans-Fatty Acid Restrictions in New York," *Journal of the American Medical Association: Cardiology* 2, no. 6 (2017): 627–634.

71. "WHO 5-Year Milestone Report on Global Trans Fat Elimination Illustrates Latest Progress up to 2023," World Health Organization, June 24, 2024,
www.who.int/news/item/24-06-2024-WHO-5-year-milestone-report-on-global
-transfat-elimination-illustrates-latest-progress-up-to-2023.

Chapter 3: Why We Are Unprepared for Retirement

1. Monique Morrissey, Siavash Radpour, and Barbara Schuster, "Chapter 2: Retirement," in *The Older Workers Retirement Chartbook* (Economic Policy Institute, 2022),
www.epi.org/publication/chapter-2-retirement/#charts.

2. Jason M. Breslow, "Teresa Ghilarducci: Why the 401(k) Is a Failed Experiment," *PBS Frontline*, April 23, 2013, www.pbs.org/wgbh/frontline/article/teresa
-ghilarducci-why-the-401k-is-a-failed-experiment/.

3. "Real Median Household Income in the United States," Federal Reserve
Bank of St. Louis, accessed May 9, 2025, https://fred.stlouisfed.org/series/MEHO
INUSA672N.

4. Sixty-seven percent of private industry workers had access to employer-provided
retirement plans in March 2020; 52 percent had access only to defined contribution
retirement plans; an additional 12 percent had access to both defined benefit and
defined contribution retirement plans; and 3 percent had access only to defined benefit
retirement plans: "Employee Benefits in the United States—March 2020," US Bureau
of Labor Statistics, news release, September 24, 2020, www.bls.gov/news.release
/archives/ebs2_09242020.pdf.

5. Stang Gappa, "Average and Median 401(k) Account Balances in 2023," Capital-
ize, March 11, 2024, www.hicapitalize.com/resources/average-401k-balance-statistics/.

6. Irena Dushi, Howard M. Iams, and Brad Trenkamp, "The Importance of Social
Security Benefits to the Income of the Aged Population," *Social Security Bulletin* 77,
no. 2 (2017), www.ssa.gov/policy/docs/ssb/v77n2/v77n2p1.html.

7. "Vanguard Viewpoints: How America Saves 2024," (Vanguard, 2024), https://
corporate.vanguard.com/content/dam/corp/research/pdf/how_america_saves
_report_2024.pdf.

8. Catherine Collinson, Patti Vogt Rowey, and Heidi Cho, *Retirement Security: A Compendium of Findings About U.S. Workers* (Transamerica Center for Retirement Studies, 2020), www.transamericainstitute.org/research/publications/details /retirement-security-a-compendium-of-findings-about-united-states-workers. The figures are also highly variable across countries. In the UK, the government-regulated auto-enrollment scheme requires employers to contribute just 3 percent of an employee's salary to their pension "pot," while the employee has to pay 5 percent. In the UK Civil Service, by contrast, employees pay roughly 4 to 8 percent (depending on their salary), while the employer contribution is a remarkable 28.97 percent (an indication of the true cost of providing a good-quality guaranteed retirement provision): "Contribution Rates," Civil Service Pensions, accessed November 4, 2024, www.civilservice pensionscheme.org.uk/your-pension/managing-your-pension/contribution-rates/.

9. Consider two people, a low-income individual taxed at a marginal rate of 10 percent and a high-income individual taxed at a marginal rate of 30 percent. Suppose that each individual saves $1,000 and gets a tax deduction (as opposed to a tax credit) for doing so. The low-income individual will get a tax break of $100, while the high-income individual gets a tax break of $300. Erik Sherman, "We All Pay for Retirement Tax Breaks That Mostly the Wealthy Use," *Forbes*, last updated April 21, 2022, www.forbes.com/sites/eriksherman/2021/11/30/we-all-pay-for-retirement-tax -breaks-that-mostly-the-wealthy-use/.

10. The Congressional Budget Office work is summarized in Kenneth Megan, "Federal Retirement Tax Benefits Mostly Go to the Wealthy: Here's How to Make Them Work for Everyone," Economic Innovation Group, November 3, 2021, https://eig.org /federal-retirement-tax-benefits-are-mostly-used-by-the-wealthy-heres-how-to -make-them-work-for-everyone/.

11. Raj Chetty, John N. Friedman, Søren Leth-Petersen, Torben Heien Nielsen, and Tore Olsen, "Active vs. Passive Decisions and Crowd-Out in Retirement Savings Accounts: Evidence from Denmark," *Quarterly Journal of Economics* 129, no. 3 (2014): 1141–1219.

12. Hazel Bateman, Jordan Louviere, Susan Thorp, Towhidul Islam, and Stephen Satchell, "Investment Decisions for Retirement Savings," *Journal of Consumer Affairs* 44, no. 3 (2010): 463–482.

13. Nari Rhee and William B. Fornia, "How Do California Teachers Fare Under CalSTRS? Applying Workforce Tenure Analysis and Counterfactual Benefit Modeling to Retirement Benefit Evaluation," *Journal of Retirement* 5, no. 2 (2017): 42.

14. E.g., Brigitte C. Madrian and Dennis F. Shea, "The Power of Suggestion: Inertia in 401(k) Participation and Savings Behavior," *Quarterly Journal of Economics* 116, no. 4 (2001): 1149–1187; Annamaria Lusardi and Olivia S. Mitchell, "Financial Literacy and Retirement Preparedness: Evidence and Implications for Financial Education," *Business Economics* 42 (2007): 35–44.

15. Sarah Meagher, "Pension Mis-Selling Review," House of Commons Library, July 9, 2002, https://commonslibrary.parliament.uk/research-briefings/sn00429/.

16. Moira O'Neill, "Why Are Fewer People Getting Financial Advice?," *Financial Times*, July 13, 2024, www.ft.com/content/6032c9f9-2297-4d29-a015-2e803f920a39.

17. An entire ecosystem of new players, of a range of moral hues, has rapidly grown up, with all the cost and complexity this entails—and with no obvious net benefit for

individual citizens or society as a whole. Indeed, pension liberalization in the UK was immediately followed by huge levels of mis-selling, and then, many years later, by a hugely expensive process of redress in which pension companies paid tens of billions of pounds back to customers: Julie Black and Richard Nobles, "Personal Pensions Misselling: The Causes and Lessons of Regulatory Failure," *Modern Law Review* 61 (1998): 789–820. Eventually the rules of the game were patched up, but only after a disaster for both individuals and the balance sheets and reputation of the pensions industry. See Lauren Wilkinson, "How Have Scams Evolved Since the Introduction of Pension Freedoms?," Pensions Policy Institute, Briefing Note 121, May 2020, www.pensions policyinstitute.org.uk/media/dc0igymj/202005-bn121-how-have-scams-evolved -since-the-introduction-of-pension-freedoms.pdf.

18. George Loewenstein and Drazen Prelec, "Negative Time Preference," *American Economic Review* 81, no. 2 (1991): 347–352; George Loewenstein, "Self-Control and Its Discontents: A Commentary on Duckworth, Milkman, and Laibson," *Psychological Science in the Public Interest* 19, no. 3 (2018): 95–101.

19. Aditya Aladangady, David Cho, Laura Feiveson, and Eugenio Pinto, "Excess Savings During the COVID-19 Pandemic," *FEDS Notes*, Board of Governors of the Federal Reserve System, October 21, 2022, www.federalreserve.gov/econres/notes /feds-notes/excess-savings-during-the-covid-19-pandemic-20221021.html.

20. George Loewenstein and Erin Carbone, "Self-Control ≠ Temporal Discounting," *Current Opinion in Psychology* 60 (2024): 101924.

21. Scott Rick and George Loewenstein, "Intangibility in Intertemporal Choice," *Philosophical Transactions of the Royal Society B: Biological Sciences* 363, no. 1511 (2008): 3813–3824.

22. Richard H. Thaler and Shlomo Benartzi, "Save More Tomorrow: Using Behavioral Economics to Increase Employee Saving," *Journal of Political Economy* 112, no. S1 (2004): S164–S187.

23. Continuing to address Thaler, Dubner concluded, "So, congratulations, and thank you. But: what does it say about the field of behavioral economics, and behavior change generally, that this largest victory took place a couple decades ago? Where are all the other victories?" Stephen J. Dubner, host, *Freakonomics*, episode 382, "How Goes the Behavior-Change Revolution?," June 19, 2019, 52 min., 54 sec., https://freakonomics .com/podcast/how-goes-the-behavior-change-revolution/.

24. John Beshears, James Choi, David Laibson, and Brigitte Madrian, "AEA/AFA Joint Luncheon—'Nudges Are Not Enough: The Case for Price-Based Paternalism,'" webcast, January 3, 2020, American Economic Association, 54 min., 11 sec., www .aeaweb.org/webcasts/2020/aea-afa-joint-luncheon-nudges-are-not-enough.

25. Madrian and Shea, "Power of Suggestion."

26. John Beshears, James J. Choi, Christopher Harris, David Laibson, Brigitte C. Madrian, and Jung Sakong, "Which Early Withdrawal Penalty Attracts the Most Deposits to a Commitment Savings Account?," *Journal of Public Economics* 183 (2020): 104144.

27. Robert Argento, Victoria L. Bryant, and John Sabelhaus, "Early Withdrawals from Retirement Accounts During the Great Recession," *Contemporary Economic Policy* 33, no. 1 (2015): 1–16.

28. Taha Choukhmane, "Default Options and Retirement Saving Dynamics," *American Economic Review*, forthcoming, https://tahachoukhmane.com/wp-content/uploads/2025/05/Default-options-and-saving.pdf.

29. James J. Choi, David Laibson, John Cammarota, Richard Lombardo, and John Beshears, "Smaller Than We Thought? The Effect of Automatic Savings Policies," no. w32828 (National Bureau of Economic Research, 2024).

30. Choi et al., "Smaller Than We Thought?" Note that (1) people not in the schemes save more than expected; (2) opt-out rates for auto-escalation are far higher than expected; (3) employee turnover rate is high, and many employees leave before their employer matching contributions are fully vested; and (4) there are high levels of leakage: more than 40 percent of 401(k) balances are cashed out on leaving the firm.

31. "Auto Enrolment Remains Resilient Through Pension Contribution Rise and Global Crisis," Nest Insight, press release, February 10, 2021, www.nestinsight.org.uk/auto-enrolment-remains-resilient/.

32. Hal E. Hershfield, Daniel G. Goldstein, William F. Sharpe, et al., "Increasing Saving Behavior Through Age-Progressed Renderings of the Future Self," *Journal of Marketing Research* 48, no. SPL (2011): S23–S37.

33. Annamaria Lusardi and Olivia S. Mitchell, "The Economic Importance of Financial Literacy: Theory and Evidence," *Journal of Economic Literature* 52, no. 1 (2014): 5–44; Lewis Mandell and Linda Schmid Klein, "The Impact of Financial Literacy Education on Subsequent Financial Behavior," *Journal of Financial Counseling and Planning* 20, no. 1 (2009): 15–24.

34. Lauren E. Willis, "Against Financial-Literacy Education," *Iowa Law Review* 94 (2008): 197–285.

35. Robert Kuttner, "The Radical Minimalist: Obama's Regulatory Czar, Cass Sunstein, Has a Complex Faith in Market Initiatives. But Sometimes a 'Nudge' Is Not Enough," *American Prospect*, March 19, 2009, https://prospect.org/features/radical-minimalist/.

36. Michael Steinberger, "Was the 401(k) a Mistake?," *New York Times Magazine*, May 8, 2024, www.nytimes.com/2024/05/08/magazine/401k-retirement.html.

37. David Hagmann, Emily H. Ho, and George Loewenstein, "Nudging Out Support for a Carbon Tax," *Nature Climate Change* 9, no. 6 (2019): 484–489.

38. Frank Pasquale, "Why 'Nudges' Hardly Help," *Atlantic*, December 4, 2015, www.theatlantic.com/business/archive/2015/12/nudges-effectiveness/418749/.

39. Greg Jericho, "In the Debate About Super, the Actual Point of a Retirement Income Policy Is Lost," *Guardian*, November 25, 2020, www.theguardian.com/business/grogonomics/2020/nov/26/in-the-debate-about-super-the-actual-point-of-a-retirement-income-policy-is-lost.

40. "Age Pension," Services Australia, Australian Government, last updated April 26, 2023, www.servicesaustralia.gov.au/age-pension. The Age Pension is "means tested." That is, the amount it pays decreases as the income of, and assets held by, an individual increase.

41. "Your Investment Options," AustralianSuper, accessed November 4, 2024, www.australiansuper.com/investments/your-investment-options.

42. Emma Wager, Matthew McGough, Shameek Rakshit, Krutika Amin, and Cynthia Cox, "How Does Health Spending in the U.S. Compare to Other Countries?," Peterson-KFF Health System Tracker, April 9, 2025, www.healthsystemtracker.org/chart-collection/health-spending-u-s-compare-countries/.

Chapter 4: Flawed Incentives: The Outsize Cost of US Health Care

1. All statistics from Emma Wager, Imani Telesford, Shameek Rakshit, Nisha Kurani, and Cynthia Cox, "How Does the Quality of the U.S. Health System Compare to Other Countries?," Peterson-KFF Health System Tracker, October 9, 2024, www.healthsystemtracker.org/chart-collection/quality-u-s-healthcare-system-compare-countries/.

2. Emma Wager, Matthew McGough, Shameek Rakshit, Krutika Amin, and Cynthia Cox, "How Does Health Spending in the U.S. Compare to Other Countries?," Peterson-KFF Health System Tracker, April 9, 2024, www.healthsystemtracker.org/chart-collection/health-spending-u-s-compare-countries/.

3. This happened largely, as we discuss in Chapter 11, as a result of the enactment of a wide range of s-frame interventions such as high taxes on tobacco and bans on smoking in public spaces.

4. "Smoking Rates by Country 2024," World Population Review, accessed November 6, 2024, https://worldpopulationreview.com/country-rankings/smoking-rates-by-country.

5. Troyen A. Brennan, *The Transformation of American Health Insurance: On the Path to Medicare for All* (Johns Hopkins University Press, 2024), 24. As the political economist Charles Lindblom wrote in a famous article in 1959, "Democracies change their policies almost entirely through incremental adjustments. Policy does not move in leaps and bounds." Lindblom characterized actual policy formation as a process of "muddling through." Charles E. Lindblom, "The Science of 'Muddling Through,'" *Public Administration Review* 19, no. 2 (1959): 84. Sometimes muddling through works out unexpectedly well; sometimes, as with US health care, it just ends in a muddle.

6. Joseph Fraiman, Shannon Brownlee, Michael A. Stoto, Kenneth W. Lin, and Alison N. Huffstetler, "An Estimate of the US Rate of Overuse of Screening Colonoscopy: A Systematic Review," *Journal of General Internal Medicine* 37, no. 7 (2022): 1754–1762; James S. Goodwin, Amanpal Singh, Nischita Reddy, Taylor S. Riall, and Yong-Fang Kuo, "Overuse of Screening Colonoscopy in the Medicare Population," *Archives of Internal Medicine* 171, no. 15 (2011): 1335–1343.

7. Mireille Jacobson, A. James O'Malley, Craig C. Earle, Juliana Pakes, Peter Gaccione, and Joseph P. Newhouse, "Does Reimbursement Influence Chemotherapy Treatment for Cancer Patients?," *Health Affairs* 25, no. 2 (2006): 437–443.

8. Donald M. Berwick and Andrew D. Hackbarth, "Eliminating Waste in US Health Care," *Journal of the American Medical Association* 307, no. 14 (2012): 1513–1516; William H. Shrank, Teresa L. Rogstad, and Natasha Parekh, "Waste in the US Health Care System: Estimated Costs and Potential for Savings," *Journal of the American Medical Association* 322, no. 15 (2019): 1501–1509.

9. Brennan, *Transformation of American Health Insurance*, 16.

10. Brennan, 16.

11. Brennan, xvi.

12. Rita F. Redberg and Sanket S. Dhruva, "The FDA's Medical Device Problem," *New York Times*, July 17, 2015, www.nytimes.com/2024/08/20/health/fda-medical -devices-ethics.html.

13. Jason Dana and George Loewenstein, "A Social Science Perspective on Gifts to Physicians from Industry," *Journal of the American Medical Association* 290, no. 2 (2003): 252–255.

14. Daylian M. Cain, George Loewenstein, and Don A. Moore, "When Sunlight Fails to Disinfect: Understanding the Perverse Effects of Disclosing Conflicts of Interest," *Journal of Consumer Research* 37, no. 5 (2010): 836–857.

15. Sunita Sah, George Loewenstein, and Daylian Cain, "Insinuation Anxiety: Concern That Advice Rejection Will Signal Distrust After Conflict of Interest Disclosures," *Personality and Social Psychology Bulletin* 45, no. 7 (2019): 1099–1112.

16. Zachariah Sharek, Robert E. Schoen, and George Loewenstein, "Bias in the Evaluation of Conflict of Interest Policies," *Journal of Law, Medicine & Ethics* 40, no. 2 (2012): 368–382.

17. Linda Babcock and George Loewenstein, "Explaining Bargaining Impasse: The Role of Self-Serving Biases," *Journal of Economic Perspectives* 11, no. 1 (1997): 109–126.

18. Linda Babcock, George Loewenstein, and Samuel Issacharoff, "Creating Convergence: Debiasing Biased Litigants," *Law & Social Inquiry* 22, no. 4 (1997): 913–925.

19. Michael A. Steinman, Michael G. Shlipak, and Stephen J. McPhee, "Of Principles and Pens: Attitudes and Practices of Medicine Housestaff Toward Pharmaceutical Industry Promotions," *American Journal of Medicine* 110, no. 7 (2001): 551–557.

20. See Brennan, *Transformation of American Health Insurance*, ix; Wendell Potter, *Deadly Spin: An Insurance Company Insider Speaks Out on How Corporate PR Is Killing Health Care and Deceiving Americans* (Bloomsbury USA, 2011).

21. Report summarized in the *Federal Register*: "60 FR 41914 Medicare Program; Physician Financial Relationships with, and Referrals to, Health Care Entities That Furnish Clinical Laboratory Services and Financial Relationship Reporting Requirements," *Federal Register* 60, no. 156 (1995), www.govinfo.gov/app/details/FR -1995-08-14/95-19647.

22. "Medicare: Higher Use of Advanced Imaging Services by Providers Who Self-Refer Costing Medicare Millions," GAO-12-966, US Government Accountability Office, September 28, 2012, www.gao.gov/products/gao-12-966.

23. Joel Lexchin, Lisa A. Bero, Benjamin Djulbegovic, and Otavio Clark, "Pharmaceutical Industry Sponsorship and Research Outcome and Quality: Systematic Review," *BMJ* 326, no. 7400 (2003): 1167–1170.

24. Liran Einav and Amy Finkelstein, *We've Got You Covered: Rebooting American Health Care* (Portfolio, 2023), 28.

25. Einav and Finkelstein, *We've Got You Covered*, 25.

26. George Loewenstein, Joelle Y. Friedman, Barbara McGill, et al., "Consumers' Misunderstanding of Health Insurance," *Journal of Health Economics* 32, no. 5 (2013): 850–862.

27. Saurabh Bhargava, George Loewenstein, and Justin Sydnor, "Choose to Lose: Health Plan Choices from a Menu with Dominated Options," *Quarterly Journal of Economics* 132, no. 3 (2017): 1319–1372.

28. "HHS and States Move to Establish Affordable Insurance Exchanges, Give Americans the Same Insurance Choices as Members of Congress," Covered California, news release, July 11, 2011, www.coveredca.com/newsroom/news-releases/2011/07/11 /HHS-and-states-move-to-establish-Affordable-Insurance-Exchanges-give-Americans -the-same-insurance-choices-as-members-of-Congress/.

29. See, e.g., Kant Patel and Mark E. Rushefsky, *Healthcare Politics and Policy in America* (Routledge, 2019).

30. Dan Wellings, "What Does the Public Think About the NHS?," King's Fund, September 16, 2017, www.kingsfund.org.uk/insight-and-analysis/long-reads /what-does-the-public-think-about-the-nhs; Matthew Lambert, "The Vast Major-ity of GPs Resisted the Founding of the NHS—Here's Why," *Conversation*, April 4, 2024, https://theconversation.com/the-vast-majority-of-gps-resisted -the-founding-of-the-nhs-heres-why-226445.

31. The strength of opposition is evident in vociferous objections by doctors at the time, e.g., E. Anthony, "BMA Opposition to the NHS 1948," Socialist Health Association, January 31, 1948, https://sochealth.co.uk/national-health-service /the-sma-and-the-foundation-of-the-national-health-service-dr-leslie-hilliard-1980 /the-start-of-the-nhs-1948/bma-opposition-to-the-nhs-1948/.

32. Barack Obama, "A President Looks Back on His Toughest Fight," *New Yorker*, October, 26 2020, www.newyorker.com/magazine/2020/11/02/barack-obama -new-book-excerpt-promised-land-obamacare.

33. Soeren Mattke, Hangsheng Liu, John Caloyeras, et al. "Workplace Wellness Programs Study," *RAND Health Quarterly* 3, no. 2 (2013), https://pubmed.ncbi.nlm .nih.gov/28083294/; Pat Redmond, Judith Solomon, and Mark Lin, "Can Incentives for Healthy Behavior Improve Health and Hold Down Medicaid Costs?," Center on Budget and Policy Priorities, accessed November 6, 2024, www.cbpp.org/research /can-incentives-for-healthy-behavior-improve-health-and-hold-down-medicaid-costs.

34. Zirui Song and Katherine Baicker, "Effect of a Workplace Wellness Program on Employee Health and Economic Outcomes: A Randomized Clinical Trial," *Journal of the American Medical Association* 321, no. 15 (2019): 1491–1501.

35. Zirui Song and Katherine Baicker, "Health and Economic Outcomes up to Three Years After a Workplace Wellness Program: A Randomized Controlled Trial," *Health Affairs* 40, no. 6 (2021): 951–960.

36. Julian Reif, David Chan, Damon Jones, Laura Payne, and David Molitor, "Effects of a Workplace Wellness Program on Employee Health, Health Beliefs, and Medical Use: A Randomized Clinical Trial," *Journal of the American Medical Association: Internal Medicine* 180, no. 7 (2020): 952–960.

37. Brennan, *Transformation of American Health Insurance*, 50.

38. Steven A. Burd, "How Safeway Is Cutting Health-Care Costs," *Wall Street Journal*, June 12, 2009, www.wsj.com/articles/SB124476804026308603.

39. Chelsea Reynolds, "Myth Surrounds Reform's 'Safeway Amendment,'" *Association of Health Care Journalists,* January 20, 2010, http://healthjournalism.org /blog/2010/01/myth-surrounds-reforms-safeway-amendment/.

40. Damon Jones, David Molitor, and Julian Reif, "What Do Workplace Wellness Programs Do? Evidence from the Illinois Workplace Wellness Study," *Quarterly Journal of Economics* 134, no. 4 (2019): 1747–1791.

41. George Loewenstein, Troyen Brennan, and Kevin G. Volpp, "Asymmetric Paternalism to Improve Health Behaviors," *Journal of the American Medical Association* 298, no. 20 (2007): 2415–2417.

42. In the UK, Drinkaware is a high-profile example: www.drinkaware.co.uk/.

43. E.g., Mitesh S. Patel, David A. Asch, Andrea B. Troxel, et al., "Premium-Based Financial Incentives Did Not Promote Workplace Weight Loss in a 2013–15 Study," *Health Affairs* 35, no. 1 (2016): 71–79.

44. Amitabh Chandra, Evan Flack, and Ziad Obermeyer, "The Health Costs of Cost-Sharing," *Quarterly Journal of Economics* 139, no. 4 (2024): 2037–2083.

45. Juliette Cubanski and Tricia Neuman, "Changes to Medicare Part D in 2024 and 2025 Under the Inflation Reduction Act and How Enrollees Will Benefit," Kaiser Family Foundation, April 20, 2023, www.kff.org/medicare/issue-brief /changes-to-medicare-part-d-in-2024-and-2025-under-the-inflation-reduction-act -and-how-enrollees-will-benefit/.

46. Jia Tolentino, "A Man Was Murdered in Cold Blood and You're Laughing?," *New Yorker*, December 7, 2024, www.newyorker.com/news/the-lede/what-the -murder-of-the-unitedhealthcare-ceo-brian-thompson-means-to-america.

47. In the aftermath of the murder of Brian Thompson, Andrew Witty, the CEO of UnitedHealth Group (the parent company of UnitedHealthcare), wrote an op-ed for *The New York Times*, which, while acknowledging "The Health Care System Is Flawed" (the headline of the piece), promulgated the same kind of i-frame perspective evident in the widespread glee in response to the killing. Witty claimed that Thompson was one of many at UnitedHealth "trying to do their best for those who they serve" and noted that Thompson was raised in an Iowa farmhouse. He lauded "the people of UnitedHealth Group" who, he noted, "are nurses, doctors, patient and client advocates, technologists and more. They all come to work each day to provide critical health services for millions of Americans in need." All very likely true, but missing the point that the anger of those who celebrated the killing would be much more productively directed against the system that consistently harms insurance subscribers.

Chapter 5: Inequality by Design

1. Melvin J. Lerner and Carolyn H. Simmons, "The Observer's Reaction to the 'Innocent Victim': Compassion or Rejection?," *Journal of Personality and Social Psychology* 4, no. 2 (1966): 203–210. For a review of early work on the "just world" hypothesis see, e.g., Melvin J. Lerner and Dale T. Miller, "Just World Research and the Attribution Process: Looking Back and Ahead," *Psychological Bulletin* 85, no. 5 (1978): 1030–1051.

2. Of course, in reality, opportunities in sport are also very unequally distributed.

3. It must be acknowledged that although globalization has almost certainly increased inequality domestically in the US, it has substantially reduced inequality at the world level. See Branko Milanovic, *Global Inequality: A New Approach for the Age of Globalization* (Harvard University Press, 2016). The broader social impact of globalization is, of course, hotly debated.

4. See, for example, Robert H. Frank and Philip J. Cook, *The Winner-Take-All Society: Why the Few at the Top Get So Much More Than the Rest of Us*, rev. ed. (Penguin, 1996).

5. In this chapter we focus on the "rich" world rather than the vast challenge of global inequality. We concentrate, too, on the general problem of inequality, rather than the specific and pernicious ways in which particular groups are treated unequally based on race, class, gender, and so on. These topics are hugely important but beyond our scope and expertise.

6. See Anand Giridharadas, *Winners Take All: The Elite Charade of Changing the World* (Alfred A. Knopf, 2018).

7. Larry M. Bartels, *Unequal Democracy: The Political Economy of the New Gilded Age*, 2nd ed. (Princeton University Press, 2016). Consistent with our argument in Part Two of this book, Bartels argues that structural features of American democracy, including campaign finance rules and legislative gridlock, contribute to a system that reinforces inequality.

8. Martin Gilens, *Affluence and Influence: Economic Inequality and Political Power in America* (Princeton University Press, 2014).

9. Paul K. Piff, Dylan Wiwad, Angela R. Robinson, Lara B. Aknin, Brett Mercier, and Azim Shariff, "Shifting Attributions for Poverty Motivates Opposition to Inequality and Enhances Egalitarianism," *Nature Human Behaviour* 4, no. 5 (2020): 496–505.

10. Giridharadas, *Winners Take All*, 7.

11. The picture looks very different when we look at the world as a whole. Based on nearly any measure of inequality, global inequality, after rising from the 1960s to 2000, has been declining dramatically as certain large, historically poor countries— most notably China, but also India and Vietnam—have developed rapidly. During the same period, within-country inequality has generally increased. Joe Hasell, Bertha Rohenkohl, Pablo Arriagada, Esteban Ortiz-Ospina, and Max Roser, "Economic Inequality," Our World in Data, accessed November 18, 2024, https://ourworldindata .org/economic-inequality.

12. "Real Personal Income," Federal Reserve Bank of St. Louis, accessed November 18, 2024, https://fred.stlouisfed.org/series/RPI.

13. Pascale Bourquin, Mike Brewer, and Tom Wernham, "Trends in Income and Wealth Inequalities," *Oxford Open Economics* 3, Supplement 1 (2024): i103–i146.

14. Daron Acemoglu, "Clarifying America's Great Inequality Debate," Project Syndicate, January 3, 2024, www.project-syndicate.org/commentary/inequality-different -metrics-but-larger-trend-still-a-problem-by-daron-acemoglu-2024-01. For a trenchant critique of this picture see Michael R. Strain, *The American Dream Is Not Dead (But Populism Could Kill It)* (Templeton Foundation Press, 2020).

15. "Wealth Inequality in the United States," Inequality.org, accessed November 18, 2024, https://inequality.org/facts/wealth-inequality/#richest-americans.

16. "The World's Real-Time Billionaires," *Forbes*, accessed May 12, 2024, www .forbes.com/real-time-billionaires/#36385b403d78. The Walton fortune is now divided among different branches of the family, with a total value of over $200 billion.

17. Thomas Piketty, *Capital in the Twenty-First Century* (Harvard University Press, 2014).

18. "Distribution of Individual Total Wealth by Characteristic in Great Britain: April 2018 to March 2020," Census 2021, UK Office for National Statistics, January 7, 2022, www.ons.gov.uk/peoplepopulationandcommunity/personal andhouseholdfinances/incomeandwealth/bulletins/distributionofindividualtotal wealthbycharacteristicingreatbritain/april2018tomarch2020.

19. Shehryar Nabi, "Thirteen Million US Households Have Negative Net Worth: Will They Ever Move from Debt to Wealth?," Aspen Institute, May 25, 2022, www .aspeninstitute.org/blog-posts/thirteen-million-us-households-have-negative-net -worth-will-they-ever-move-from-debt-to-wealth/.

20. The details are somewhat controversial and only partly resolved. It has sometimes been claimed that additional income, beyond a point around or above the median income in a society, has no effect on emotional well-being: Daniel Kahneman and Angus Deaton, "High Income Improves Evaluation of Life but Not Emotional Well-Being," *Proceedings of the National Academy of Sciences* 107, no. 38 (2010): 16489–16493. But recent work suggests that additional income continues to provide some benefit even to the wealthy: Matthew A. Killingsworth, Daniel Kahneman, and Barbara Mellers, "Income and Emotional Well-Being: A Conflict Resolved," *Proceedings of the National Academy of Sciences* 120, no. 10 (2023): e2208661120. Nonetheless, it is uncontroversial that the marginal impact of money is much greater for the poor than for the wealthy, whatever one's methodology or theoretical standpoint.

21. Journalist Robert Frank (not to be confused with Robert Frank the Cornell University economics professor) has talked, not implausibly, about the creation of something close to a state-within-a-state, which he dubs "Richistan." Robert Frank, *Richistan: A Journey Through the American Wealth Boom and the Lives of the New Rich* (Crown, 2007). On the impact of wealth differences on health outcomes, Harvard economist Raj Chetty references a remarkable statistic in a recent seminar at the University of Pennsylvania: The gap in life expectancy between the poorest and richest white Americans is between 12 and 14 years. To drive home the immensity of these numbers, he notes that the approximate gain in life-expectancy were cancer to be eradicated would be just 3 years! www.youtube.com/watch?v=yqb7oW8Q8a4 (minute 14).

22. Emily Haisley, Romel Mostafa, and George Loewenstein, "Subjective Relative Income and Lottery Ticket Purchases," *Journal of Behavioral Decision Making* 21, no. 3 (2008): 283–295.

23. This viewpoint is particularly associated with what is sometimes called the "populist right." "Beyond Red vs. Blue: The Political Typology," Pew Research Center, November 9, 2021, www.pewresearch.org/politics/2021/11/09/beyond-red-vs-blue -the-political-typology-2/.

24. For a recent discussion of how the accidental invention of the 401(k) pension scheme in the US around 1980 has boosted inequality see Michael Steinberg, "Was the 401(k) a Mistake?," *New York Times Magazine*, May 8, 2024, www.nytimes .com/2024/05/08/magazine/401k-retirement-crisis.html, and Teresa Ghilarducci, *Work, Retire, Repeat: The Uncertainty of Retirement in the New Economy* (University of Chicago Press, 2024).

25. For a remarkable exposé see Jesse Eisinger, Jeff Ernsthausen, and Paul Kiel, "The Secret IRS Files: Trove of Never-Before-Seen Records Reveal How the Wealthiest Avoid

Income Tax," *ProPublica*, June 8, 2021, www.propublica.org/article/the-secret-irs-files-trove-of-never-before-seen-records-reveal-how-the-wealthiest-avoid-income-tax.

26. Richard Bilton, "Panama Papers: Mossack Fonseca Leak Reveals Elite's Tax Havens," *BBC News*, April 4, 2016, www.bbc.com/news/world-35918844.

27. Russ Buettner, Susanne Craig, and Mike McIntire, "The President's Taxes: Long-Concealed Records Show Trump's Chronic Losses and Years of Tax Avoidance," *New York Times*, September 27, 2020, www.nytimes.com/interactive/2020/09/27/us/donald-trump-taxes.html.

28. The Rebel Accountant, *Taxtopia: How I Discovered the Injustices, Scams and Guilty Secrets of the Tax Evasion Game* (Monoray, 2023).

29. "How Did the TCJA Affect the Federal Budget Outlook?," Tax Policy Center, accessed November 18, 2024, www.taxpolicycenter.org/briefing-book/how-did-tcja-affect-federal-budget-outlook#.

30. The Nobel Prize–winning economist Paul Krugman stresses that the decline in unionization in the US resulted from government policies and was not the product of globalization or other inexorable forces. See Paul Krugman, *The Conscience of a Liberal* (W. W. Norton, 2009); for a recent summary see Paul Krugman, "Paul Krugman on Unions," Big Think, accessed November 18, 2024, 1 min., 39 sec., https://bigthink.com/videos/paul-krugman-on-unions/. Krugman notes that unionization rates in the US and Canada were 32 percent and 30 percent respectively in 1960. By 1999, while Canadian unionization was unchanged, US unionization had plummeted to 13 percent. The 2023 US figure is around 10 percent. See Andrea Hsu, "Union Membership Grew Last Year, But Only 10% of U.S. Workers Belong to a Union," NPR, January 23, 2024, www.npr.org/2024/01/23/1226034366/labor-union-membership-uaw-hollywood-workers-strike-gallup#. UK unionization is about 23 percent, down from a high of roughly half the workforce in 1980: John Moylan, "Union Membership Has Halved Since 1980," *BBC News*, September 7, 2012, www.bbc.co.uk/news/business-19521535.

31. Anton Korinek and Jonathan Kreamer, "The Redistributive Effects of Financial Deregulation," *Journal of Monetary Economics* 68 (2014): S55–S67.

32. Of course there are many other forces determining political allegiances, and these may work against disadvantaged voters who back parties committed to reducing inequality. For discussion of some recent viewpoints see Thomas B. Edsall, "Why Aren't You Voting in Your Financial Self-Interest?," *New York Times*, September 14, 2022, www.nytimes.com/2022/09/14/opinion/elites-populists-political-beliefs.html. We see the increasing influence of populist and socially conservative sentiments not merely arising bottom-up among working people but as being actively encouraged by some of the powerful concentrated interests who benefit from reducing any pressure to combat rising inequality (see Chapter 7).

33. Esteban Ortiz-Ospina, "Is Trade a Major Driver of Income Inequality?," Our World in Data, October 22, 2018, https://ourworldindata.org/trade-and-income-inequality.

34. Zaid Jilani, "Average Japanese CEO Earns One-Sixth as Much as American CEOs," *ThinkProgress*, July 8, 2010, https://archive.thinkprogress.org/average-japanese-ceo-earns-one-sixth-as-much-as-american-ceos-9d95cf97af34/.

35. Alyssa Davis and Lawrence Mishel, "CEO Pay Continues to Rise as Typical Workers Are Paid Less," Economic Policy Institute, Issue Brief #380, press release, June 12, 2014, www.epi.org/publication/ceo-pay-continues-to-rise/.

36. Jerusalem Demsas, "The Obvious Answer to Homelessness (and Why Everyone's Ignoring It)," *Atlantic*, December 12, 2022, www.theatlantic.com/magazine/archive/2023/01/homelessness-affordable-housing-crisis-democrats-causes/672224/.

37. Rebecca Montacute, "Socio-Economic Diversity and the Educational Background of Boris Johnson's Cabinet," *LSE BPP*, July 29, 2019, https://blogs.lse.ac.uk/politicsandpolicy/the-educational-background-of-boris-johnsons-cabinet/.

38. "List of Prime Ministers of the United Kingdom by Education," Wikipedia, accessed November 18, 2024, https://en.wikipedia.org/wiki/List_of_prime_ministers_of_the_United_Kingdom_by_education#.

39. "Inheriting Is Becoming Nearly as Important as Working," *Economist*, February 27, 2025, www.economist.com/leaders/2025/02/27/inheriting-is-becoming-nearly-as-important-as-working.

40. Susan K. Urahn, Erin Currier, Diana Elliot, Lauren Wechsler, Denise Wilson, and Daniel Colbert, *Pursuing the American Dream: Economic Mobility Across Generations* (Pew Charitable Trusts, 2012), Figure 3, www.pewtrusts.org/-/media/legacy/uploadedfiles/wwwpewtrustsorg/reports/economic_mobility/pursuingamericandreampdf.pdf.

41. Raj Chetty, John N. Friedman, Emmanuel Saez, Nicholas Turner, and Danny Yagan, "Income Segregation and Intergenerational Mobility Across Colleges in the United States," *Quarterly Journal of Economics* 135, no. 3 (2020): 1567–1633.

42. For an in-depth analysis of one county: Jennifer Berry Hawes, Nat Lash, and Mollie Simon, "The Story of One Mississippi County Shows How Private Schools Are Exacerbating Segregation," *ProPublica*, December 19, 2024, www.propublica.org/article/segregation-academies-public-schools-amite-county-mississippi.

43. Jesse Singal, *The Quick Fix: Why Fad Psychology Can't Cure Our Social Ills* (Farrar, Straus and Giroux, 2021).

44. Singal, *Quick Fix*, 137; Angela L. Duckworth, Christopher Peterson, Michael D. Matthews, and Dennis R. Kelly, "Grit: Perseverance and Passion for Long-Term Goals," *Journal of Personality and Social Psychology* 92, no. 6 (2007): 1087.

45. Marcus Credé, Michael C. Tynan, and Peter D. Harms, "Much Ado About Grit: A Meta-Analytic Synthesis of the Grit Literature," *Journal of Personality and Social Psychology* 113, no. 3 (2017): 492.

46. Sule Alan, Teodora Boneva, and Seda Ertac, "Ever Failed, Try Again, Succeed Better: Results from a Randomized Educational Intervention on Grit," *Quarterly Journal of Economics* 134, no. 3 (2019): 1121–1162.

47. Indhira Santos, Violeta Petroska-Beska, Pedro Carneiro, et al., "Can Grit Be Taught? Lessons from a Nationwide Field Experiment with Middle-School Students," IZA Discussion Paper no. 15588, September 2022.

48. Claude M. Steele and Joshua Aronson, "Stereotype Threat and the Intellectual Test Performance of African Americans," *Journal of Personality and Social Psychology* 69, no. 5 (1995): 797.

49. Oren R. Shewach, Paul R. Sackett, and Sander Quint, "Stereotype Threat Effects in Settings with Features Likely Versus Unlikely in Operational Test Settings: A Meta-Analysis," *Journal of Applied Psychology* 104, no. 12 (2019): 1514.

50. Carol S. Dweck and Ellen L. Leggett, "A Social-Cognitive Approach to Motivation and Personality," *Psychological Review* 95, no. 2 (1988): 256–273.

51. Jeni L. Burnette, Joseph Billingsley, George C. Banks, et al., "A Systematic Review and Meta-Analysis of Growth Mindset Interventions: For Whom, How, and Why Might Such Interventions Work?," *Psychological Bulletin* 149, nos. 3–4 (2023): 174.

52. Elif G. Ikizer and Hart Blanton, "Media Coverage of 'Wise' Interventions Can Reduce Concern for the Disadvantaged," *Journal of Experimental Psychology: Applied* 22, no. 2 (2016): 135.

53. Sendhil Mullainathan and Eldar Shafir, *Scarcity: Why Having Too Little Means So Much* (Macmillan, 2013).

54. Colin F. Camerer, Anna Dreber, Felix Holzmeister, et al., "Evaluating the Replicability of Social Science Experiments in *Nature* and *Science* Between 2010 and 2015," *Nature Human Behaviour* 2, no. 9 (2018): 637–644; Anuj K. Shah, Sendhil Mullainathan, and Eldar Shafir, "An Exercise in Self-Replication: Replicating Shah, Mullainathan, and Shafir (2012)," *Journal of Economic Psychology* 75 (2019): 102127.

55. Singal, *Quick Fix*, 161.

56. Jacob Hacker, "How to Reinvigorate the Centre-Left? Predistribution," *Guardian*, June 12, 2013, www.theguardian.com/commentisfree/2013/jun/12/reinvigorate-centre-left-predistribution.

57. Gavin Kelly and Hannah Slaughter, "Towards a Fairer Britain: The Case for 'Predistribution' Policies," *LSE Blog*, February 27, 2024, https://blogs.lse.ac.uk/inequalities/2024/02/27/towards-a-fairer-britain-the-case-for-predistribution/#.

58. David Card and Alan B. Krueger, "Minimum Wages and Employment: A Case Study of the Fast-Food Industry in New Jersey and Pennsylvania," *American Economic Review* 84, no. 4 (1994): 772–793; David Neumark and William Wascher, "Minimum Wages and Employment: A Case Study of the Fast-Food Industry in New Jersey and Pennsylvania: Comment," *American Economic Review* 90, no. 5 (2000): 1362–1396; Arindrajit Dube, T. William Lester, and Michael Reich, "Minimum Wage Effects Across State Borders: Estimates Using Contiguous Counties," *Review of Economics and Statistics* 92, no. 4 (2010): 945–964; *The Effects on Employment and Family Income of Increasing the Federal Minimum Wage* (Congressional Budget Office, 2019), www.cbo.gov/system/files/2019-07/CBO-55410-MinimumWage2019.pdf. For a recent discussion see José Azar, Emiliano Huet-Vaughn, Ioana Marinescu, Bledi Taska, and Till von Wachter, "Minimum Wage Employment Effects and Labour Market Concentration," *Review of Economic Studies* 91, no. 4 (2024): 1843–1883.

59. "Economic Impact Payments," US Department of the Treasury, accessed November 18, 2024, https://home.treasury.gov/policy-issues/coronavirus/assistance-for-american-families-and-workers/economic-impact-payments#.

60. *Statement on a Two-Pillar Solution to Address the Tax Challenges Arising from the Digitalisation of the Economy*, OECD/G20 Base Erosion and Profit Shifting Project (Organization for Economic Co-operation and Development, 2021), www.oecd.org

/tax/beps/statement-on-a-two-pillar-solution-to-address-the-tax-challenges-arising
-from-the-digitalisation-of-the-economy-october-2021.pdf.

61. Emma Agyemang and Paola Tamma, "Global Tax Deal Under Threat from US Politics and Fraying Consensus," *Financial Times*, February 28, 2024, www.ft.com/content/cd88500d-a063-4f15-b6ad-e453a1d8b16d.

Chapter 6: The Pattern Is Everywhere!

1. "The Facts," Plastic Oceans, accessed November 18, 2024, https://plasticoceans.org/the-facts/.

2. "Plastic Pollution," United Nations Environment Programme, accessed May 9, 2025, www.unep.org/interactives/beat-plastic-pollution/.

3. Damian Carrington, "Microplastics Found in Human Blood for First Time," *Guardian*, March 24, 2022, www.theguardian.com/environment/2022/mar/24/microplastics-found-in-human-blood-for-first-time#.

4. Yongfeng Deng, Yan Zhang, Bernardo Lemos, and Hongqiang Ren, "Tissue Accumulation of Microplastics in Mice and Biomarker Responses Suggest Widespread Health Risks of Exposure," *Scientific Reports* 7, no. 1 (2017): 46687; Dick A. Vethaak and Juliette Legler, "Microplastics and Human Health," *Science* 371, no. 6530 (2021): 672–674.

5. Roland Geyer, Jenna R. Jambeck, and Kara Lavender Law, "Production, Use, and Fate of All Plastics Ever Made," *Science Advances* 3, no. 7 (2017): e1700782.

6. Quoted in Max Liboiron, *Pollution Is Colonialism* (Duke University Press, 2021).

7. Lloyd Stouffer, "Plastics Packaging: Today and Tomorrow," in *National Plastics Conference, Nov. 1963, Chicago: Proceedings*, 1–3, Society of the Plastics Industry Chicago, 1963. Cited in Max Liboiron, "Modern Waste as Strategy," *Lo Squaderno: Explorations in Space and Society* 29 (2013): 9–12.

8. "Garnier's 'One Green Step' Campaign to Promote Greener Living," L'Oreal Groupe, www.loreal.com/en/news/commitments/garnier-one-green-step/.

9. Keep Britain Tidy, accessed November 18, 2024, www.keepbritaintidy.org/.

10. Melissa Bateson, Daniel Nettle, and Gilbert Roberts, "Cues of Being Watched Enhance Cooperation in a Real-World Setting," *Biology Letters* 2, no. 3 (2006): 412–414; Kevin J. Haley and Daniel M. T. Fessler, "Nobody's Watching? Subtle Cues Affect Generosity in an Anonymous Economic Game," *Evolution and Human Behavior* 26, no. 3 (2005): 245–256, https://doi.org/10.1016/j.evolhumbehav.2005.01.002; Melissa Bateson, Rebecca Robinson, Tim Abayomi-Cole, Josh Greenlees, Abby O'Connor, and Daniel Nettle, "Watching Eyes on Potential Litter Can Reduce Littering: Evidence from Two Field Experiments," *PeerJ* 3 (2015): e1443.

11. "Green Nudge: Nudging Litter into the Bin," iNudgeYou, accessed November 18, 2024, https://inudgeyou.com/en/green-nudge-nudging-litter-into-the-bin/.

12. "Litter and Flytipping," Zero Waste Scotland, accessed November 18, 2024, www.zerowastescotland.org.uk/litter-flytipping/nudge-study.

13. Silvia Saccardo, Hengchen Dai, Maria Han, Naveen Raja, Sitaram Vangala, and Daniel Croymans, *Assessing Nudge Scalability* (SSRN, 2023), https://ssrn.com/abstract=3971192. There has been some controversy over the general replicability of

"watching eyes" interventions, though a recent meta-analysis concludes in favor of the effect: Keith Dear, Kevin Dutton, and Elaine Fox, "Do 'Watching Eyes' Influence Antisocial Behavior? A Systematic Review and Meta-Analysis," *Evolution and Human Behavior* 40, no. 3 (2019): 269–280.

14. Bateson et al., "Watching Eyes." Littering is also a focus of *Nudge*. On page 79 of *Nudge: The Final Edition*, Thaler and Sunstein extol the huge success of the "Don't Mess with Texas" campaign, citing it as an example of identity-based nudges and crediting it with "a remarkable 72 percent reduction in visible roadside litter." What they don't note is that the campaign was accompanied by well-publicized and very large fines for littering, and coincided with Texas's pioneering of the "adopt-a-highway" program.

15. "State Plastic Bag Legislation," National Conference of State Legislatures, accessed November 18, 2024, www.ncsl.org/environment-and-natural-resources /state-plastic-bag-legislation.

16. "City of San Jose Releases 'Bring Your Own Bag' Ordinance Implementation Results," Plasticbaglaws.org, January 20, 2013, www.plasticbaglaws.org/blog/city-of -san-jose-releases-bring-your-own-bag-ordinance-implementation-results. The publication claimed an 89 percent reduction in bags in the storm drain system, but a website titled "Fight the Plastic Bag Ban: Protect the Environment Through Reason, Common Sense, and Practical Solutions" claimed to find an error in the calculation (we present the more conservative figure): Anthony van Leeuwen, "San Jose Miscalculates Plastic Bag Litter Reduction in Storm Drain System," *Fight the Plastic Bag Ban*, February 12, 2015, https://fighttheplasticbagban.com/wp-content/uploads/2015/09/san-jose -miscalculates-plastic-bag-litter-reduction-in-storm-drain-system.pdf. Interestingly, "Fight the Plastic Bag Ban" does not disclose its funding sources.

17. "Plastic Bag Preemption Conflicts Between State and Local Governments," Ballotpedia, last updated March 14, 2022, https://ballotpedia.org/Plastic _bag_preemption_conflicts_between_state_and_local_governments.

18. Margaret Walls, "Extended Producer Responsibility and Product Design: Economic Theory and Selected Case Studies," Resources for the Future, Discussion Paper 06-08 (2006).

19. Carola Hanisch, "Is Extended Producer Responsibility Effective?," *Environmental Science & Technology* 34, no. 7 (2000): 170A–175A.

20. Sergio Rubio, Tânia Rodrigues Pereira Ramos, Manuel Maria Rodrigues Leitão, and Ana Paula Barbosa-Povoa, "Effectiveness of Extended Producer Responsibility Policies Implementation: The Case of Portuguese and Spanish Packaging Waste Systems," *Journal of Cleaner Production* 210 (2019): 217–230.

21. "Germany Tops EU for Automobile Recovery," Waste Management World by International Solid Waste Association, July 13, 2021, https://waste-management -world.com/artikel/germany-tops-eu-for-automobile-recovery/.

22. Katelyn Harrop and Meghna Chakrabarti, "Is This Ancient Process the Future of Plastics Recycling?," WBUR, August 16, 2024, www.wbur.org/onpoint/2024/08/16 /pyrolysis-oil-company-plastics-recycling-propublica; Lisa Song, "Selling a Mirage," *ProPublica*, accessed November 18, 2024, www.propublica.org/article /delusion-advanced-chemical-plastic-recycling-pyrolysis.

23. Anthony Schiavo is senior director and principal analyst at Lux Research and host of the *Innovation Matters* podcast.

24. Although the General Data Protection Regulation, or GDPR, is state-of-the-art when it comes to privacy regulation, it has been argued that it has been co-opted and hijacked by industry. Christine Utz, Martin Degeling, Sascha Fahl, Florian Schaub, and Thorsten Holz, "(Un)informed Consent: Studying GDPR Consent Notices in the Field," *Proceedings of the 2019 ACM SIGSAC Conference on Computer and Communications Security (CCS '19)* (London, 2019): 973–990.

25. Rachel Welch, "Statement of Rachel Welch, Senior Vice President Policy and External Affairs, Charter Communications on Examining Safeguards for Consumer Data Privacy Before the Senate Committee on Commerce, Science, and Transportation," September 26, 2018, www.commerce.senate.gov/services/files/9cb79c7e-815c-4091-80d0-f425105b110b.

26. Laura Brandimarte, Alessandro Acquisti, and George Loewenstein, "Misplaced Confidences: Privacy and the Control Paradox," *Social Psychological and Personality Science* 4, no. 3 (2013): 340–347.

27. George Loewenstein, Cass R. Sunstein, and Russell Golman, "Disclosure: Psychology Changes Everything," *Annual Review of Economics* 6, no. 1 (2014): 391–419.

28. Athina Ioannou, Iis Tussyadiah, Graham Miller, Shujun Li, and Mario Weick, "Privacy Nudges for Disclosure of Personal Information: A Systematic Literature Review and Meta-Analysis," *PLOS ONE* 16, no. 8 (2021): e0256822; Sofia Schöbel, Torben Barev, Andreas Janson, Felix Hupfeld, and Jan Marco Leimeister, "Understanding User Preferences of Digital Privacy Nudges: A Best-Worst Scaling Approach," in *Proceedings of the 53rd Hawaii International Conference on System Sciences 2020*, 1–10.

29. Susan B. Barnes, "A Privacy Paradox: Social Networking in the United States," *First Monday* 11, no. 9 (2006); Spyros Kokolakis, "Privacy Attitudes and Privacy Behaviour: A Review of Current Research on the Privacy Paradox Phenomenon," *Computers & Security* 64 (2017): 122–134.

30. Alessandro Acquisti, Laura Brandimarte, and George Loewenstein, "Privacy and Human Behavior in the Age of Information," *Science* 347, no. 6221 (2015): 509–514.

31. Martin Moore and Damian Tambini, eds., *Regulating Big Tech: Policy Responses to Digital Dominance* (Oxford University Press, 2021). In practice, the biggest steps so far have come from the EU's 2022 measures, the Digital Markets Act and Digital Services Act (Ilaria Buri and Joris van Hoboken, *The Digital Services Act (DSA) Proposal: A Critical Overview*, Digital Services Act Observatory, October 28, 2021, https://dsa-observatory.eu/wp-content/uploads/2021/11/Buri-Van-Hoboken-DSA-discussion-paper-Version-28_10_21.pdf), and Australia's ban on social media for the under-16s (Hannah Ritchie, "Australia Approves Social Media Ban on Under-16s," BBC News, November 28, 2024, www.bbc.co.uk/news/articles/c89vjj0lxx9o).

32. Tim Carmody, "Facebook's 'Letter from Zuckerberg': The Annotated Version," *Wired*, February 1, 2012, www.wired.com/2012/02/facebook-letter-zuckerberg-annotated/.

33. Merianne R. Spencer, Matthew F. Garnett, and Arialdi M. Miniño, "Drug Overdose Deaths in the United States, 2002–2022," National Center for Health Statistics, Data Brief, no. 491 (2024), www.cdc.gov/nchs/products/databriefs/db491.htm.

34. Andrew Kolodny, David T. Courtwright, Catherine S. Hwang, et al., "The Prescription Opioid and Heroin Crisis: A Public Health Approach to an Epidemic of Addiction," *Annual Review of Public Health* 36, no. 1 (2015): 559–574.

35. Marion S. Greene and R. Andrew Chambers, "Pseudoaddiction: Fact or Fiction? An Investigation of the Medical Literature," *Current Addiction Reports* 2 (2015): 310–317.

36. Julia Lurie, "The Untold Story of Purdue Pharma's Cozy Relationship with the American Medical Association," *Mother Jones*, August 5, 2021, www.motherjones .com/politics/2021/08/purdue-pharma-american-medical-association-relationship -opioid-crisis-public-health/.

37. "Pain Management CME Online," American Medical Association, archived version, accessed October 13, 2007, https://ama-cmeonline.com/.

38. Katie Zezima and Lenny Bernstein, "'Hammer on the Abusers': Mass. Attorney General Alleges Purdue Pharma Tried to Shift Blame for Opioid Addiction," *Washington Post*, January 15, 2019, www.washingtonpost.com/national/hammer-on-the-abusers -mass-attorney-general-alleges-purdue-pharma-tried-to-shift-blame-for-opioid-addic tion/2019/01/15/4af25c4c-190c-11e9-88fe-f9f77a3bcb6c_story.html.

39. The story is told in detail in the 2021 Hulu special *Dopesick* (dir. Barry Levinson) and in books: Sam Quinones, *Dreamland: The True Tale of America's Opiate Epidemic* (Bloomsbury, 2015), and Patrick Radden Keefe, *Empire of Pain: The Secret History of the Sackler Dynasty* (Doubleday, 2021).

40. Carole Gan, "Surgeon General: 'Connect with Community,'" June 27, 2019, remarks at special Grand Rounds for UC Davis Health personnel, www.ucdavis.edu /news/surgeon-general-connect-community.

41. Kris N. Kirby, Nancy M. Petry, and Warren K. Bickel, "Heroin Addicts Have Higher Discount Rates for Delayed Rewards Than Non–Drug-Using Controls," *Journal of Experimental Psychology: General* 128, no. 1 (1999): 78–87.

42. Andrew Kolodny, "How FDA Failures Contributed to the Opioid Crisis," *AMA Journal of Ethics* 22, no. 8 (2020): 743–750; Linda A. Suydam, "Anesthetic and Life Support Drugs Advisory Committee: Notice of Meeting," *US Food and Drug Administration*, notice, April 24, 2002, www.federalregister.gov/documents /2002/05/01/02-10708/anesthetic-and-life-support-drugs-advisory-committee -notice-of-meeting. In a recent book that details the myriad misdeeds of the pharmaceutical company Johnson and Johnson, Gardiner Harris's *No More Tears: The Dark Secrets of Johnson & Johnson* (Random House, 2025) notes that "every FDA commissioner of the modern era has worked for drugmakers after leaving government service, and many worked for them beforehand" (page 102).

43. Ludwig Kraus, Nicki-Nils Seitz, Bernd Schulte, et al., "Estimation of the Number of People with Opioid Addiction in Germany," *Deutsches Ärzteblatt International* 116, no. 9 (2019): 137–143.

44. Deborah Dowell, Elizabeth Arias, Kenneth Kochanek, et al., "Contribution of Opioid-Involved Poisoning to the Change in Life Expectancy in the United States, 2000–2015," *Journal of the American Medical Association* 318, no. 11 (2017): 1065–1067.

45. Here we follow those who see "behavioral" addictions of all kinds as continuous with addictions to nicotine, alcohol, or recreational drugs: Halley M. Pontes,

ed., *Behavioral Addictions: Conceptual, Clinical, Assessment, and Treatment Approaches (Studies in Neuroscience, Psychology and Behavioral Economics)* (Springer, 2022).

46. Natasha Dow Schüll, *Addiction by Design: Machine Gambling in Las Vegas* (Princeton University Press, 2014).

47. David Stewart, "Demystifying Slot Machines and Their Impact in the United States," American Gaming Association (2010), www.scribd.com/document /460066651/Demystifying-Slot-Machines-and-Their-Impact-in-the-United-States -Stewart-2010-pdf.

48. For a recent review see Rosanna Smart, Andrew R. Morral, James P. Murphy, Rupa Jose, Amanda Charbonneau, and Sierra Smucker, "The Science of Gun Policy: A Critical Synthesis of Research Evidence on the Effects of Gun Policies in the United States," *RAND Health Quarterly* 12, no. 1 (2024): 3.

49. On UK mass shootings see "List of Mass Shootings in the United Kingdom," Wikipedia, last modified March 14, 2025, https://en.wikipedia.org/wiki/List_of _mass_shootings_in_the_United_Kingdom; for the US, "List of Mass Shootings in the United States in 2023," Wikipedia, last modified March 2024, https://en .wikipedia.org/wiki/List_of_mass_shootings_in_the_United_States_in_2023 (here a mass shooting is an incident in which four or more people are shot, not necessarily fatally). Second Amendment advocates are fond of pointing out that Switzerland has high levels of gun ownership (as a result of individuals holding on to guns after leaving the military) but low rates of violence. However, the case of Britain shows how an s-frame policy can make a difference.

50. Aaron Karp, *Estimating Global Civilian-Held Firearms Numbers* (Small Arms Survey, 2018), www.smallarmssurvey.org/sites/default/files/resources/SAS-BP-Civilian -Firearms-Numbers.pdf.

51. The NRA also receives considerable funding from public donations and membership fees: "Who Funds the NRA?," A-Mark Foundation, accessed November 18, 2024, https://amarkfoundation.org/reports/who-funds-the-nra/.

52. Sara B. Heller, Anuj K. Shah, Jonathan Guryan, Jens Ludwig, Sendhil Mullainathan, and Harold A. Pollack, "Thinking, Fast and Slow? Some Field Experiments to Reduce Crime and Dropout in Chicago," *Quarterly Journal of Economics* 132, no. 1 (2017): 1–54; Monica P. Bhatt, Sara B. Heller, Max Kapustin, Marianne Bertrand, and Christopher Blattman, "Predicting and Preventing Gun Violence: An Experimental Evaluation of READI Chicago," *Quarterly Journal of Economics* 139, no. 1 (2024): 1–56.

53. Monica P. Bhatt, Jonathan Guryan, Jens Ludwig, and Anuj K. Shah, *Scope Challenges to Social Impact* (no. w28406), National Bureau of Economic Research, 2021, www.nber.org/system/files/working_papers/w28406/w28406.pdf.

54. For road safety statistics see Harvard Global Health Education and Learning Incubator, *Global Status Report on Road Safety 2023* (World Health Organization, 2023), https://iris.who.int/bitstream/handle/10665/375016/978924 0086517-eng.pdf?sequence=1; "Fatality Facts 2023: Pedestrians," Insurance Institute for Highway Safety/Highway Loss Data Institute, updated July 2025, www.iihs .org/topics/fatality-statistics/detail/pedestrians; and "List of Countries by Traffic-Related Death Rate," Wikipedia, last modified 2024, https://en.wikipedia.org/wiki/List _of_countries_by_traffic-related_death_rate.

55. Tom Standage, *A Brief History of Motion: From the Wheel, to the Car, to What Comes Next* (Bloomsbury, 2021).

56. "Automakers' Intransigence Has Blocked Progress: At a Key Moment for Vehicle Standards, Automakers Could Fall into Old Patterns—Or Innovate to Succeed," Union of Concerned Scientists, December 6, 2017, www.ucs.org/about/news /automakers-intransigence-has-blocked-progress; Jerry L. Mashaw and David L. Harfst, *The Struggle for Auto Safety* (Harvard University Press, 1990).

57. Richard Weingroff, "A Moment in Time: Highway Safety Breakthrough," US Department of Transportation, Federal Highway Administration, FHWA News 2021, last updated June 30, 2023, https://highways.dot.gov/highway-history /general-highway-history/moment-time-highway-safety-breakthrough.

58. Sean O'Connell, *The Car in British Society: Class, Gender and Motoring, 1896–1939* (Manchester University Press, 1998); Ralph Nader, *Unsafe at Any Speed: The Designed-In Dangers of the American Automobile* (Pocket Books, 1966).

59. Arthur Neslen, "Car Lobby Opposes EU Safety Bid That Would Save 1,300 Lives a Year," *Guardian*, December 13, 2018, www.theguardian.com/business/2018 /dec/13/car-lobby-opposes-eu-safety-bid-that-would-save-1300-lives-a-year.

60. "Behavioral Insights for Traffic Safety," Behavia, accessed November 18, 2024, https://behavia.de/post-behavioral-insights-for-traffic-safety/. These are closely related to ideas discussed in Richard H. Thaler and Cass R. Sunstein, *Nudge: Improving Decisions About Health, Wealth, and Happiness* (Penguin, 2008).

61. "Vision Zero: No Fatalities or Serious Injuries Through Road Accidents," Vision Zero Initiative, accessed November 18, 2024, www.roadsafetysweden.com/about-the -conference/vision-zero---no-fatalities-or-serious-injuries-through-road-accidents/.

62. Gwyn Topham, "'Hard to Argue Against': Mandatory Speed Limiters Come to the EU and NI," *Guardian*, July 5, 2024, www.theguardian.com/technology /article/2024/jul/05/hard-to-argue-against-mandatory-speed-limiters-come-to-the -eu-and-ni. The UK government, picking up the individualist theme, long opposed this legislation when the UK was still an EU member state. For example, back in 2013 a "government source" was quoted as saying, "To be forced to have automatic controls in your car amounts to Big Brother nannying by EU bureaucrats": Press Association, "U.K. Fights EU Bid to Introduce Speed Limit Devices," *Guardian*, September 1, 2013, www.theguardian.com/world/2013/sep/01/uk-fights-eu-speed-limit-devices.

63. Topham, "'Hard to Argue Against.'"

Chapter 7: The Big Myth

1. Joseph E. Stiglitz, *Globalization and Its Discontents* (W. W. Norton, 2003). George witnessed this firsthand during a recent trip to Peru, where he was informed by his hosts that there is for practical purposes *no* public transportation. The reason dates back to the rule of the late Alberto Fujimori (who later served sixteen years of a twenty-five-year prison sentence for human rights abuses: See "Peruvian Constitutional Court Orders Release of Former President Alberto Fujimori," Associated Press, last updated December 5, 2023, https://apnews.com/article/alberto-fujimori -expresident-peru-released-4a9c8a0159ac9bf170a15338fa860937). During his term as president, 1990–2000, Fujimori, paralleling the famous deregulation of Chile at the

hands of the "Chicago boys" (an influential group of Chicago-educated Chilean economists), deregulated public transportation. The result was chaos. *Anyone* could take whatever vehicle they liked and put it into service as a taxi. Bus companies formed and competed with one another in a wild struggle; when one of their buses found itself behind the bus of another company, it attempted to race past to be first in line to pick up customers. Competition between bus companies (and buses) led to a natural race to the bottom when it comes to safety and reliability of service: See Ana María Fernández-Maldonado, "Attempting to Bridge the Urban Divide in Cities of the Developing World: The Case of Lima, Peru," Academia.edu, accessed November 25, 2024, www.academia.edu/593091/Attempting_to_bridge_the_urban_divide_in_cities _of_the_developing_world_The_case_of_Lima_Peru.

2. The landmark ruling that corporations should be treated as individuals for the purposes of free speech (hence clearing away restrictions on corporate campaign financing) is *Citizens United v. Federal Election Commission*, 558 U.S. 310 (2010).

3. Jacob Hacker and Paul Pierson argue that some of the policy shifts that are commonly attributed to Reagan can actually be traced further back, to Jimmy Carter (e.g., the deregulation of the trucking and airline industries and in finance). Jacob S. Hacker and Paul Pierson, "Winner-Take-All Politics: Public Policy, Political Organization, and the Precipitous Rise of Top Incomes in the United States," *Politics & Society* 38, no. 2 (2010): 152–204.

4. Max Boot, *Reagan: His Life and Legend* (Liveright, 2024), chap. 40.

5. Boot, *Reagan*, chap. 45.

6. The Clinton quotations are from Bill Clinton, "1992 Clinton VS. Bush VS. Perot (presidential campaign ad)," The Living Room Candidate, Museum of the Moving Image, 32 sec., 1992, www.livingroomcandidate.org/commercials/1992 /second-chance; and Bill Clinton, "State of the Union Address," Clinton White House Archives, January 23, 1996, accessed March 20, 2025, https://clintonwhitehouse4 .archives.gov/WH/New/other/sotu.html.

7. For insightful discussion see Rogé Karma, "Why America Abandoned the Greatest Economy in History," *Atlantic*, November 25, 2023, www.theatlantic.com/ideas /archive/2023/11/new-deal-us-economy-american-dream/676051/.

8. Susan Dudley, "Jimmy Carter: The Great Deregulator," *Regulatory Review*, March 6, 2023, www.theregreview.org/2023/03/06/dudley-jimmy-carter-the-great-deregulator/.

9. "General Electric Theater (TV Series 1953–1962)," IMDb, accessed November 25, 2024, www.imdb.com/title/tt0045395/.

10. Erik M. Conway and Naomi Oreskes, *The Big Myth: How American Business Taught Us to Loathe Government and Love the Free Market* (Bloomsbury, 2023), 8–9, Kindle.

11. Jim Powell, "Why Has Liberty Flourished in the West?," *Cato Policy Report* 22, no. 5 (2000): 1–4, www.cato.org/sites/cato.org/files/serials/files/policy-report/2000/9 /cpr-22n5.pdf. Powell's broader argument is that the fight for liberty has often been carried through by lone individuals over many centuries. More recently, though, the influence of big business backing has become dominant.

12. Milton Friedman, "The Role of Government in Education," in *Economics and the Public Interest*, ed. Robert A. Solo (Rutgers University Press, 1955).

13. "Too Much of a Good Thing: Americans Love Big Cars, But New Analysis Suggests That the Heaviest Vehicles Kill More People Than They Save," *Economist*, August 31, 2024, www.economist.com/interactive/united-states/2024/08/31/americans-love-affair-with-big-cars-is-killing-them.

14. Chicago school economists were well aware of these effects, of course, but tended to downplay their importance. Indeed, Friedman noted that what he terms "neighborhood effects" (which sound rather innocuous and perhaps even positive), by which one person's action may harm another, are a potential justification for government intervention. But the Chicago school tended to assume that such interventions would usually do more harm than good in practice. For example, see Milton Friedman, *Capitalism and Freedom* (University of Chicago Press, 1962).

15. Albert O. Hirschman, "Reactionary Rhetoric," *Atlantic*, May 1989, www.theatlantic.com/magazine/archive/1989/05/reactionary-rhetoric/668595/; Albert O. Hirschman, "The Rhetoric of Reaction—Two Years Later," *Government and Opposition* 28, no. 3 (1993): 292–314; Albert O. Hirschman, *The Rhetoric of Reaction: Perversity, Futility, Jeopardy* (Harvard University Press, 1991).

16. Sam Peltzman, "The Effects of Automobile Safety Regulation," *Journal of Political Economy* 83, no. 4 (1975): 677–725.

17. Leon S. Robertson, "A Critical Analysis of Peltzman's 'The Effects of Automobile Safety Regulation,'" *Journal of Economic Issues* 11, no. 3 (1977): 587–600; Alma Cohen and Liran Einav, "The Effects of Mandatory Seat Belt Laws on Driving Behavior and Traffic Fatalities," *Review of Economics and Statistics* 85, no. 4 (2003): 828–843.

18. Peltzman claimed that improved safety measures were *completely* offset by riskier behavior. The general idea that "risk compensation" can somewhat offset safety measures may apply to a limited degree in some contexts, but systematic reviews have found little to no evidence of risk compensation in domains as diverse as helmet-wearing in cycling and skiing, and sexual behavior and mask-wearing to reduce the spread of COVID-19. See Eleni Mantzari, G. James Rubin, and Theresa M. Marteau, "Is Risk Compensation Threatening Public Health in the COVID-19 Pandemic?," *BMJ* 370 (2020).

19. George J. Stigler, "The Theory of Economic Regulation," in *The Political Economy: Readings in the Politics and Economics of American Public Policy* (Routledge, 1984), 67–81.

20. This rollback has been tied to later financial instability, and especially to the 2023 collapse of Silicon Valley Bank. Todd Phillips, "How 2018 Regulatory Rollbacks Set the Stage for the Silicon Valley Bank Collapse—and How to Change Course," *Roosevelt Institute Blog*, March 15, 2023, https://rooseveltinstitute.org/blog/how-2018-regulatory-rollbacks-set-the-stage-for-the-silicon-valley-bank-collapse-and-how-to-change-course/.

21. Conway and Oreskes, *Big Myth*, 8–9.

22. More precisely, "Greed, for lack of a better word, is good," a line that seems to have been adapted by director Oliver Stone from a speech by later-convicted insider trader Ivan Boesky. Newsweek Staff, "The Return of Greed," *Newsweek*, last updated March 13, 2010, www.newsweek.com/return-greed-146987. The shortened form has become a catchphrase for the excesses of the era.

Chapter 8: Sleepwalking into the Enemy's Ranks

1. The first paper—Daniel Kahneman and Amos Tversky, "Prospect Theory: An Analysis of Decision Under Risk," *Econometrica* 47, no. 2 (1979): 263–292—provided a theory of how people actually make risky decisions, which diverges from the theory of ideally rational decision-makers typically assumed in economics. The second paper—Richard H. Thaler, "Toward a Positive Theory of Consumer Choice," *Journal of Economic Behavior & Organization* 1, no. 1 (1980): 39–60—showed how this psychological theory provided deep insights into a wide range of otherwise puzzling economic phenomena: i.e., how an infusion of psychology could strengthen economic theory.

2. At one seminar, for example, a group of researchers from the Harvard Kennedy School came to present their paper arguing that the incentives of CEOs are not sufficiently contingent on the performance of the firms they lead—seemingly a message that free-marketers should be strongly supportive of. They were wrong. Embracing the Panglossian view that we are already in the best of possible worlds, those in the room proposed that if such contingent incentives were beneficial they would already be in place. Gary Becker, for example, argued that the presenters were likely failing to appreciate existing incentives already in place, including the ego gratification of performing well.

3. George would say not that people are *irrational* but that they are far more psychologically interesting and complicated, as well as cognitively limited, than traditional economics has assumed. People do their best given their emotional makeup and cognitive limitations.

4. At our regular Thursday afternoon get-together, we collectively agreed to name the new field "behavioral economics," and it was at one of these weekly get-togethers that Rabin proposed the idea that has since come to be known by the term "nudge." Rabin never intended for the approach he proposed to be a substitute for traditional regulation. Indeed, simultaneously with proposing it, he and Ted O'Donoghue proposed an agenda that promoted "sin taxes"—a decidedly heavy-handed paternalistic policy.

5. Colin Camerer, Samuel Issacharoff, George Loewenstein, Ted O'Donoghue, and Matthew Rabin, "Regulation for Conservatives: Behavioral Economics and the Case for 'Asymmetric Paternalism,'" *University of Pennsylvania Law Review* 151, no. 3 (2003): 1211–1254; Richard H. Thaler and Cass R. Sunstein, "Libertarian Paternalism," *American Economic Review* 93, no. 2 (2003): 175–179; Cass R. Sunstein and Richard H. Thaler, "Libertarian Paternalism Is Not an Oxymoron," *University of Chicago Law Review* 70, no. 4 (2003): 1159–1202. Neither team argued, of course, that all regulation should have this form—indeed, as a leading lawyer Sunstein has continued to be actively and extensively involved in conventional nonlibertarian regulation.

6. Underlining the desire for the new approach to public policy to appeal to conservatives, the Camerer et al. paper also proposes that the term "asymmetric" could be understood in a second, related, way. These policies were designed to appeal to conservatives, who believe that interventions such as defaults and framing effects will not influence consequential choices but will retain the freedom of choice that they (conservatives) see as so crucial.

7. Camerer et al., "Regulation for Conservatives," 1212.

8. Richard H. Thaler and Cass R. Sunstein, *Nudge: The Final Edition* (Penguin Books, 2021), 7.

9. *Nudge* also helped to win Thaler a Nobel Prize, which was, in any case, much deserved for his crucial role in helping to create the field of behavioral economics.

10. While the origin of the term is difficult to discern, some trace it to Nikolas Rose and Peter Miller, "Political Power Beyond the State: Problematics of Government," *British Journal of Sociology* 61 (2010): 271–303, where, on page 293, they refer to a "responsibilizing mode of government."

11. Markus Giesler and Ela Veresiu, "Creating the Responsible Consumer: Moralistic Governance Regimes and Consumer Subjectivity," *Journal of Consumer Research* 41, no. 3 (2014): 840–857.

12. Craig J. Thompson and Gokcen Coskuner-Balli, "Countervailing Market Responses to Corporate Co-Optation and the Ideological Recruitment of Consumption Communities," *Journal of Consumer Research* 34, no. 2 (2007): 138.

13. "Office of Information and Regulatory Affairs," Wikipedia, accessed November 28, 2024, https://en.wikipedia.org/wiki/Office_of_Information_and_Regulatory _Affairs.

14. "Social and Behavioral Sciences Team," Wikipedia, accessed November 28, 2024, https://en.wikipedia.org/wiki/Social_and_Behavioral_Sciences_Team.

15. See, for example, Zeina Afif, "'Nudge Units'—Where They Came from and What They Can Do," *World Bank Blogs*, October 25, 2017, https://blogs.worldbank org/en/developmenttalk/nudge-units-where-they-came-and-what-they-can-do#.

16. George has a (possibly faulty) memory of attending a meeting in Downing Street where he presented preliminary, but seemingly very promising, research he was doing testing the impact of traffic-light labels on food purchases. Not long after, he saw that the UK had in fact adopted such labels, and he worried, in light of subsequent, less encouraging, results he obtained from further research on the topic, that his presentation may have made a—or even *the*—difference.

17. George Loewenstein and Peter Ubel, "Economics Behaving Badly," *New York Times*, July 14, 2010, www.nytimes.com/2010/07/15/opinion/15loewenstein.html.

Chapter 9: The Way Forward

1. Samuel Bowles, "Behavioral Mechanism Design," *Behavioral & Brain Sciences* 46 (2023).

2. Cédric Carbonnier, Alexis Direr, and Ihssane Slimani Houti, "Do Savers Respond to Tax Incentives? The Case of Retirement Savings," *Annals of Economics and Statistics / Annales d'Économie et de Statistique*, no. 113/114 (2014): 225–256; Eric M. Engen, William G. Gale, and John Karl Scholz, "The Illusory Effects of Saving Incentives on Saving," *Journal of Economic Perspectives* 10, no. 4 (1996): 113–138; Andrew G. Biggs, Alicia H. Munnell, and Michael Wicklein, "The Case for Using Subsidies for Retirement Plans to Fix Social Security," no. wp2024-1 (Center for Retirement Research, Boston College, 2024), https://crr.bc.edu/wp-content/uploads/2024/01 /wp_2024-1-2.pdf.

3. Daniel Kahneman, Terrance Odean, and Brad Barber, "Privatizing Pensions: An Irrational Choice," *Global Agenda Magazine* (World Economic Forum, 2005).

4. Henrik Cronqvist and Richard H. Thaler, "Design Choices in Privatized Social-Security Systems: Learning from the Swedish Experience," *American Economic Review* 94, no. 2 (2004): 424–428. We note that if people are able to amass savings above and beyond those in their retirement accounts, they should certainly have the option of investing it themselves (though most would probably do best simply investing in index or target-date funds).

5. Those making nonsensical choices were disproportionately poor and uneducated, which meant that they effectively provided "money on the table" that the company could use to lower the premiums of those who made informed choices. This pattern of low-income, low-education individuals subsidizing high-income, high-education individuals is a common one. For example, credit card users who miss payments or amass a credit balance pay for the rewards—e.g., airline miles or cash back—received by the generally more affluent credit card holders who pay their cards off in full each month. Saurabh Bhargava, George Loewenstein, and Justin Sydnor, "Choose to Lose: Health Plan Choices from a Menu with Dominated Options," *Quarterly Journal of Economics* 132, no. 3 (2017): 1319–1372.

6. Eliminating or vastly simplifying insurance choice is only one of a diversity of needed reforms in the domain of health insurance. We are in accord with Einav and Finkelstein's masterly and informed argument that a wholesale, ground-up reform of health coverage is sorely needed. Liran Einav and Amy Finkelstein, *We've Got You Covered: Rebooting American Health Care* (Portfolio, 2023).

7. Benjamin R. Handel, "Adverse Selection and Inertia in Health Insurance Markets: When Nudging Hurts," *American Economic Review* 103, no. 7 (2013): 2643–2682.

8. Sunstein and Thaler refer to the use of nudges against citizens' interests for purposes of exploitation and manipulation as "sludge"—e.g., defaulting consumers into products they are unlikely to want, or auto-renewal of services that individuals would naturally want to terminate: Cass R. Sunstein, "Sludge Audits," *Behavioural Public Policy* 6, no. 4 (2022): 654–673, and Richard H. Thaler, "Nudge, Not Sludge," *Science* 361, no. 6401 (2018): 431.

9. Punam Anand Keller, Bari Harlam, George Loewenstein, and Kevin G. Volpp, "Enhanced Active Choice: A New Method to Motivate Behavior Change," *Journal of Consumer Psychology* 21, no. 4 (2011): 376–383.

10. "Federal Trade Commission Announces Final 'Click to Cancel' Rule Making It Easier for Consumers to End Recurring Subscriptions and Memberships," Federal Trade Commission, press release, October 16, 2024, www.ftc.gov /news-events/news/press-releases/2024/10/federal-trade-commission-announces -final-click-cancel-rule-making-it-easier-consumers-end-recurring.

11. Handel, "Adverse Selection."

12. Keyvan Kasaian, B. P. S. Murthi, and Erin Steffes, "Effects of Teaser Rates on New Credit Card Customers' Spending and Borrowing: An Empirical Analysis," *International Journal of Bank Marketing* 40, no. 7 (2022): 1555–1574; Brad M. Barber, Terrance Odean, and Lu Zheng, "Out of Sight, Out of Mind: The Effects

of Expenses on Mutual Fund Flows," *Journal of Business* 78, no. 6 (2005): 2095–2120.

13. Note, however, that eventual (mandated) *withdrawals* are taxed as regular income, albeit at an individual's post-retirement marginal tax rate.

14. Biggs et al., "Case for Using Subsidies for Retirement Plans."

15. "Change the Tax Treatment of Capital Gains from Sales of Inherited Assets," *Options for Reducing the Deficit, 2021 to 2030* (Congressional Budget Office, 2020), www.cbo.gov/budget-options/56851.

16. "Wyden, Whitehouse Bill Ensures Private Equity Moguls Pay Fair Share in Taxes," US Senate Committee on Finance, press release, August 5, 2021, www.finance .senate.gov/chairmans-news/wyden-whitehouse-bill-ensures-private-equity-moguls -pay-fair-share-in-taxes.

17. "Saving America's Family Enterprises (SAFE) Relaunches to Oppose Taxing Unrealized Gains," *Saving America's Family Enterprises*, February 8, 2023, https:// protectfamilysavings.org/saving-americas-family-enterprises-safe-relaunches -to-oppose-taxing-unrealized-gains/.

18. Robert Reich, "This Tax Loophole Costs $180bn a Decade. Why Won't Democrats Close It?," *Guardian*, December 14, 2021, www.theguardian .com/commentisfree/2021/dec/14/carried-interest-tax-loophole-close-it; Alexandra Heal, "How Will UK Tax Rises on Private Equity's Carried Interest Work?," *Financial Times*, October 31, 2024, www.ft.com/content/46375cc4-bcf5-44b4 -b87d-761aaa5676ba; "Investment Groups Oppose Trump's Carried-Interest Tax Hike Plan," Reuters, last updated February 7, 2025, www.reuters.com/world/us /investment-group-opposes-trumps-carried-interest-tax-hike-plan-2025-02-07/.

19. Kevin Lane Keller, "Brand Synthesis: The Multidimensionality of Brand Knowledge," *Journal of Consumer Research* 29, no. 4 (2003): 595–600.

20. Parliament of Canada, LEGISinfo, C-8, 41st Parliament, 2nd session, www .parl.ca/legisinfo/en/bill/41-2/C-8.

21. David Aaker, *Creating Signature Stories: Strategic Messaging That Energizes, Persuades and Inspires* (Morgan James, 2018).

22. Americus Reed II, Joel B. Cohen, and Amit Bhattacharjee, "When Brands Are Built from Within: A Social Identity Pathway to Liking and Evaluation," in *Handbook of Brand Relationships*, ed. Deborah J. MacInnis, C. Whan Park, and Joseph W. Priester (Routledge, 2014): 124–150; Jonah Berger and Katherine L. Milkman, "What Makes Online Content Viral?," *Journal of Marketing Research* 49, no. 2 (2012): 192–205.

23. The official phrasing is almost as punchy: Federal Trade Commission, "Trade Regulation Rule on Unfair or Deceptive Fees," *Federal Register* 88, no. 216 (November 9, 2023): 77420–85 (FR Doc. 2023-24234), www.federalregister.gov /documents/2023/11/09/2023-24234/trade-regulation-rule-on-unfair-or-deceptive -fees.

24. Lina M. Khan, "Statement of Chair Lina M. Khan Regarding the Trade Regulation Rule on Unfair or Deceptive Fees, Commission File No. R207011," Federal Trade Commission, December 17, 2024, www.ftc.gov/system/files/ftc_gov/pdf/statement-khan -trade-regulation-rule_-unfair-deceptive-fees.pdf.

25. On the possible defunding of the CFPB see John H. Henson, "Disappearing CFPB? What's Happened and What's Next," *National Law Review*, February 10, 2025, www.natlawreview.com/article/disappearing-cfpb-whats-happened-and-whats-next. On the undermining of the FTC see David McCabe and Cecilia Kang, "Trump Fires Democrats on Federal Trade Commission," *New York Times*, March 18, 2025, www.nytimes.com/2025/03/18/technology/trump-ftc-fires-democrats.html.

26. Jason Fichtner, William Gale, and Jeff Trinca, *Tax Administration: Compliance, Complexity, and Capacity* (Bipartisan Policy Center, 2019), https://bipartisan policy.org/download/?file=/wp-content/uploads/2019/04/Tax-Administration -Compliance-Complexity-Capacity.pdf.

27. George Loewenstein, Cass R. Sunstein, and Russell Golman, "Disclosure: Psychology Changes Everything," *Annual Review of Economics* 6, no. 1 (2014): 391–419.

28. Donald A. Norman, *The Design of Everyday Things* (Basic Books, 2013); Richard H. Thaler and Cass R. Sunstein, *Nudge: Improving Decisions About Health, Wealth, and Happiness* (Penguin Books, 2009); Richard H. Thaler and Cass R. Sunstein, *Nudge: The Final Edition* (Penguin Books, 2021).

29. Daylian M. Cain, George Loewenstein, and Don A. Moore, "The Dirt on Coming Clean: Perverse Effects of Disclosing Conflicts of Interest," *Journal of Legal Studies* 34, no. 1 (2005): 1–25; Daylian M. Cain, George Loewenstein, and Don A. Moore, "When Sunlight Fails to Disinfect: Understanding the Perverse Effects of Disclosing Conflicts of Interest," *Journal of Consumer Research* 37, no. 5 (2011): 836–857; Ian Larkin, Desmond Ang, Jonathan Steinhart, et al., "Association Between Academic Medical Center Pharmaceutical Detailing Policies and Physician Prescribing," *JAMA* 317, no. 17 (2017): 1785–1795; Genevieve P. Kanter and George Loewenstein, "Evaluating Open Payments," *JAMA* 322, no. 5 (2019): 401–402.

30. Although the factors that impact support for antismoking measures are numerous and not well understood, see, e.g., Shyanika W. Rose, Sherry L. Emery, Susan Ennett, Heath Luz McNaughton Reyes, John C. Scott, and Kurt M. Ribisl, "Public Support for Family Smoking Prevention and Tobacco Control Act Point-of-Sale Provisions: Results of a National Study," *American Journal of Public Health* 105, no. 10 (2015): e60–e67.

31. "How Carbon Pricing Works," Government of Canada, accessed December 9, 2024, www.canada.ca/en/environment-climate-change/services/climate-change /pricing-pollution-how-it-will-work/putting-price-on-carbon-pollution.html. Despite its revenue neutrality, Canada's carbon tax has still proved to be politically controversial, and the Conservative opposition has vowed to repeal it. See Eric Van Rythoven, "A Conservative Government May Axe the Carbon Tax But Then May Have to Bring It Back," Institute for Research on Public Policy, *Policy Options*, May 23, 2024, https://policyoptions.irpp.org/magazines/may-2024 /conservative-carbon-tax/. Taxes, even revenue-neutral ones, are rarely vote winners.

32. In the framework of behavioral economics, this is because people treat opportunity costs (in this case, not selling their flight credit) very differently from out-of-pocket costs (i.e., paying more for a flight): e.g., Richard H. Thaler, "Toward a Positive Theory of Consumer Choice," *Journal of Economic Behavior and Organization* 1, no. 1 (1980): 39–60.

33. Amos Tversky and Daniel Kahneman, "Loss Aversion in Riskless Choice: A Reference-Dependent Model," *Quarterly Journal of Economics* 106, no. 4 (1991): 1039–1061.

34. Tatiana A. Homonoff, "Can Small Incentives Have Large Effects? The Impact of Taxes Versus Bonuses on Disposable Bag Use," *American Economic Journal: Economic Policy* 10, no. 4 (2018): 177–210.

35. It is probably also important that, with a suitable level of prior public concern about the proliferation of plastic waste, the small cost is viewed as a legitimate reminder that using disposable plastic bags is widely agreed to be a "bad thing." Indeed, where such small charges are used, as in the UK, people often feel guilty rather than outraged when they need to purchase a plastic bag.

36. Kevin Keane, "Scottish Government Scraps Climate Change Targets," *BBC News*, April 18, 2024, www.bbc.co.uk/news/uk-scotland-68847434.

37. Cynthia E. Cryder, George Loewenstein, and Richard Scheines, "The Donor Is in the Details," *Organizational Behavior and Human Decision Processes* 120, no. 1 (2013): 21.

38. Scott Rick and George Loewenstein, "Intangibility in Intertemporal Choice," *Philosophical Transactions of the Royal Society B: Biological Sciences* 363, no. 1511 (2008): 3813–3824.

39. Daniel J. Connolly, George Loewenstein, and Nick Chater, "An s-Frame Agenda for Behavioral Public Policy Research," *Behavioural Public Policy* 9, no. 3 (2025): 593–613. The present chapter draws extensively on this paper, and we thank Dan Connolly for helping to develop these ideas.

40. Laura Haynes, Owain Service, Ben Goldacre, and David Torgerson, "Test, Learn, Adapt: Developing Public Policy with Randomised Controlled Trials," *Cabinet Office Behavioural Insights Team* (2012); Michael Luca and Max H. Bazerman, *The Power of Experiments: Decision-Making in a Data-Driven World* (MIT Press, 2020); and in the domain of development economics, Esther Duflo, Michael Kremer, and Jonathan Robinson, "How High Are Rates of Return to Fertilizer? Evidence from Field Experiments in Kenya," *American Economic Review* 98, no. 2 (2008): 482–488.

41. Thomas. R. Frieden, "Evidence for Health Decision Making—Beyond Randomized, Controlled Trials," *New England Journal of Medicine* 377, no. 5 (2017): 465–475.

42. Angus Deaton and Nancy Cartwright, "Understanding and Misunderstanding Randomized Controlled Trials," *Social Science & Medicine* 210 (2018): 2–21.

43. Michelle Jackson, "The Social Sciences Are Increasingly Ill-Equipped to Design System-Level Reforms," *Behavioral and Brain Sciences* 46 (2023): e162. See also Michelle Jackson, *Manifesto for a Dream: Inequality, Constraint, and Radical Reform* (Stanford University Press, 2020).

44. Dani Rodrik, "The New Development Economics: We Shall Experiment, but How Shall We Learn?," in *What Works in Development? Thinking Big and Thinking Small*, ed. Jessica Cohen and William Easterly (Brookings Institution, 2009).

45. Janet Currie, Lucas Davis, Michael Greenstone, and Reed Walker, "Environmental Health Risks and Housing Values: Evidence from 1,600 Toxic Plant

Openings and Closings," *American Economic Review* 105, no. 2 (2015): 678–709; Olivier Deschênes, Michael Greenstone, and Joseph S. Shapiro, "Defensive Investments and the Demand for Air Quality: Evidence from the NOx Budget Program," *American Economic Review* 107, no. 10 (2017): 2958–2989.

46. Alexander T. J. Barron, Jenny Huang, Rebecca L. Spang, and Simon DeDeo, "Individuals, Institutions, and Innovation in the Debates of the French Revolution," *Proceedings of the National Academy of Sciences* 115, no. 18 (2018): 4607–4612; Marten Scheffer, Ingrid van de Leemput, Els Weinans, and Johan Bollen, "The Rise and Fall of Rationality in Language," *Proceedings of the National Academy of Sciences* 118, no. 51 (2021): e2107848118; Sandeep Soni, Lauren F. Klein, and Jacob Eisenstein, "Abolitionist Networks: Modeling Language Change in Nineteenth-Century Activist Newspapers," *Journal of Cultural Analytics* 6, no. 1 (2021).

47. We are not the first to make this point: Newell made a parallel critique of experimental methods in cognitive psychology, though with a rather different focus: Allen Newell, "You Can't Play 20 Questions with Nature and Win: Projective Comments on the Papers of This Symposium," in *Machine Intelligence* (Routledge, 2012): 121–146. Irzik makes a related critique of Karl Popper's advocacy for "piecemeal engineering": Gürol Irzik, "Popper's Piecemeal Engineering: What Is Good for Science Is Not Always Good for Society," *British Journal for the Philosophy of Science* 36, no. 1 (1985): 1–9. Popper's view is outlined in Karl R. Popper, *The Poverty of Historicism* (Routledge & Kegan Paul, 2002). Similar arguments have been persuasively advanced in the context of economic development: Ricardo Hausmann and Dani Rodrik, "Economic Development as Self-Discovery," *Journal of Development Economics* 72, no. 2 (2003): 603–633.

48. "Franklin D. Roosevelt Speeches: Oglethorpe University Address; the New Deal," May 22, 1932, Pepperdine School of Public Policy, https://publicpolicy.pepperdine.edu/academics/research/faculty-research/new-deal/roosevelt-speeches/fr052232.htm.

49. Geoff Mulgan, *Another World Is Possible: How to Reignite Social and Political Imagination* (Hurst, 2022).

50. See Robert Proctor's lecture, April 2022, to Gonville & Caius College, Cambridge: "Fisher in the 21st Century," YouTube, 49 min., 1 sec., www.youtube.com/watch?v=S9eiEJOPMOA.

51. Paul D. Stolley, "When Genius Errs: R. A. Fisher and the Lung Cancer Controversy," *American Journal of Epidemiology* 133, no. 5 (1991): 416–425.

52. Proctor lecture, 2022, minute 13:11.

53. Fred Panzer, "The Roper Proposal," Tobacco Institute, May 1, 1972, p. 1, http://legacy.library.ucsf.edu/tid/vhu92f00. For background see Clive Bates and Andy Rowell, *Tobacco Explained: The Truth About the Tobacco Industry . . . in Its Own Words*, (Action on Smoking and Health, 1999).

54. Panzer, "Roper Proposal."

55. For discussion of the original report and its consequences, see "Reducing the Health Consequences of Smoking: 25 Years of Progress, A Report of the Surgeon General," *DHHS publication* no. (CDC) 89-8411 (1989), https://stacks.cdc.gov/view/cdc/13240; "Text: S.559—89th Congress (1965–1966): Federal Cigarette Labeling

and Advertising Act," congress.gov, July 27, 1965, www.congress.gov/bill/89th-congress/senate-bill/559/text.

56. "Reducing the Health Consequences of Smoking."

57. Note, though, that an ad ban is an s-frame mandate from the point of view of advertisers.

58. Max Roser, "Smoking: How Large of a Global Problem Is It? And How Can We Make Progress Against It?," *Our World in Data*, July 14, 2021, https://ourworldindata.org/smoking-big-problem-in-brief.

Chapter 10: Democracy Hacked

1. That has changed in recent years with action taken against the merger of giant publishers Penguin Random House and Simon & Schuster, rumblings about a possible breakup of Google for having a near monopoly over internet search, and the pushback against the merger of US grocery chains Kroger and Albertsons. Running up to the 2024 US election, the *Financial Times* had credible reports that billionaire backers of the Democratic campaign were exerting pressure to replace the strongly antitrust Lina Khan as chair of the Federal Trade Commission. See Stefania Palma, "Alexandria Ocasio-Cortez Warns of 'Brawl' If Kamala Harris Removes Lina Khan," *Financial Times*, October 9, 2024, www.ft.com/content/dc2eb9a0-1cbd-4f39-98af-b4c86673db0b.

2. Filippo Lancieri, Eric A. Posner, and Luigi Zingales, "The Political Economy of the Decline of Antitrust Enforcement in the United States," Working Paper no. w30326 (National Bureau of Economic Research, 2022).

3. The Rebel Accountant, *Taxtopia: How I Discovered the Injustices, Scams and Guilty Secrets of the Tax Evasion Game* (Monoray, 2023). For a recent lobbying success by private equity see Sebastian McCarthy and Justin Cash, "Back from the Brink: Private Equity's Lobbying Effort on Carried Interest Pays Off," *Financial News*, October 30, 2024, www.fnlondon.com/articles/back-from-the-brink-private-equitys-lobbying-effort-on-carried-interest-pays-off-5b99a638.

4. "Citizens United v. FEC," Federal Election Commission, accessed December 10, 2024, www.fec.gov/legal-resources/court-cases/citizens-united-v-fec/.

5. Daniel I. Weiner and Tim Lau, "Citizens United Explained," Brennan Center for Justice, last updated January 29, 2025, www.brennancenter.org/our-work/research-reports/citizens-united-explained.

6. Daniel I. Weiner, *Citizens United Five Years Later* (Brennan Center for Justice, 2015), www.brennancenter.org/our-work/research-reports/citizens-united-five-years-later.

7. See, e.g., Lawrence Lessig, *Republic, Lost: The Corruption of Equality and the Steps to End It* (Twelve Books, 2015), for discussion of reform in the US. For background on the situation in the UK, see a 2011 parliamentary committee report on reform: Committee on Standards in Public Life, "Political Party Finance: Ending the Big Donor Culture," no. 13 (2011), www.gov.uk/government/publications/political-party-finance-ending-the-big-donor-culture.

8. See, e.g., Marcel Mauss, *The Gift: The Form and Reason for Exchange in Archaic Societies*, trans. W. D. Halls (W. W. Norton, 2000); John W. Thibaut and Harold H. Kelley, *The Social Psychology of Groups* (John Wiley, 1959).

9. Brett Murphy and Alex Mierjeski, "Clarence Thomas' 38 Vacations: The Other Billionaires Who Have Treated the Supreme Court Justice to Luxury Travel," *ProPublica*, August 10, 2023, www.propublica.org/article/clarence -thomas-other-billionaires-sokol-huizenga-novelly-supreme-court.

10. Critics have argued that the rules are also easy to circumvent. Several regulations target lobbying but allow officials to engage in related roles. "Cooling off periods" that restrict cycling between government and businesses for a limited period have been criticized as too short. And even with the existing regulations in place, revolving-door practices remain widespread. For example, in 2023, out of 708 lobbyists working for defense companies, at least 517 had previously held government positions. See, e.g., Taylor Giorno, "'Revolving Door' Lobbyists Help Defense Contractors Get Off to 'Strong' Start in 2023," Open Secrets, May 4, 2023, www.opensecrets.org /news/2023/05/revolving-door-lobbyists-help-defense-contractors-get-off-to-strong -start-in-2023/?utm_source=chatgpt.com.

11. This includes Supreme Court justices (see Joshua Kaplan, Justin Elliott, and Alex Mierjeski, "Clarence Thomas Secretly Participated in Koch Network Donor Events," *ProPublica*, September 22, 2023, www.propublica.org/article /clarence-thomas-secretly-attended-koch-brothers-donor-events-scotus); former US treasury secretaries (William D. Cohan, "Big Profits, Big Questions," *New York Times*, April 14, 2009, www.nytimes.com/2009/04/15/opinion/15cohan.html); and UK prime ministers (Rose Whiffen, "Managing Revolving Door Risks in Westminster," Transparency International UK, www.transparency.org.uk/news/managing-revolving -door-risks-westminster).

12. Yasha Levine, "All EFF'd Up: Silicon Valley's Astroturf Privacy Shakedown," *Baffler*, no. 40 (2018), https://thebaffler.com/salvos/all-effd-up-levine.

13. Quotes retrieved from the EFF website, www.eff.org/, in March 2025.

14. The 4th Viscount Rothermere has been reported in *Private Eye* to have complex tax arrangements ("Rothermere's Patriot Games," October 18, 2013, https:// web.archive.org/web/20131021212813/http://www.private-eye.co.uk/sections.php ?section_link=street_of_shame&issue=1351) which seem largely to have evaded public scrutiny.

15. Rupert Murdoch's *Sun* certainly proclaimed itself to be crucial to general election outcomes. In the previous and closely fought election in 1992, the newspaper had backed the successful Conservative campaign and posted the now-famous headline "It's The Sun Wot Won It" on its front page on April 11, 1992. At minimum, Murdoch, owner of *The Sun* (and not a UK citizen), has probably had more influence on UK elections, and the political platforms presented to the electorate, than thousands and perhaps even millions of individual UK citizens.

16. Fran Abrams and Anthony Bevins, "Murdoch's Courtship of Blair Finally Pays Off," *Independent*, February 11, 1998, www.independent.co.uk/news/murdoch-s -courtship-of-blair-finally-pays-off-1144087.html.

17. Anthony Hilton, "Stay or Go: The Lack of Solid Facts Means It's All a Leap of Faith," *The Standard*, February 25, 2016, www.standard.co.uk/comment /comment/anthony-hilton-stay-or-go-the-lack-of-solid-facts-means-it-s-all-a-leap -of-faith-a3189151.html; Karl Macdonald, "Rupert Murdoch References 'Fake News'

in Guardian Letter over Influence on Prime Minister," *iPaper*, last updated July 2, 2020, https://inews.co.uk/news/politics/rupert-murdoch-says-never-asks-anything-prime-minister-37419?srsltid=AfmBOorAWzZJR6bvIUfs4RNJAiCI3wIioKHSdLQS_6f-AREZd7BuVS-y.

18. Phillip Longman, "How Fighting Monopoly Can Save Journalism," *Washington Monthly*, January 16, 2024, https://washingtonmonthly.com/2024/01/16/how-fighting-monopoly-can-save-journalism/.

19. There are, of course, exceptions, such as *The New York Times* in the US and *The Guardian* in the UK, among others. But relatively independent outlets are in the minority.

20. Susie Alegre, "We're Dangerously Close to Giving Big Tech Control of Our Thoughts," *Time*, June 29, 2022, https://time.com/6191973/big-tech-freedom-of-thought/.

21. Max Boot, *Reagan: His Life and Legend* (Liveright, 2024), chap. 52.

22. Longman, "How Fighting Monopoly Can Save Journalism."

23. Matthew d'Ancona, *Post-Truth: The New War on Truth and How to Fight Back* (Ebury Press, 2017).

24. Lulu Garcia-Navarro, "The Interview: John Oliver Is Still Working Through the Rage," *New York Times*, September 28, 2024, www.nytimes.com/2024/09/28/magazine/john-oliver-interview.html.

25. Hilary Beaumont and Nina Lakhani, "Revealed: How the Fossil Fuel Industry Helps Spread Anti-Protest Laws Across the US," *Guardian*, September 26, 2024, www.theguardian.com/us-news/2024/sep/26/anti-protest-laws-fossil-fuel-lobby.

26. The 2022 Police, Crime, Sentencing and Courts (PCSC) Act was introduced by then–Home Secretary Suella Braverman; the tougher antiprotest rules were openly justified as combating protests by the Just Stop Oil activist group. Some aspects of the bill were watered down in the House of Lords. The later Public Order Act (2023) was amended to include the power "to apply for injunctions against anyone [the home secretary] deems 'likely' to carry out protests that could cause 'serious disruption' to 'key national infrastructure,' prevent access to 'essential' goods or services, or have a 'serious adverse effect on public safety.' The proposal would also give police the power to arrest anyone they suspect to be breaching such an injunction." See Adam Bychawski, "Suella Braverman Quietly Gives Herself Fresh Anti-Protest Powers," *Open Democracy*, October 18, 2022, www.opendemocracy.net/en/public-order-bill-suella-braverman-anti-protest/.

27. Bethany Bell, "Just Stop Oil Sentences Condemned by Celebrities," *BBC News*, July 23, 2024, www.bbc.co.uk/news/articles/cz9xr4q3rk6o#.

28. Dan Bloom, "Braverman Jets in, but Will Migrants Fly Out?," *Politico*, June 29, 2023, www.politico.eu/newsletter/london-playbook/braverman-jets-in-but-will-migrants-fly-out/.

29. Anita Mureithi, "Rishi Sunak Admits Oil-Funded Think Tank Helped Write Anti-Protest Laws," *Open Democracy*, June 30, 2023, www.opendemocracy.net/en/dark-money-investigations/rishi-sunak-right-wing-think-tank-anti-protest-laws-policy-exchange/.

Chapter 11: Green Eggs and Ham

1. Dr. Seuss [Theodor Seuss Geisel], *Green Eggs and Ham* (Beginner Books, 1960).

2. For US readers of George's generation this theme will also inevitably evoke a ubiquitous advertisement for Alka-Seltzer from the 1970s: "Try It, You'll Like It," 1971, YouTube, 48 sec., www.youtube.com/watch?v=OHdPwRZt8_k.

3. Shane Frederick and George Loewenstein, "Hedonic Adaptation," in *Well-Being: The Foundations of Hedonic Psychology*, ed. Daniel Kahneman, Edward Diener, and Norbert Schwarz (Russell Sage Foundation, 1999).

4. Philip Brickman, Dan Coates, and Ronnie Janoff-Bulman, "Lottery Winners and Accident Victims: Is Happiness Relative?," *Journal of Personality and Social Psychology* 36, no. 8 (1978): 917.

5. Peter A. Ubel, George Loewenstein, and Christopher Jepson, "Disability and Sunshine: Can Hedonic Predictions Be Improved by Drawing Attention to Focusing Illusions or Emotional Adaptation?," *Journal of Experimental Psychology: Applied* 11, no. 2 (2005): 111; George Loewenstein and Peter A. Ubel, "Hedonic Adaptation and the Role of Decision and Experience Utility in Public Policy," *Journal of Public Economics* 92, nos. 8–9 (2008): 1795–1810.

6. Adam Smith, *The Theory of Moral Sentiments* (London, 1759).

7. William Samuelson and Richard Zeckhauser, "Status Quo Bias in Decision Making," *Journal of Risk and Uncertainty* 1 (1988): 7–59.

8. In the UK, for example, the proportion of smokers supporting restrictions on smoking grew steadily after their implementation, to the point that most smokers supported restrictions on their own smoking behavior. "Smokefree: The First Ten Years," Action on Smoking and Health GB, July 1, 2017, http://ash.org.uk/wp-content/uploads/2017/06/170107-Smokefree-the-first-ten-years-FINAL.pdf.

9. Rob Davies and Matthew Chapman, "Revealed: How Sunak Dropped Smoking Ban amid Lobbying from Tobacco Firms," *Guardian*, June 29, 2024, www.theguardian.com/business/article/2024/jun/29/rishi-sunak-smoking-ban-bill-backlash-tobacco-firms.

10. Maarten Wolsink, "Wind Power Implementation: The Nature of Public Attitudes; Equity and Fairness Instead of 'Backyard Motives,'" *Renewable and Sustainable Energy Reviews* 11, no. 6 (2007): 1188–1207; Robert L. Thayer and Carla M. Freeman, "Altamont: Public Perceptions of a Wind Energy Landscape," *Landscape and Urban Planning* 14 (1987): 379–398; Martin J. Pasqualetti, "Wind Energy Landscapes: Society and Technology in the California Desert," *Society & Natural Resources* 14, no. 8 (2001): 689–699; Dan van der Horst, "NIMBY or Not? Exploring the Relevance of Location and the Politics of Voiced Opinions in Renewable Energy Siting Controversies," *Energy Policy* 35, no. 5 (2007): 2705–2714.

11. Geertje Schuitema, Linda Steg, and Sonja Forward, "Explaining Differences in Acceptability Before and Acceptance After the Implementation of a Congestion Charge in Stockholm," *Transportation Research Part A: Policy and Practice* 44, no. 2 (2010): 99–109.

12. "Stockholm Congestion Pricing," Tools of Change, accessed December 9, 2024, https://toolsofchange.com/en/case-studies/detail/670.

13. Nicholas Janusch, Stephan Kroll, Christopher Goemans, Todd L. Cherry, and Steffen Kallbekken, "Learning to Accept Welfare-Enhancing Policies: An Experimental Investigation of Congestion Pricing," *Experimental Economics* 24 (2021): 59–86.

14. In some cases, part of the opposition arises from people's underappreciation of the importance of good policies. One very clever paper studies this experimentally by having people play a standard economic "Prisoner's Dilemma" game, in which two individuals independently choose between cooperating and "defecting" (i.e., betraying the other person) without knowing the other's choice. If both cooperate, they receive a moderate reward. If one defects while the other cooperates, the defector gets a high reward and the cooperator gets a severe penalty. If both defect, they receive a low reward. In one version of the experiment, they started everyone off in the Prisoner's Dilemma game but gave them the opportunity to pay to play a modified game in which they would be taxed 1 point if they cooperated and 4 points if they betrayed. This was deliberately made to seem like an extraordinarily bad deal—if one didn't take account of how this change in payoffs would affect players' behavior. The taxes were, in fact, beneficial because they modified the game in a way that led almost everyone to cooperate, but a majority of players rejected the modified game and earned lower payoffs as a result. Summarizing their finding, the authors conclude that people "systematically underappreciate the extent to which policy changes affect other people's behavior, and that these mistaken beliefs exert a causal effect on the demand for bad policy." See Ernesto Dal Bó, Pedro Dal Bó, and Erik Eyster, "The Demand for Bad Policy When Voters Underappreciate Equilibrium Effects," *Review of Economic Studies* 85, no. 2 (2018): 964–998 (quotation on 964).

15. "Soft Drinks Industry Levy Statistics Commentary 2024," HM Revenue & Customs, UK Government Statistics, accessed December 9, 2024, www.gov.uk /government/statistics/soft-drinks-industry-levy-statistics/soft-drinks-industry-levy -statistics-commentary-2021#. Initially it was proposed that the additional tax revenue would be funneled into programs to tackle childhood obesity. Controversially, but perhaps not surprisingly, the money was rapidly subsumed into general taxation. Tom Sasse and Sophie Metcalfe, "Sugar Tax," Institute for Government, accessed December 9, 2024, www.instituteforgovernment.org.uk/explainers/sugar-tax.

16. Of course, to some degree if people consume less sugar in soft drinks, they may consume more sugar and, more broadly, more calories in other aspects of their diet. It is difficult to estimate the size of this effect—but unlikely that any compensation obliterated the positive effects of the missing sugar.

17. "Retail Banking Consumer Duty Multi-Firm Work," Financial Conduct Authority, last updated December 14, 2023, www.fca.org.uk/publications/multi-firm-reviews /retail-banking-consumer-duty-multi-firm-work#.

18. Robert H. Frank, "Frames of Reference and the Quality of Life," *American Economic Review* 79, no. 2 (1989): 80–85.

19. In the US, tax rules have actually favored larger vehicles, although at the time of writing it is unclear whether this might be set to change. "Why American Cars Are So Big," *Economist*, March 11, 2024, www.economist.com/the-economist-explains/2024 /03/11/why-american-cars-are-so-big.

20. The economist Robert Frank has stressed another, closely related, force at work—that a lot of consumption is focused on social comparison, so that what really matters is not the size of my car, but the size of my car in comparison with everyone else's. This can lead to a costly and futile "arms race" in which people compete to have more, and more luxurious, goods than others; but overall, no one is better off. Robert H. Frank, "Positional Externalities Cause Large and Preventable Welfare Losses," *American Economic Review* 95, no. 2 (2005): 137–141.

21. Daniel Schwartz and George Loewenstein, "The Chill of the Moment: Emotions and Proenvironmental Behavior," *Journal of Public Policy & Marketing* 36, no. 2 (2017): 255–268.

Conclusion: Taking Back Control

1. Bill McKibben, "It's Easy to Feel Pessimistic About the Climate. But We've Got Two Big Things on Our Side," *Guardian*, October 15, 2021, www.theguardian.com /commentisfree/2021/oct/15/climate-crisis-cop26-bill-mckibben.

2. Cass R. Sunstein, "Conspiracy Theory," *Behavioral & Brain Sciences* 46 (2023): e176. Our response to Sunstein is Nick Chater and George Loewenstein, "Where Next for Behavioral Public Policy?," *Behavioral and Brain Sciences* 46 (2023). We're not sure how seriously the "conspiracy theory" allegation was meant; Sunstein has himself defined conspiracy theories as beliefs that "powerful people *have worked together* in order to withhold the truth" (Cass R. Sunstein and Adrian Vermeule, "Conspiracy Theories," Working Paper No. 387 (John M. Olin Program in Law and Economics, 2008), https://chicagounbound.uchicago.edu/law_and_economics/119/), but our argument is very different. There need be no "powerful people" secretly working together. Rather, corporations are independently pursuing PR and lobbying tactics that will, as conventional economic logic would dictate, promote their interests. And, of course, "real" conspiracy theories are notable for their complexity, inconsistency, and failure to fit agreed facts; think of QAnon as a paradigm example: Monica K. Miller, ed., *The Social Science of QAnon: A New Social and Political Phenomenon* (Cambridge University Press, 2023). By contrast, the present account is simple and coherent and, we believe, fits the facts all too well.

3. David Hume, *Essays and Treatises on Several Subjects*, part 1, essay 6, "Of the Independency of Parliament," https://davidhume.org/texts/empl1/ip.

4. Richard H. Thaler, "Nudging Is Being Framed," *Behavioral and Brain Sciences* 46 (2023).

5. Anand Giridharadas, *Winners Take All: The Elite Charade of Changing the World* (Alfred A. Knopf, 2018), 3.

6. Giridharadas, *Winners Take All*, 10.

7. David Cole, *Engines of Liberty: The Power of Citizen Activists to Make Constitutional Law* (Basic Books, 2016). Cole's account of how social change really happens contrasts starkly with the market-based model of change that, according to Giridharadas, is increasingly prevalent among the young. Some prominent psychologists appear to share this individualistic viewpoint: Giridharadas reproduces a radio segment where Krista Tippett interviews Jonathan Haidt, a professor of psychology at New York University, who states optimistically that "people our age grew up expecting that the point

of civic engagement is to be active, so we can make the government fix civil rights or something—we've got to make the government do something. And young people have grown up never seeing the government do anything except turn the lights off now and then. And so their activism is not going to be to get the government to do things. It's going to be to invent some app, some way of solving problems separately. And that's going to work." Inventing an app is, we would argue, unlikely to have anything like the impact of the types of concerted movements for change, orchestrated through existing governmental institutions, documented in Cole's book.

8. Tim Harford, "What Nudge Theory Got Wrong," *Financial Times*, May 6, 2020, www.ft.com/content/a23e808b-e293-4cc0-b077-9168cff135e4. In the interests of full disclosure, the author of this piece is a friend of one of the authors; but it was written unprompted.

INDEX

Warwick Business School

Billy Delfs

Nick Chater is a professor of behavioral science at Warwick Business School. **George Loewenstein** is the Herbert A. Simon University Professor of Economics and Psychology at Carnegie Mellon University. Both have written and edited a number of books in their respective fields. Chater resides in Oxford, UK, and Loewenstein resides in Pittsburgh, Pennsylvania.